GURKHA

Better to Die
Than Live a Coward:
My Life with the Gurkhas

GURKHA

Better to Die
Than Live a Coward:
My Life with the Gurkhas

KAILASH LIMBU

Little, Brown

LITTLE, BROWN

First published in Great Britain in 2015 by Little, Brown

Copyright © A.R. Norman 2015

Maps © John Gilkes 2015

A CIP catalogue record for this book
is available from the British Library.

Hardback ISBN 978-1-4087-0535-3
Trade Paperback ISBN 978-1-4087-0536-0

Typeset in Garamond by M Rules
Printed and bound in India by
Manipal Technologies Ltd, Manipal

Papers used by Little, Brown are from well-managed forests
and other responsible sources.

Little, Brown
An imprint of
Little, Brown Book Group
Carmelite House
50 Victoria Embankment
London EC4Y 0DZ

An Hachette UK Company
www.hachette.co.uk

www.littlebrown.co.uk

UK MOD review of this work has been undertaken for security
purposes only and should not be construed as an endorsement.

*Dedicated to the memory of Lance Corporal
Gajbahadur Gurung, born 16 April 1985,
died Afghanistan, 27 January 2012, and
to all my comrades at Now Zad*

Contents

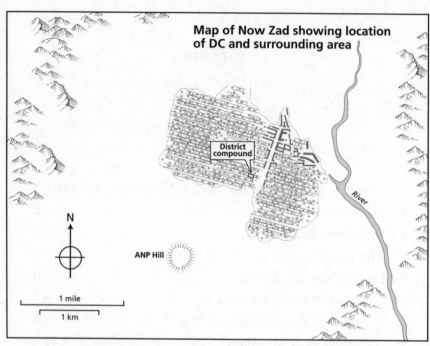

Map of Now Zad showing location of DC and surrounding area

District compound

River

N

ANP Hill

1 mile

1 km

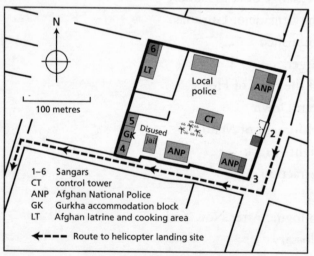

N

100 metres

6
LT

Local
police

ANP

1

5
GK

Disused
jail

CT

2

4

ANP

ANP

3

1–6   Sangars
CT   control tower
ANP   Afghan National Police
GK   Gurkha accommodation block
LT   Afghan latrine and cooking area

◀---- Route to helicopter landing site

The District Compound (DC)

Introduction

This is one man's story, the story of a Gurkha soldier serving in the British Army. Probably, it could have been written by almost any of my comrades, except that some have had more distinguished careers than me. Although I have been mentioned in despatches, I have won no major gallantry awards, nor am I one of those heroes who fought, kukri in hand, after all their ammunition ran out. I have never been last man standing. My story is just that of an ordinary hill boy from Nepal whose ambition was to be a Gurkha from as far back as I can remember. I therefore feel very privileged to have been chosen as the first serving Gurkha soldier to tell his life story in his own words.

The idea for writing this book as part of the celebration of two hundred years' unbroken service to the British crown came from Brigadier Ian Rigden OBE, former Colonel Brigade of Gurkhas, and I am very grateful to him for supporting me throughout the project.

This, then, is the story of a Gurkha soldier who was lucky enough to serve alongside the allied forces during the recent war in Afghanistan and to have survived, as many did not. It is also,

in part, the story of an action which has not much been written about – the siege of Now Zad.

Now I am quite sure that everyone present in Now Zad during
July 2006 could write their own book, and it could easily be that
theirs is more accurate and better written than mine. What I have
tried to do is to give a sense of what it was like to be a soldier on
the ground in the situation we faced. Above all, I have tried to the
best of my ability to give a straightforward and truthful account
of my experiences. As such, this is a personal record of how a few
dozen men of the 2nd Battalion, The Royal Gurkha Rifles held
out against the combined forces of the Taliban insurgency at a
time when Helmand province was largely under their control.
What we went through was something like an old-fashioned
siege – a bit like the siege that brought the British Army and
Nepal's Gurkhas together for the first time. On that occasion, the
Gurkhas drove off the British and their attempted invasion of
Nepal failed.

But the story goes that, during this first encounter, a small band
of Gurkhas captured a British officer who had been deserted by
the force of Indian soldiers he was leading. They were so afraid of
the Gurkhas they dared not stay and fight. But their commander,
Lieutenant Frederick Young, stood his ground. When the
Gurkhas took him prisoner, they were astonished with the reply
he gave when they asked him why he had not also fled:

'I didn't come this far just to run away.'

'We could serve under an officer like you!' they said in return.

And that, according to legend, is how the Gurkhas and the
British came together. It was – as it remains – a relationship
based on mutual respect, a relationship that has endured
through many wars and countless actions since Gurkhas first

fought as members of the British Army in 1815, a relationship that I for one hope will last another two hundred years and more.

There are some others I would also like to thank for their help. First, Lieutenant Colonel Dan Rex MVO for making available his chronology of major Troops in Contact during the siege. In some places, my recollection of events has not quite been the same as this log, but I have chosen to record my memories and I hope he and others will forgive any differences between my account of what happened in Now Zad and what they remember of it. Any mistakes I have made are of course my responsibility.

I must also say a word of thanks to all members of the team who I had the privilege to fight alongside in Now Zad. Without them, without their courage and their determination, it is doubtful I would have survived to tell my story. Some I have mentioned by name, many more I have not. Where I have not mentioned names, this is no reflection on the role those soldiers played but only of the fact that we were not always on the ground together.

For the part of my story where I speak about my childhood and growing up in Nepal, I wish to thank my parents, Duryodhan and Mina Kumari, my sister Gudiya, also my teachers at school and all my family and friends in Khebang village.

Finally, I would like to express my sincere devotion to my wife Sumitra and to my children Alisa and Anish.

Kailash Khebang Limbu
Sir John Moore Barracks, Shorncliffe, Kent
March 2015

1

Death at a Hundred
and Twenty Metres per Second

We were already under attack when I saw something that really frightened me.

In a split second I registered a smoke trail and a loud pshh-hhhhhhhhhhhhhhhhhh as it approached.

What was it? It was death hurtling towards me at a hundred and twenty metres per second.

Aare! RPG!

Flinging myself back, I watched as the fireball flashed over the top of the sangar.

'*Bloody hell*, that was close ... Baren, did you see that?' I shouted. For Gurkhas, this is really bad language, but I was seriously alarmed. Not for myself, you understand. It doesn't feel like that. You don't think about yourself. You are frightened for your men. You are concerned for them, and for their families. If they get hurt, it will be on your watch – even if it isn't your fault.

Baren was busy firing an extended burst from the Browning.

'I saw him! I saw who fired it!' he yelled excitedly, pausing for a second before releasing another salvo.

TAKTAKTAK TAKTAKTAK TAKTAKTAK

With my heart raging in my chest, I followed the tracer with my eye. Baren on the .50-cal machine gun was engaging a doorway about halfway along the alleyway directly in front of our position, no more than 150 metres away. I quickly added to the weight of fire with my rifle. We needed to tell the *jatha* we were onto him.

'OK, keep at it!' I yelled as, scrambling off the platform and back into our sangar position – our 3 metre by 2 metre outpost overlooking the town – I lunged for the field telephone.

'Zero, this is Sangar Three. CONTACT! RPG. Enemy seen in alleyway directly in front. One hundred and fifty metres. Doorway on left.'

'Roger. Looking.'

I slammed the receiver down and, grabbing a UGL (underslung grenade launcher), threw myself out onto the platform in front of the position.

'KEEP ME COVERED!' I yelled as I took aim at the enemy fire position. Not a difficult target so long as I remembered my basic principles of marksmanship.

Taking several deep breaths, I squeezed the trigger. The downside of deploying a UGL was that I had to fire it kneeling and therefore expose the upper part of my body, but it was a risk worth taking. If they were this close, it wouldn't be long before they got lucky. They needed stopping.

An instant later, the target building was enveloped in white smoke. Of course, there was no way of telling whether I actually hit anyone, but if they were in there, their ears would definitely be bleeding.

Half crawling, half running, I threw myself back inside the sangar and picked up the field telephone again.

'Zero, this is Sangar Three. Possible enemy FP engaged with UGL. Continuing to observe.'

'Zero, roger. Well done, Kailash. Good work.'

It was just after 3.15 in the afternoon of 16 July 2006. The first indication of trouble we'd had was when an Afghan National Police patrol got attacked. This was the first patrol to leave the district centre for several days. They'd taken a vehicle and got as far as the old cemetery on the other side of town.

The sound of gunfire in the distance had put us all on maximum alert.

'Looks like the patrol has been ambushed!' exclaimed Rifleman Lal.

'Or it could be them firing,' said Baren.

'Yeah, ANP firing!' agreed Lal. This was an in-joke. It referred to our Afghan allies' tendency to let off rounds randomly, often just for fun as it seemed to us.

'I don't think so,' I said. 'My guess is they've been hit.'

A moment later, we came under attack ourselves. As soon as we realised what was happening, we'd opened up with the .50-cal and the GPMG (General Purpose Machine Gun, or 'jimpy') on our preselected targets – places we'd been contacted from before. With heavy small-arms fire still striking the sangar, Baren on the .50-cal and Lal supporting, and me using both my assault rifle and the jimpy, we fought back, desperate not to let the enemy gain the initiative.

'Anybody see anything?' I demanded.

'Nothing, *guruji*.'

'No, nothing.'

'OK keep it up. Short bursts onto all identified firing positions.'

I took out my binos and began looking and looking. It was the same old story. You're the target of a serious attack and yet you can't see a thing.

The rounds continued to strike the sangar and little puffs of sand filled the air as sandbags were holed, but it was impossible to work out exactly where it was coming from.

It was scary, for sure. But we'd been there long enough and under attack often enough not to seize up like the first time we came under fire this heavy. It was more about your nerves being stretched taut, almost to breaking point, and your main focus is just to stay on top of things. It's hotter than hell itself: you are dripping with sweat as fast as you can replace it with snatches from your water bottle between bursts. The sound is intense and the air is filled with the smell of propellant and burning oil from your ammunition.

Occasionally there'd be a flash of the enemy's tracer, but this wasn't enough to give a definite target indication. So while I scanned and scanned, the *bhai*s continued firing in short bursts at their targets, all of us getting more and more frustrated by the second.

It was at that moment that I'd spotted the RPG – our biggest fear. Fired from a shoulder-mounted launcher, the rocket-propelled grenade was one of the most effective weapons in the enemy's arsenal. For a start, at ranges of less than two hundred metres it is almost impossible to miss your target – so we'd just been very, very lucky. The other thing about an RPG is that all it would take would be for them to land a round on one of our roof supports and that would be end-ex: all our ammunition would go off. Twenty grenades at least, not to mention the two anti-tank weapons we had.

After discharging the grenade launcher, there was no let-up in the weight of fire coming in at us, but for the next several minutes we had no further indication of the enemy on the ground. Suddenly, Lal let out a shout.

'*Guruji!* I can see smoke! Take a look over there!'

He pointed in the direction of Sniper's House.

'Sniper's House!' This small building built on top of a nearby compound about 200 metres away, or a bit less, was an AOI – an Area of Interest – we'd identified in the past few days as a definite enemy-fire position.

'You sure?'

'Yes, *guruji*. Definitely.'

Without bothering to confirm for myself, I grabbed the field telephone again, shouting to Baren at the same time.

'Leave the .50-cal. Get over the other side! . . . Zero, this is Sangar Three. Enemy firing position identified in Sniper's House. Engaging with GPMG and rifles.'

'Zero, roger.'

Unfortunately, Sniper's House was out of arc to the .50-cal. There were sandbags in the way. In fact, our use of the .50-cal in Sangar 3 was severely restricted. Because of the bracket the heavy machine gun was mounted on, you couldn't point it down either. But the reality of our situation was that we really needed to be able to bring it to bear on the alleyway directly below.

On the other hand, Sniper's House was an ideal target for the anti-tank weapon, the ILAW.

Using the radio this time, I called the control tower.

'Zero, this is Sangar Three. Suggest deploy ILAW.'

'Roger. Are you sure?' demanded Mathers *sahib*, the 2 i/c (second-in-command).

'Yes sure.'

'OK, but be careful. Make sure you get maximum covering fire. Also, be advised that Sunray has called for air support.'

'Roger out.'

That was good news, but in the meantime we had to fight back. We mustn't let the enemy gain the initiative.

'Come on, *bhai haru*! We need to keep going! I'm going to fire the ILAW,' I shouted, lifting it out of its box. 'Lal, I need you over here too now. Cover me while I go forward, OK?'

The key thing in all these engagements was not to let the enemy get on top. If we could put Sniper's House out of action, even just for a short time, that would be a big plus. Of course, in doing so I'd have to expose myself again and take the risk. But that's just the way it goes. At least this time I had ear-defenders and knew what to expect, unlike the first time I'd fired it. It was a straightforward target too – just about on the same level as we were.

Lal and Baren both opened up as I scrambled out with the ILAW to where I could get a good shot. As I took aim, I could clearly see a barrel-end poking out of a small hole in the wall of the building I was targeting. That was the *jatha* who was trying to kill me.

BLAM!

There was a huge flash and a cloud of white smoke engulfed the building, giving me a few seconds to scramble back inside the sangar and get out my binos to inspect the damage as it cleared.

YES! Target! The round had left a gaping hole exactly where I'd seen the barrel.

'Zero, this is Sangar Three. TARGET! Sniper's House successfully engaged!'

'Roger. Well done, Kailash.' It was the Officer Commanding's voice this time. 'And by the way, air support in approx fifteen minutes.'

'Roger, out.'

I turned to the two riflemen.

'OK, *bhai haru*, it isn't over yet. We need to concentrate. Baren, you get back onto the .50-cal. Lal, you stay this side with me. Engage all known fire positions but remember your discipline.'

'*Hasur, guruji.*'

Not many minutes later, I was just in the process of fitting a new magazine to my rifle when Baren fell back with a loud cry.

2

Limbuwan

My full name is Kailash Khebang and I am a Limbu. Limbu is my caste, Khebang is my village and Kailash is what people call me. Kailash is also the name of a holy mountain in Tibet. When I was just a few days old, my mother's father measured me with his hand and said I was going to be tall and strong as a mountain.

I was born in 1981 on my family's small farm in Taplejung district in the far east of Nepal. Taplejung lies among the foothills of Mount Kanchenjunga, on the border with India still further east and Tibet to the north. At more than 28,000 feet, Kanchenjunga is the third-highest peak in the world, and from where we lived on the steep slopes of the valley you could see the snows of the Himalayas in the near distance.

We Nepalese are made up of many different castes, or tribes. Apart from Limbus, there are Chetris, Gurungs, Magars, Rais,

Sunwars and Thakurs, plus a few other smaller groups. Broadly you can divide us into highlanders and lowlanders – the Limbus, of course, are highlanders. And it is from the hill-dwelling castes that traditionally the Gurkhas have been recruited – although this rule is no longer hard and fast.

The Limbus live not just in the eastern part of Nepal but also in Sikkim, and the Darjeeling area of West Bengal (both part of India) and Bhutan, which is autonomous. Collectively, this is known as Limbuwan, and there are thought to be around three quarters of a million of us; so, though not as numerous as the Gurungs, we are still quite a large group.

Just like each of the other castes, we have our own language, and within this several distinct dialects, although almost everyone nowadays speaks Gorkhali as well. Gorkhali, also known as Nepali, is the main language of the whole country. English is quite widely spoken too – even in Khebang village, it is taught from year 5 onwards – but during my earliest years I spoke only in dialect, and it wasn't until I began school that I learned Nepali. Today I don't get much opportunity to speak *yakthungba bahsa*, as we call our language, and I am a bit rusty. But when I leave the Army and return to my village, as I fully intend, I look forward to taking it up again properly.

Originally, the Limbu people came to Nepal from Tibet. In our own language we refer to ourselves as *yakthumba*, which translates as 'yak herders'. There are no yaks in Nepal, so this shows that our ancestors came from the Tibetan plateau. Yet while Tibetans are almost all Buddhists, and while there are some Limbus who are Buddhist, my family follows the ancient Kirat religion. Unlike Tibetans, we believe in a god whom we call Bhagawan.

Until the age of seven, I lived with my parents in my paternal grandfather's house, which is situated at the upper end of Khebang village. These days my aunt and uncle and several cousins still live there, as my grandfather and grandmother have both passed away. It is a traditional house built with mud walls and a wooden veranda running round the first floor, and a single attic room in the roof. Like most of the other houses in the village, the outside is painted – in this case brown at the bottom and cream above, with the veranda painted blue. Overall, the effect is very colourful. But while today the roof is of corrugated iron, when I was younger it was thatched with straw. We replaced the roof with tin at my expense when I went home on my first leave as a Gurkha. I felt very proud to be able to repay my grandfather for all his kindness to me in this way. Thatch may look better, but the old style of roof has to be changed every two years – a very big and dirty job. Also, thatch is a fire hazard, so tin is much preferred.

Inside the house were six rooms, one large and two small ones on each floor. I suppose the ground-floor area was about the same size as a double garage, so it was a bit above average compared with other houses in our district. This was just as well because, amazing as it may seem, it was home to more than thirty people in total! My father had several brothers and they all stayed with us, along with their wives and children, so that these kids could go to school locally. As a result, my grandmother spent her whole life cooking vast amounts of food. I remember that she had three enormous pots – one for *bhaat* (rice), one for *makai* (maize) and one for *dhal* (lentils). We didn't eat meat very often, but sometimes – maybe once a month, or if guests came – we would kill an animal and have a proper feast.

Looking back on my childhood, I see that it was something quite remarkable in this day and age. We had no electricity and hence no TV or telephones or household appliances. And because the nearest motorable road was so far away, I was fifteen before I saw my first car. It's different today, as there are several generators in the area, and the school and several other buildings have light. Some families even have satellite television. Also, a lot of people now have mobile phones, though there are still no iPods or computers. But during my childhood we had none of these things and my life was all about playing – and fighting – with other children as we accompanied our elders to the fields. It was a really healthy outdoor life out in the clean mountain air. We didn't lack for entertainment, as there were lots of religious festivals and dances and picnics in the forest, and in the evening stories about ghosts and witches and the glorious deeds of our ancestors.

One of my favourite stories as a very young boy was about how our family came to Khebang. There were two ladies from Lhasa, the capital of Tibet, who travelled together on pilgrimage to a place called Kashi near Benares, the holy city of India. One of the ladies got married there and stayed. The other did not and returned to Tibet. The one who stayed had a son, and it was he who eventually came to our district in Nepal. On arrival, he learned that there were two rajas who ruled the place between them. One was a good raja, generous to his people and just. The other was a bad raja, who thought only of himself and how much money he could extort from the people. My family's forefather made an alliance with the good raja and, taking a bow and arrow, he went into battle and shot the bad raja. As a result, the good raja rewarded him with a lot of land. To celebrate their victory, this raja called the best ladies to his palace and offered our forefather the choice of any one of them. At that point, my ancestor tried to refuse, and it was only when the raja insisted that he reluctantly made his choice. Unfortunately, it turned out that he had chosen the raja's own brother's wife. But the raja gave this lady to him anyway. After that, our forefather and his descendants ruled the family lands as *subba*, one who is the next rank below raja in authority.

The place where my ancestor settled was given the name *Kingba*, a word that comes from the Limbu word for 'ambitious', in recognition of our forefather's ambition. You could say it's a characteristic I have inherited myself.

The village of Khebang lies more than a day's trek from the nearest road, even if you are very fit. If you are not so fit, the journey can take two or even three days. It is about the same distance to Tibet, which we call Bothe, although this track is very difficult and only open at certain times of year because of the snow and danger from avalanches and rockfalls. There is also a track that leads to the Indian border about one day's walk away. This one is much easier and a lot of people use it to get to Sikkim, where they take jobs for six months of the year. Part of that time they spend harvesting medicinal plants, such as the *alchi* grass, which grows in the area and fetches a very good price.

There are several other villages in the same valley as Khebang. The closest of these, called Surukim, is right opposite and it takes only twenty minutes to walk there, except that to do so you have to use a narrow rope bridge which has a drop of at least 400 metres. This bridge is really flimsy and it often has to be repaired after heavy rain. Even when it is in a good state, it sways a lot as you go over and every so often there are accidents. I remember one time when I was young there was a mother crossing with her baby in a basket on her back. The bridge moved so violently that, tragically, the baby fell out. There was no chance of saving it. Even if by some miracle a person could survive the fall, the torrent in the river below is so strong that you would be swept away and drowned instantly.

Most of my earliest memories involve fighting, which I really enjoyed. I particularly remember one night when I was about three or four. At that time, as the youngest children in the house, I and my aunt Radika, who was only a few years older than me, had the privilege of sleeping with our grandparents in their warm bed. The problem was that she always got to sleep in between them – which was, of course, the warmest place of all. So one night, I woke up and started pulling Radika out of bed with the idea of taking her place. I thought that because my grandmother had given her some *raksi* (a traditional drink made from fermented rice, and quite alcoholic) before she went to bed, she would not wake up. But actually she did and I discovered then what a good fighter she was.

It was in fact my grandmother who did not wake up, as she herself was completely drunk. Luckily, our grandfather took my side and he let me move in and made my aunt sleep on the outside. As a result, Radika and I became sworn enemies.

Like I say, my grandmother was completely drunk – as often happened. I remember one time she drank so much that when she was serving our food, she dropped it on the floor – a huge pot of *dhal*. There was a shocked silence as we all turned to look at my grandfather. He was very strict and we were all waiting for the explosion. I was afraid he was going to chase my grandmother out of the house. But he just laughed and told us to clear up the mess. The truth was, he really loved his wife, and even when she was like this, he forgave her.

It may seem surprising to say that my grandmother always gave us children alcohol at night time, but it is true.

'This will help you sleep,' she used to say, although I never liked the stuff. Radika, on the other hand, developed a taste for it and I remember once when she became very drunk during daytime. She was about nine years old, and for no reason that I could tell she came up and slapped me in the face.

'What did you do that for?' I demanded.

'Because you're a pig!' she screamed.

I hit her straight away, and we had another big fight that left her in tears. Luckily for both of us, everyone else was outside working in the fields, so nobody saw.

My father too was a big drinker. Unlike my grandfather, who was very even-tempered, Dad had an extremely aggressive side to him. It never lasted and most of the time he was kind and warmhearted and took really good care of his family. But when he was drunk, he got angry very easily, and when this happened he would chase after me, stumbling and shouting.

'Come to me you little *jatha*! I'll show you who's boss round here!'

That was one of the reasons I became such a good runner. I knew that if he ever caught up with me, he'd thrash me hard. I suppose it is also one reason why I personally never touch alcohol. I am afraid that if I did, I might become one of the bad guys myself. Luckily for me, when I was in Class Seven my dad went to work in the Gulf States for two years. A lot of Nepalese men do this, as the money is quite good, though in my father's case he didn't do very well out of it. He said it was hard work for not much reward.

My grandfather was a very impressive man and highly respected in our community. For a short time he had served as a Gurkha in the British Army in India, around the time of Partition in 1947. Unfortunately his military career was cut short by the death of his father, as he had to return home to look after his family. He was also a very religious man, very pure in his habits, and, unlike my grandmother and father, never touched alcohol. It was a rule that no one ever drank in his presence.

In a lot of ways, I grew up closer to my grandfather than to my father, and I shall never forget his example. Every morning he would get up early and walk the 200 metres to the spring where we used to get our water. There, after washing, he would pray for a while before coming back to the house and praying some more at the little shrine he kept in one corner of the room next to my parents'. This was very simple, with just a small altar, a picture of the god and, hanging on the wall, a special kukri.

During his prayers, my grandfather would light a small fire and burn a mixture of aromatic leaves and sit cross-legged on the floor, where he would recite the names of the saints and all our family members, including our ancestors. I can hear him now, softly chanting while the rest of the house slept.

Bhagawan, Bhagawan, Bhagawan . . .

Bishnu, Bishnu, Bishnu . . .

Patibharai Devi, Patibharai Devi, Patibharai Devi . . .

Mohadeb Bhagawan, Mohadeb Bhagawan, Mohadeb Bhagawan . . .

It was very soothing to listen to.

My grandfather always kept this part of the house very tidy, and once every two weeks, without fail, on the day of the full moon and on the day of the new moon, he used to sweep it carefully with a cowpat. This may sound strange, but dried dung works very effectively as a brush.

The special kukri – to which we all used to pray on certain occasions – was only ever taken down from the wall once a year for the purpose of sacrificing an animal, usually a goat. Once the blade was drawn, we believed that it could not be returned to its scabbard until it had tasted blood.

I am not sure how common this practice of worshipping the kukri is among the other castes, but among Limbus it is very strong. First my grandfather would light some special herbs and start chanting. After a while, when the spirit of the god was inside him, he would start to shake. At that point, he would take the weapon and withdraw the blade and hand it to the person chosen to actually kill the animal. When I was about ten or eleven years old, I remember, he handed it to me. I felt very proud, though also quite nervous. It is considered very unlucky if the person doing the sacrifice cannot do so with a single stroke.

Happily I succeeded, and in fact it is not difficult for someone used to handling a kukri – as any hill boy is from a very early age. But if you are not skilled and you don't know what you are doing, they are not very effective. Most of the weight of the blade is at the tip end, so you need to keep your wrist straight.

As everyone knows, the kukri blade is curved and at its thinnest where it tapers and joins the handle. With most, there is also a notch, called a *kaudi*, just in front of the handle. This is to stop the blood running onto your hand and making it slippery to hold.

Kukris come in many different shapes and sizes. The *sirupathi* blade used by Limbus is longer and thinner than the blade you see in other parts of the country. Also, we Limbus tend to decorate both the blades and the handles more than people in other parts of Nepal. The one in my grandfather's house was particularly ornate. However, although the kukri is very important in our culture as a symbol of power and as a weapon of war, it is also a very practical tool. Besides being used for sacrifices, they have more ordinary uses such as in harvesting crops, felling trees, chopping firewood, skinning animals, and even opening bottles.

After the kukri, the most important things my grandfather kept in his shrine were some precious stones that had been found on our land. When I say they were precious, I don't mean they were valuable like jewels, but that they had special powers. The most important of them was the *mothi* stone from a snake. There are certain snakes in the Himalayas which are believed to possess magical abilities. These snakes are blind by day but, using *mothi*, are able to generate light from inside themselves at night and so to see in the dark. We believe that if you can catch one of the snakes and extract the *mothi* stone from it, you will possess something of great power. One day when I was very young, an Indian Nagaman – that is to say, someone with knowledge of snakes – came to our village. It seems he had some supernatural indication of one of these special snakes living near our house. Eventually he succeeded in capturing it and was able to extract the *mothi* stone from its mouth. He then sold it to my grandfather for an enormous sum of money – something like forty thousand rupees, which in those days was easily enough to buy a field or to build a house such as ours. Yet although this sounds like a crazy amount, the *mothi* stone brings such good fortune and prosperity to the one who possesses it, my grandfather explained that it was not too high a price to pay. You could say it is just coincidence based on superstition, but looking back on his life – he died a few years ago at the time of writing – I have to say that I cannot disagree with him. We certainly did prosper, and throughout my childhood the harvests were good and the animals stayed healthy and productive.

As a result of this prosperity, my grandfather was able to use his wealth to benefit others in the community. He built a small hostel for the poor and gave money to help build the school in our village. This was a fine two-storey building about half an hour's walk downhill from the house, very simple, and painted colourfully in blue and white. He also paid for better roads in our area (though of course I don't mean motorable roads) and for the construction of a pipeline to bring water to people who lived far from the nearest stream.

My grandfather also used to say that another reason for his success in life was the jackal horns that he had obtained when younger. Like the *mothi* stone, these also have special powers. They came from a kind of jackal found in the Himalayas which has horns not on the front, but on the back of its head. Now the peculiar thing about these horns is that they only appear when the jackal is howling. If you see one of these animals when it is just roaming in the daytime, they are not visible.

It was late one night when he was walking home from the fields along a road that took him past a graveyard that my grandfather had his opportunity. From a long distance away, he could hear some wild animals howling in the moonlight. Sure enough, when he got close to the graveyard, he saw three jackals sitting there, their heads upturned to the moon. Keeping as quiet as he could, my grandfather crept behind them and when he had got into a good position, hurled his stick with all his strength. With a great yelp, all three ran off but, just as he'd hoped, the horns of one had fallen off and he picked them up and took them home. My grandfather told me that if ever I had the chance, I should try to get hold of some jackal horns for myself. Unfortunately, I have not been lucky enough so far.

Of course, not all the wildlife in our area possessed magical powers, but there were some that were also quite rare. From time to time, people reported bears in the jungle nearby, and every so often a tiger would appear. I've never actually seen a bear, but I did see several tigers when I was young. Because I was armed with my kukri, I wasn't too scared. In fact I remember on one occasion how, when I saw one, I picked up a stone and threw it at the tiger. It turned and ran away.

All in all, mine was a happy childhood. I lived the typical life of a hill boy, little different from that of my ancestors for hundreds of years, if not a thousand and more. It was a simple life and in some respects also quite hard. From a very early age, I had to help out on the family farm. We grew mainly rice and maize, but also some wheat and potatoes, as well as fodder for the cattle. Together with the other children, I had to cut and collect firewood and to help at harvest time and plough the fields afterwards. I had to take the bullocks into the jungle to forage and to carry baskets of hay for them home on my back. I spent hours up to my knees in water in the rice paddies and many more bent over repairing the earth mounds that ran round the sides to keep the water from running away. But the worst time was in winter, when the cold came. When it gets into your bones as it does when the only heat you have is a small open fire in the house, it is almost impossible to get warm again. Yet the difficulties we experienced were eased by the fact that we bore them all together as a family – a fact that has helped me a lot in later life. As a Gurkha, you do the same. When we face hardship, we do not face it just as one person, but as a member of a group – a section, a platoon, a company, a battalion, and finally a whole brigade. You are never alone. In fact you could say that to be a Gurkha is to be a member of one very big family, of which your section is the closest part.

3

Into Now Zad

I'll never forget the flight into Now Zad, and nor will anyone else who was on that helicopter.

'Ready, *guruji haru*? Ready, *bhai haru*?' It's too loud inside a Chinook to be heard, but they each got my meaning. One by one, my seven brothers, the seven men under my command, nodded as I looked into their eyes.

'Ready, *guruji*,' they mouthed in reply, each in turn. 'Yes, Kailash *bhai*. Ready.' Seven times.

Even at times of maximum stress, we Gurkhas remember our manners. *Bhai* means 'younger brother'. *Guruji* means, literally, 'honourable teacher'. It is used by juniors towards their seniors. But it is also used by soldiers senior in rank towards someone lower in rank if the junior person joined up before you. Rank does not confer more honour than age.

Haru, by the way, just signifies more than one.

We had been airborne since 1300 local time – just about fifteen minutes by now, so we were more than two thirds of the 40 miles to the HLS, the Helicopter Landing Site – and I needed to be sure everyone was ready. The thing is, when you are on the journey out to an operation, you are keyed up to the maximum. That doesn't have to be said. But your mind can wander. You start thinking about home, about your family and loved ones. In my own case, I was thinking about Anish, my son born just two weeks earlier. I wondered whether I was ever going to see him again. I realised I might not.

But there comes a moment when you need to focus. You have to snap out of your thoughts about home and about what might happen. And we had reached that moment. The point when we needed to be fully alert to the task in hand, when we needed to let go of those warm thoughts, and the nervous thoughts too. Because when we got there, we had just one minute. The Chinook was carrying twenty-seven men with full kit and we were packed tight. We had a lot of gear with us, but only one minute. Could we do it?

Because at sixty seconds, the pilot was going to firewall the throttle and head for home.

Sixty seconds. Not sixty-one. Sixty seconds for all us of us to get out with every item we needed for a full-scale operation, and for the men we were relieving to get on board. That isn't long when you've got as much stuff with you as we were carrying then.

It would not matter if you had to go back to get something. It wouldn't matter if your bergen – your rucksack – got stuck, maybe snagged on one of the fittings on the floor. At sixty-one seconds you would be on your way back to Bastion. At sixty-one seconds, if you're not off the helicopter you'll have let everyone down. They were relying on you to play your part, and now you have let them down, your younger brothers and your honourable teachers.

It would not matter if you were standing at the edge of the ramp, just about to jump. At sixty-one seconds, you would have to jump thirty feet. If not fifty, or even a hundred.

So I had to be sure my *bhai*s and *guruji*s were fully focused and not thinking about the possibility of going back in a box or, worse, with some of their body parts missing. And yes, I could see now that they were ready, as ready as it was possible to be.

Two days back we'd practised on the ground. We'd practised the exit, so everyone knew exactly what to do the moment we touched down, and what to do next. Basically, you had to grab your weapons and a bergen – it didn't matter whose – and just go for it. Down the ramp, 20-metre dash and hit the deck, take up firing position, observe. Move only when instructed to do so. Then patrol the 800 metres to the safe house, bearing in mind we could be being engaged from the moment the helicopter appeared in the sky.

Satisfied that the *bhai*s were all set, I ran through different scenarios in my head. How precisely I was going to get out, which of the *bhai*s was to go where when we were on the ground, what kit I was going to need to hand. My personal weapon, obviously. But binoculars, map, compass, chinagraph too. And having done this, I began to ask myself the questions all commanders ask themselves on the way into an operation. Did we have enough ammunition? How long would it last if there was a big contact on landing? What about water? Temperatures at this time of year regularly hit 50 degrees celsius. What about food? How many days could we go if we found ourselves cut off and no resupp could get in? Would we be able to buy some food locally? How long before we would need to go looking for it? And what about purification tablets? Yes, I had mine. And yes, I had checked the *bhais'* kit: they all had plenty. OK, so what happens if we're contacted on landing? Or ambushed on our way to the safe house? And what was I going to do if my PRR – my Personal Radio Relay – failed? In answer to my own questions, first I ran over all the IAs in my mind – all the immediate actions – and then all the SOPs – the standard operating procedures – for each of the different possible scenarios. What I would do if separated from the rest of the platoon, for example.

Kit, procedures, drills. There was plenty to think about. No room for being scared, that's for sure. A bit anxious for the *gurujis* and *bhais* under my command, maybe. For myself, no.

I glanced at my watch. Five minutes more, maximum. Five minutes and then sixty seconds.

But I couldn't stop asking questions. What if one of the vehicles waiting for us was hit? What if the vehicles weren't waiting at all? What if one of my riflemen got hit? The possibilities were endless. One thing I didn't have to worry about, though, was the loyalty of my men.

I glanced once more at each of them. There was Gaj, who we all called Gaaz, nineteen years old and the youngest and best of them all. Tough, totally dependable, totally committed, with a big sense of humour. He caught my eye and we both smiled. Then there was Lance Corporal Shree, my section 2 i/c, an experienced soldier and solid as they come. There was Nagen, only a bit older than Gaaz and reliable and solid as a mountain. Then Amrit – a real hard worker and totally straight-forward. There was Nani, our WMIK driver. A WMIK (it stands for Weapons Mount Installation Kit) is basically an armoured Land Rover – not the quickest of vehicles at the best of times, and not good at all for surviving an IED (an impro-vised explosive device, i.e. a remotely triggered mine), but great for getting round the desert in. I never understood how he did it, but luckily Nani seemed to be able to get a WMIK to go 20 per cent faster than anyone else. He was three years senior to me, although junior in rank, so I called him *guruji*. Next to him was Nabin, wiry and fit as anything, another young rifleman who had joined around the same time as Gaaz. At the end sat Ambika. We called him the Smiley Man – but you wouldn't want to get in a fight with him.

They were a great bunch, a great team. The younger ones would need some looking after, but, as some officer *sahib* once said, the Gurkha is a pack animal. We work together and fight together as a team. Everyone helps everyone else: that's how we operate. We'd be fine just so long as we remembered what we'd been taught.

Suddenly, I felt the helicopter start to descend. Now began the most dangerous part of the flight. It was nerve-racking, I have to admit. We knew the enemy had brought down a Chinook carrying a US Navy SEAL team with an RPG the year before. And what they'd done once they could do again. You're big and not very fast. Not so difficult if the enemy can get in range. That's why we flew high to begin with and why, now we were descending, we had to manoeuvre constantly. Banking first left then right, we dropped steeply down. Like this you make it as hard for the enemy as possible.

We were a platoon plus of the 2nd Battalion of the Royal Gurkha Regiment on our way to conduct a Relief in Place of a safe house that 10 Platoon had been holding for the past three weeks. This was an operation in support of the 3 PARA Battlegroup that had been deployed to counter the Taliban insurgency in Helmand province. We were bringing enough supplies with us to last a week. Ten days at a stretch, though we were told we could be relieved within seventy-two hours if all went well, so it was unlikely to be a big deal. Our main job, it had been explained to us, was the battle for hearts and minds – although to judge by 10 Platoon's experience, there was a good chance we were going to find ourselves in a real battle. We'd heard they had been ambushed while out on patrol and were lucky not to take any casualties.

And to tell you the truth, we were quite looking forward to it. Since late April, we had been providing close defence for Camp Bastion, the British battlefield headquarters in Helmand. During that time, the lads from 48 Engineer Squadron had improved the place a lot, but conditions remained quite tough, as these were still early days. There was no air conditioning at that point, and by day it was hot enough to fry an egg in a mess tin that had been left out in the sun. Then there was the fine powder of the desert dust. Every time you moved, a little cloud of it would form. When you went on patrol you'd come back caked in it. Dust, dust everywhere. Dust in your eyes, dust in your ears, and dust under your foreskin if you weren't careful. But apart from everyone's personal battle with the elements, there hadn't been much to do. Day patrols, night patrols, ambush patrols, vehicle checkpoints, that sort of thing. We'd seen a few cars blown up, but we hadn't come under fire ourselves, so we were keen to see a bit of action. After all, that's what we'd joined up for.

As we swooped lower, time seemed to slow down. It goes like that when you're pumped up. It's strange, though. I hardly even knew I was feeling a bit queasy from all the manoeuvring of the chopper, but thinking back, I realise I was. It's different what you notice depending on your state of mind. You might think that when time seems to move more slowly you'd notice everything around you. It's not like that, I found. I wasn't focused on myself at all, but entirely alert to what the next few minutes would bring.

There was a sudden change of engine note.

'GOGGLES!' I shouted, and looked round to make sure everyone had them pulled down.

This was it! The door was already open. I began to look for the ground. But it was hopeless. All you could see was the swirling dust. Dust and more damned dust, billowing up all around us, stirred into angry life by the rotor blades.

As soon as we felt the Chinook touching down, the *bhais* nearest the exit got moving. In a hurry, but not in a panic. Out they went. Our bergens weighed 30 kilos each and we had another 15 kilos strapped to our bodies – ammunition, water, rations, mess tin, field dressings. Weapons were on top of that. In my own case, I had my SA80 personal weapon plus UGL grenade launcher, radio, binos, night-vision sight, tactical aide memoire. In all, probably 50 kilos. Some of the *bhais* and *guru-jis* had still more than that: between us we were carrying a section GPMG (7.62 calibre General Purpose Machine Gun), an LSW (the bipod-mounted version of the SA80 5.65 calibre rifle), a 51 mm mortar and two ILAWs (Interim Light Anti-Tank Weapon) – not to mention our kukris.

No Gurkha is ever without his kukri.

But you don't register the weight in a situation like this. You just pick it up and run.

As we heaved our gear out of the chopper, I hardly noticed the platoon we were relieving standing ready to board as soon as we were clear. I was focused entirely on the job in hand and launched myself into the swirling dust cloud, mouth tight shut. Thank God for those goggles.

We fanned out, just as we had practised. My section was out first and we were to go left. Fifteen, twenty paces then down. Already the Chinook was getting airborne again, and the dust storm intensified so we were running blind. It was like a blizzard in the mountains, only worse, because when it got into your mouth and nose and ears, it didn't dissolve like snow does. I threw myself down and waited.

No sooner had the sound of the heli started to fade than I heard machine-gun fire.

Aayo! We were being engaged.

But where from?

First you hear the TAK TAK TAK of the rounds as they fly past, then the TUM TUM TUM of the report.

'CONTACT WAIT OUT!' I screamed into the PRR.

If you hear the rounds in the air before you hear the sound of them being fired, you can be fairly certain they're being fired at you.

TAK TAK TAK TAK TAK. TUM TUM TUM TUM TUM.

Aare jatha! But where was it coming from?

'Anybody see anything?' I shouted.

'*Kahi pani chaina!* Can't see anything at all,' someone yelled.

'Can I fire?' someone else shouted.

'Not until you can see something definite!' I shouted back.

'Zero, this is Two One Charlie.' I steadied my voice as I spoke into the PRR. 'Contact! Small-arms fire. Position unknown. Looking.'

'Zero, roger. We're in contact too. Keep observing.'

Major Rex's voice was calm, though I could hear shouts coming from his position.

The enemy couldn't see anything either of course, because the dust hadn't settled yet. But they knew we were in there somewhere and the rounds kept coming.

Slowly the air started to clear. As it did so, the fire intensified. But it was still completely impossible to work out where the enemy position was. This was terrible. My heart was raging in my chest. Every so often I was popping my head up and looking round 360 degrees. But they were too well concealed. The only clue was the sound of the rounds flying towards us.

And it was at this moment that I learned the hardest thing in any combat situation. The hardest thing is to know where you are being engaged from. It's the hardest thing, and also the most frustrating. Because if you can't see the enemy, you can't engage him. It's no good just shooting back blindly. You waste ammunition and have a big chance of blue on blue contact. And yet your whole body, your whole mind, is screaming at you to hit back. You want to see the *jatha haru*. You want to take the fight to them. You want to kill them.

Here I should say that Gurkhas do not like swearing too much, and when we do, it is a matter of embarrassment. Also, the words will seem strange to English readers – *jatha*, which we use when a British squaddie might say 'fu**ers', actually means 'pubic hair', which, for us, is not so rude.

But you can't hit back at the *jatha* because you don't know where they are.

So I was lying there in the prone position, using my bergen for cover, trying hard to work out where the fire was coming from – looking for any clue. The sight of tracer. Muzzle flash. Smoke from a barrel. Movement. Any clue at all. I suppose that if I'd been frightened, I'd have felt it then. But I didn't feel any fear. Just excitement. Real excitement. This was my first-ever contact and I desperately wanted to fight, to take them on. So all I was thinking was: Where are they? Who are they? What are they wearing? What kind of weapons do they have?

I was just totally focused on returning fire.

At the same time, I was shouting to the *bhai*s and *guruji*s.

'Keep down! OBSERVE! . . . Use your bergen for cover! . . . Hold fire unless you get a PID [positive identification].'

I could feel the *bhai*s' frustration. Just like me, they were desperate to hit back. They too were coiled like springs. But they remembered their discipline and there was no panic. Of course not. We are Gurkhas. This is what we are trained for. This is what we are bred to do.

After two or three minutes of enforced inaction, I became aware of answering fire coming from another position, up on the high ground nearby. That must be ANP Hill. It was a mound about 150 metres high that we'd been briefed beforehand was held by ISAF – friendly forces – who were to provide fire support for us. So that was a big plus, but I still couldn't see what they were firing at. You might think that you'd be able to see their tracer, but because it was daytime, that was impossible. It's extremely difficult to see tracer by day unless you're looking straight at it. And if you're looking straight at it, obviously you need to get your head down, because it's you it's aimed at.

As I lay there, I took out my map to orientate myself. I was expecting orders any moment, but in the meantime I would try to get a grip on our surroundings. The other section was no more than 30 or 40 metres distant, but they were partially out of sight, as there was some dead ground in-between our positions. Up ahead, as expected, there were the two WMIKs, not more than 20 metres away, engines running. They were there to transport the gear. Inside, they had a crew of just two, the driver and a commander. That meant there was no gunner to fire the top cover. Those *bhais* and *gurujis* were in the Chinook on their way back to Bastion.

There was also a quad bike with a trailer. I could see its driver was on the ground taking cover next to it.

I made a quick appreciation. If we could get someone up onto the nearest WMIK, he could get a much better view and also make use of its .50-cal heavy machine gun. The only problem with this was that he would be very vulnerable, as there was no protection.

I shouted to my men.

'*Guruji haru! Bhai haru!* Over here! On me now!'

I got up, grabbed my bergen and made a dash for the vehicle and the *bhais* and *gurujis* followed. They yelled at me as we ran.

'Where are they? Where are they?'

'Can you see them, *guruji*?'

'Can we fire, *guruji*?'

'Shall I set up the jimpy now, *guruji*?'

They were all pumped up and aching to return fire, but still I had to tell them no.

Instead I made them take cover either side of the vehicle with me while I put one man on top cover.

'Gaaz,' I said. 'Get up there and take control of that Browning.'

'Yes, *guruji*.'

I felt really nervous watching him climb onto the vehicle. If he was hit, it would be my fault, but I felt I had to take the risk. I told him he wasn't to fire until I gave him the order. It was vital we followed the Rules of Engagement. Besides, the last thing I wanted was blue on blue contact. The .50-cal is a serious weapon.

'And Nagen, I want you to get the ILAW out and make ready.'

He nodded acknowledgement.

'Yes, *guruji*.'

If we could only spot the enemy position I'd get Nagen to drop a round on it. Gaaz could take care of any runners.

Meanwhile, the enemy fire was still coming at us.

TAK TAK TAK TAK TAK TAK. TUM TUM TUM TUM TUM TUM.

It seemed like there were at least two separate weapons to judge by the weight of fire, but for now there was nothing we could do.

I pulled out my map again. With ANP Hill on our right, Now Zad town and the safe house we were to occupy were directly ahead of us. It was just as I expected. The pilot had landed spot on. The only thing that hadn't gone quite according to plan was the fact that he had deposited us bang on top of a hornets' nest. Right now it looked like we were going to have to fight every step of the 800 metres between the HLS and our objective.

Now Zad is the name of both a town and its surrounding district. Situated in Helmand province, the population was around ten thousand, we'd been told, and that looked about right, judging by what I could see of it in the near distance.

Between the HLS and the town itself, there were quite a few buildings lying on our route, and I wondered if the enemy was engaging us from inside one of these. But then, looking towards them and up to ANP Hill, although it was impossible to be sure, I began to get the idea that the section occupying ANP Hill was firing down not at the buildings themselves but onto the open ground between them and the high ground. That would mean the enemy position was at something like two o'clock of our route to the police compound.

So now I was using the sight on my rifle to try to see if the enemy could have dug a trench somewhere, and I told Gaaz up on the WMIK to do the same.

'Reference buildings directly ahead. Go right. Open ground. Can you see anything? Anything at all?' I shouted up to him.

The .50-cal's sight is no better than the sight on an SA80, but he had a better view because he was higher up.

'Nothing, *guruji*. Can't see a thing. But can I shoot? Just a few rounds, *guruji*? To show them we mean business.'

It was massively tempting to say yes. It's always tempting to lash out when you're under fire. It must have been ten minutes since we'd landed now and the enemy was continuing to put up a non-stop hail of bullets. It was lucky no one had been hit. But

I knew that if Gaaz opened up with the .50-cal, we'd lose all possibility of picking up clues. We'd also be wasting ammo we might need later.

'No,' I said. 'Not until we're sure.'

I was gathering my thoughts to send a sitrep, a situation report, to Rex *sahib*, the OC, when suddenly it dawned on me that it had all gone quiet. The gunfire had stopped. Why? I didn't know. Maybe they got hit by fire from ISAF up on ANP Hill. Maybe they were relocating. Maybe they thought they'd done all they could for now, and if they stayed longer they would be putting themselves in danger.

Well, they had that bit right. As soon as we'd got onto them, the .50-cal and the ILAW between them would have wiped out just about any kind of defensive position short of a nuclear bunker. That or the mud-brick wall of some of the larger Afghan houses.

So now the question was, were they going to engage us from somewhere else? We waited, still looking, everyone trying desperately to see any movement there might be. Then after a few moments of quiet, together with Corporal Ramesh the acting platoon sergeant, and Corporal Santos, the other section commander, I received the order over the radio to RV (rendezvous) with the platoon commander, Lieutenant Mathers. He'd moved up so that he was only about 30 metres away from my position. Leaving my kit where it was, I made my way over, moving tactically. Running a few steps, I threw myself down, observed, crawled, got up, ran, and dropped down again in a series of short bursts to cover the distance. There was no question of just heading over, as there was no cover anywhere. You had to hug the ground as much as possible.

Mathers *sahib* gave us a QBO, a Quick Battle Order. We needed to be ready to move on his signal, so we should get our bergens on the vehicles right away and prepare to patrol our way in: full fighting patrol, that is. That meant tactical movement the whole way, with the vehicles providing top cover.

I made my way back to my section, gave them their orders and we threw our kit into the back of the vehicles. The trouble was, there wasn't room for all of it. Maybe if we took it all off and repacked it more carefully, but there wasn't time for that. We were too good a target to be standing up and messing about with kit. We got a couple more bergens onto the trailer behind the quad bike, though that still left two of the *bhai*s carrying theirs, which wasn't ideal for them. But at least their stuff could give them some protection if we came under fire again.

On hearing the command to move, I signalled to the *bhai*s and *guruji*s that we should start patrolling, four to the left, three to the right of the vehicle, Gaaz still on top, manning the .50-cal. The other section spread out round the other WMIK, with the command group and the quad bike slightly behind.

Although the firing had stopped, after an arrival like that you're still on maximum alert. You're looking out all the time for the smallest sign of the enemy. More than anything else, you want to hit the *jatha* back.

'Make sure you still do a three-sixty lookout,' I told the *bhai*s, not that it was necessary – they were already doing so, just as they'd been trained. But command and control in a battle situation is often as much about reassurance as it is about coming up with brilliant ideas. You need to reassure the *bhai*s and *guruji*s under your command that you are in charge of the situation – even when you're not.

Slowly but steadily, we made our way towards the town, ready to drop down at the first sign of trouble. There was still no cover whatsoever. The ground was completely flat, with nothing bigger than a few rocks strewn here and there. But mostly it was just compacted sand. It was like this all round, except that far up ahead, on the other side of the town, there were mountains. Mountains to remind us of home.

As we approached the outskirts of Now Zad, we continued to move slowly and cautiously. I fully expected to be engaged again – as did the OC, who kept reminding us over the radio that the enemy were out there and it was only a matter of time.

There began to be a few buildings skirting the road, and it was these I was watching, watching. This was a point of serious risk of ambush. But all was quiet. There was just the sound of our vehicles and, in the distance, the occasional hooting of a car horn, or the tinny toot of a motorbike's. As we continued, the number of buildings to the left and right of us increased, and now we were being channelled up a narrow alleyway between houses. These were low, mud-brick and mostly with open doors and windowless.

Aayo! This was serious grenade territory. There could be enemy inside ready just to lob one out at us as we went past. In a built-up area, that's always going to be a serious worry. I told the *bhai*s to be extra careful, to scan every door, every window and every compound we passed.

'If you see anything suspicious, immediate action is get down and cover with your weapon.'

Altogether, it took maybe about half an hour to cover the 800 metres of ground from where we'd first been engaged to our present position. But now that we were getting inside the town proper, we couldn't be far from our objective. I looked up and suddenly saw a sangar position on top of a wall. This must be it! We'd been told the police station was set in a compound about 200 metres square with sangars in each corner. As we came up to it, I saw the nearest one was occupied by two British soldiers providing cover. Signallers, both.

We reached a T-junction and turned left along the perimeter wall. Up ahead, I could see the main street running through the town, a road in quite a good state. There were one or two vehicles and a lot of people moving along it, together with loads of small motorbikes weaving in and out of the crowds. I noticed there were a lot of shops, all still open with people going in and out, buying and selling. I say people – I mean men and boys mostly. Few women, and those women that were there walked a few steps behind their male relatives. As for the shops themselves, they were a bit like the shops we have back in Nepal. A single room with a roll-down metal door. There was a display at the front of fruit and vegetables or whatever it was the shop sold, and the shopkeeper sitting there, talking with passers-by or smoking. Strangely, they didn't react much to the sight of us and just shot a few sly glances in our direction. But there were some children in the street too, kicking a plastic ball around. As we came towards them, they stopped their game and stared at us like we'd landed from the moon.

It was like two different worlds, side by side. For them, normal life. For us, the threat of enemy action at any moment.

But here we were now. This had to be the main entrance – a flimsy metal gate pushed open and a compound inside. This was to be our home for the next few days – or maybe for ever, if it was here we were going to die.

4

The DC

We walked up to the gate and the vehicles drove inside and parked, with us following. We'd got there with no further engagement after that first attack, but we still all felt very suspicious as we unloaded our kit and put our bergens in a pile.

So this was Now Zad's police station. It didn't look like any police station I'd seen before, just an ordinary Afghan compound with a jumble of buildings, most of them built up against the outer walls. I looked round and took stock. Besides ourselves, there must have been twenty or so people already in the compound. Of these, there were maybe ten British soldiers. The rest were Afghans. We'd been told there was a contingent of ANP – Afghan National Police – and some local police, but there was no way to tell the difference. None of them was wearing anything in the way of uniform. They all looked like ordinary civilians. But we didn't take a lot of notice of these people at first, although they were staring at us and were obviously excited about our arrival.

Our first priority was rehydration. It must have been at least 50 degrees and we all took out our water bottles while the OC spoke to the two police chiefs through the local interpreter who came forward now, the *torjeman* as we called him.

As we quenched our thirst, I looked more closely at the position. We'd been bumped on arrival in the HLS, and there was nothing to say we weren't going to be attacked again at any moment. So the first thing you do in a situation like this is make an appreciation. What are the weak points? Where are you going to take cover if you come under fire? Who is going to go where? One thing that stood out at once was that this was a very large compound for just a platoon to defend, even for a platoon plus. A compound 200 metres square has got a lot of wall round it. The distance between the sangar positions meant that you would only just be heard at the far end of the compound if you shouted at the top of your voice. We were going to depend heavily on our radios and on the field telephone.

Having glanced round, I started to tell the riflemen what we would do in the event of attack. But every time I tried to say something, some of the local militiamen would come up and interrupt. Just who were these people? I wondered. Which were ANP and which were local police? And could we trust them? The *bhai*s looked at them equally suspiciously. Several came forward to shake hands.

'*Assalam-u-alaikum. Assalam-u-alaikum,*' they said. 'How are you, how are you?'

Because Urdu is close to the Hindi language, which I speak

OK, I could understand them quite a bit, and we exchanged a few words.

'*Wa'alaikum assalam*,' I replied. 'Very well thanks.' This surprised them. I suppose they hadn't met many foreign soldiers, let alone soldiers who spoke to them in a language they could understand. But I could also see they weren't all showing the same enthusiasm about our arrival. Either that or some were just very shy.

At this point, the British NCO who had stayed behind to hand over the position came over to show the platoon sergeant Corporal Ramesh and the two section leaders – myself and Corporal Santos – round the compound. On close inspection, we saw that it was in a shocking state. Really *sarai pohor* – full of dirt and rubbish, with bits of paper and discarded tins and empty plastic bottles just thrown on the floor without any care. I was a bit surprised that 10 Platoon hadn't cleared the place up more. This suggested they'd been under a lot of pressure, as normally you'd expect them to have left the place tidy. As it turned out, we had a similar situation on handover – for the same reason.

Altogether there were maybe twelve or fifteen buildings: a central one with a dome on top like a mosque, which was something like eight metres square, while the remainder were built up in different places against the perimeter wall. These buildings were mostly windowless with small rooms, all full of sand and rubbish and badly in need of cleaning out. Several were obviously occupied by the ANP and their local counterparts, but even these were not well kept. In all, the only thing in a good state of repair was the perimeter wall. That and two obviously new portable cabins painted white and blue. But these were too flimsy to survive a direct hit and, stuck out in the middle of the compound, too vulnerable to be any use to us, so after a quick look in through the windows we ignored them.

But as I say, the perimeter wall looked to be in a good state. This was encouraging, because when they are intact about the only thing that can get through them is a Hellfire missile fired from an Apache helicopter. Against small arms and even RPGs, they are completely secure. But that was the only positive thing about the place. Compared with any other police station I'd ever seen, it was a real dump.

But here was one surprise. I noticed on the southern side of the central block that there was a small area, no more than six metres by six, of beautiful garden. There was grass and flowers, mainly red and white, growing in neatly laid beds. It was obviously well looked after – in stark contrast to the rest of the compound. There were even some small trees.

The main points of interest, though, were the sangars. These were small fortified positions, one in each corner plus two extra ones halfway along the longest walls. Sangar 1 was in the north-western corner, Sangar 2 in the south-eastern, Sangar 3 in the north-eastern corner and Sangar 4 in the south-western. Sangars 1 and 3 were therefore the ones that looked down onto the main, metal, road and faced the shops that stood on the other side of it. It was also these that were the most vulnerable to engagement from close quarters. There were also two other temporary sangar positions – not fully protected, that is – about midway along the eastern and western perimeter walls. These were designated sangars number 5 and 6 respectively.

One problem struck me at once. The only way up to these positions was by climbing onto the roof of the buildings they were built on top of, and the only way to do this was by using outside steps. This meant you'd be exposed going in and out. We'd need to do something about that – screen them with some hessian or something. Otherwise a sniper could just sit outside and take a pop every time the sangar duties changed.

The NCO showing us round explained that they'd been contacted – that's to say shot at – several times in the past week.

'It's practically impossible to know where they're hitting you from,' he explained as he pointed out the various places they'd identified as probable fire positions.

That sounded familiar. It clearly wasn't going to be any easier up here to identify where the enemy was than it had been out in the open.

To make matters worse, I saw straight away that some of the buildings outside the compound were on two storeys. As the compound wall was not more than 4 metres high, that gave a big advantage to any enemy occupying the upper rooms of these places. They would be looking down on us.

Our guide, a tough-looking guy, not very tall and with a week's beard growth, also pointed out where the danger zones were along the alleyways. There were lots of them. This was all useful information, but what struck me immediately was how narrow the arcs of fire were. If you swung your weapon too far in any direction, there was going to be serious danger of blue on blue contact. I made a mental note that we would need to put up marker posts for day operations and Cyalume infrared markers each night.

After our tour of the compound, we headed back to the central building, where we found the rest of the platoon now completely surrounded by Afghans. Even the ones who had been hanging back before had obviously lost their shyness.

Although 10 Platoon had been here before us, they all wanted to know where we came from. Were we Chinese? Japanese?

'Nepalese? Where is Nepal?'

The questioning was friendly, but while it was going on I noticed that some of the Afghans still hung back a bit, not really joining in but – it looked to me – sizing us up.

There wasn't time to investigate this suspicion any further, because now a platoon O-group (an orders group) was called inside the central building which Rex *sahib*, the Company Commander who was in overall charge, had already decided would be platoon HQ. The word *sahib*, by the way, is a term of endearment. Although it's an old-fashioned word, not much in use in everyday Gorkhali, it's what you would use to a member of your family – your grandfather, perhaps. It's a term of respect, but not a cringing word. It implies closeness. The OC began by reminding us that the main purpose of Op Herrick 4 was to win hearts and minds. We had to show the local people we were on their side. It would weaken the appeal of the Taliban if we could convince the locals that they had our support. He then went on to say that for now, the top priority was the question of how we were going to make the compound secure, given we were so few.

'As you know, Ten Platoon had a major contact while out on patrol last week. And as we saw ourselves, not everybody here welcomes us. It's vital we don't take any chances.'

He went on to explain that Company Tactical Head-quarters – that's to say himself, the 2 i/c Lieutenant Mathers, the platoon sergeant and an orderly – would occupy the central building along with the J Tac (the tactical air controller), the doctor and his orderly. Everyone else would have to help build up the positions with more sandbags.

'It's going to be hard work in this heat, I'm afraid. But all the intelligence we're getting tells us there's a lot of enemy in the area. We need to make sure we can defend ourselves properly.'

We all looked at each other, nodding.

The OC's other big concern was ANP Hill.

'I've already asked for another section to reinforce it,' the OC continued. 'Probably it will be from your platoon, Kailash.'

'*Hasur, sahib,*' I replied. 'Yes sir.'

He hoped they would be here tomorrow or the next day, depending on helicopter availability.

The OC went on to emphasise the importance of holding the high ground, and in fact it was obvious that it was going to be crucial to holding the compound in the event of attack, as it was close enough to dominate the ground in-between. The positions were mutually supporting.

At this point, Mathers *sahib* took over the O-group to give us detailed instructions on where each section was to go and what their duties were. The most important information from my point of view was his decision to run both my section of seven men (eight including myself) and Corporal Santos's section of another seven as a single unit. It made better sense that way, given the shortage of manpower. The upshot of this was that Corporal Santos and I would be responsible for the two main sangars, 1 and 3.

Mathers *sahib* then gave orders for my section's .50-cal to be placed in Sangar 3. That was where its fire looked likely to be most effective. The other .50 was left on top of a vehicle in case of a need to go out – on resupp for example – while the remaining three corner sangars were to have one GPMG each. The WMIK itself would form part of Sangar 5, one of the temporary sangars, while Sangar 6, the other, would be manned by the QRF – the Quick Reaction Force – together with the ANP and their local counterparts. Next, Mathers *sahib* gave the immediate actions we were to take on engagement by the enemy. Finally he did a walk-through, talk-through of the compound, which included showing us our stand-to positions.

'So commanders, I want you to go away now and organise a sentry rota. We'll have three men for each of the main sangars, that is, One and Three, and two each for the other two. The Quick Reaction Force will be under Corporal Ramesh and HQ will be under command of myself. Are there any questions?'

We all had several – the role of the ANP and that of the local police prominent among them. Mathers *sahib* repeated what he said about the ANP manning Sangar 6 while the local police would join the QRF and provide reinforcements as necessary. But he added that we should not expect too much from them. I glanced at my fellow NCOs. We both understood from this that we would be lucky to get any help from them. In fact, quite likely *kohi pani hoina* – none at all.

With the O-group complete, and after passing on the relevant information to the *bhais* and *gurujis*, the first thing to do was to draw up the list of sentry duties. That done, I took my riflemen up to our sangars to relieve the remaining members of 10 Platoon, i.e. the Signallers, who were due to be picked up and flown out when our reinforcements came in. I took special care to go over arcs of fire with my section and to point out the likely enemy firing positions we'd been told about.

'We'll get some posts up as soon as possible, so you don't go out of arc, but for now you need to be really careful. Have you got that, Gaaz? Nabin? Nagen?'

'Yes, *guruji*,' they all answered in turn.

'And report anything suspicious, OK, *bhai haru*? Anything at all,' I said as I left.

'OK, *guruji*. We'll let you know right away,' they replied, getting themselves into a comfortable position behind the sandbags.

I could tell they were all excited. They were longing for an opportunity to prove themselves.

After that, I showed the remaining members of my section quickly round the rest of the compound, including the building along the eastern wall that Mathers *sahib* had decided was to be our accommodation. They immediately started making jokes about where they were going to sleep. Of course, everyone wanted the best room, or if not the best room, to sleep in a corner. I had to remind them that the best places belonged to the section commanders. After all, we were going to be up in the night longer than they were. So after that they tried to persuade me to let them sleep next to their best friends. In some cases this meant *bhai*s from the other section. I reminded them that they didn't have a choice. They would go where I put them according to my assessment.

But before we could actually occupy the accommodation block, we would have to give it a good sweep out. Not only was the building full of sand and all kinds of rubbish, part of it had obviously been used as a latrine as well. It stank of urine.

The most urgent task, however, was to repair the sangars and make them as secure as possible. This meant filling the sandbags we'd brought with us and putting them round each position. Our platoon sergeant, Corporal Ramesh, told us he wanted each sangar to be protected to a height of six sandbags by nightfall, so there was plenty to do in the next few hours before it got dark. Accordingly, I gave the *bhai*s and *guruji*s orders to take it in turns to clean out the buildings and fill sandbags.

We quickly realised that the sandbag filling was a much bigger job than we at first thought. Although it looked easy work, the sand was so compacted that it was like digging into solid rock. It was at least as bad as Salisbury Plain, where it can take four men all night to sink a trench four feet deep.

'It's worse than digging into the mountainside back home!' exclaimed Gaaz with a weary smile after twenty minutes of solid hacking.

But morale was high and the *bhai*s all laughed and joked. In typical Gurkha style, it had immediately been decided that the one who filled the least number of sandbags should be the one who cooked the evening meal.

Stripped to the waist, they all put their backs into the task at hand. Even so, it wasn't long before the *bhai*s started to slow down. It had been a long day already.

'*Guruji*, this is too hard. Maybe we could try digging somewhere else?' said one.

'What about going outside? It's got to be easier there,' said another.

'Let's do three more bags,' I replied, grabbing a spade. 'Then we'll stop and take a break.'

The Afghans meanwhile stood or sat around watching as we worked.

'*Kalli, bhai?*' they asked, every so often coming up and patting us on the back. 'How are you?'

'*Tik hai, dost,*' we replied. 'Fine thanks, friend.'

'*Za pora murkar maanche,*' said Gaaz under his breath. Roughly translated this means: 'Now shuffle off and go away.'

It soon became obvious that we weren't going to be able to get all the sandbags filled before night time, and that worried me. Already the temperature was starting to drop and soon it would be dark. When night comes, it falls fast in this part of the world. The sangars were in a bad state, and if the enemy could give us a reception like the one they gave us in the HLS, the sentries were going to be very vulnerable. But there was nothing to be done except keep on going as long as possible.

At approximately 5 p.m., we stood-to. This involved everyone turning out and taking up positions as directed at the O-group. There were three riflemen in sangars 1 and 3, two each in sangars 4, 5 and 6. Three more were posted on the roof of the Control Tower, or CT – the name we had already given to the central building – together with the OC. There were another four or five men in the QRF posted outside one of the buildings along the perimeter wall, with the balance of the platoon – the command group – remaining inside the Control Tower. This included the 2 i/c, Lieutenant Mathers, the Platoon Sergeant, Corporal Ramesh, the FOO (Forward Observation Officer), two signallers and the two medics.

After we had stood-to for fifteen to twenty minutes, night routine began. The sentries were to change at two-hourly intervals, so that meant that at any one time, half the combined section would be off duty. Until it was actually dark, we would carry on filling sandbags. In the event that meant until around 7 p.m., after which there just wasn't enough ambient light. There was no proper electrical power at this stage, and anyway we kept use of light after dark to an absolute minimum. This was for reasons of field discipline – we did not want to give the enemy any help whatsoever. We used battery-powered lanterns just enough to let us do our evening routine of cooking and weapon cleaning, which was what we now got on with. It was the job of those not in the sangars to prepare the evening meal – the loser of the sandbag-filling contest was the one to actually cook it.

Truthfully, it wasn't the cooking that was the issue. Gurkhas are keen cooks – we like to try to outdo each other in making the best of what's available. It was the knowledge, unspoken but not forgotten, that that person had filled one less sandbag than anyone else. It might not even have been quite fair. It might have been that the rifleman in question had hit a particularly hard bit of ground. That wasn't the point either. The point was that we like to compete with each other. It's how you build a team. You might get the hard patch today, but hopefully it will be your turn to be lucky tomorrow.

The prospect of our first food at the end of a long day was a real morale boost for us all, and we began to relax a bit.

'Wow, *guruji*! That was really something, *hunza*?' said Gaaz as we waited for the rice to cook. *Hunza* is Gorkhali for 'isn't it?' or 'wasn't it?' The proper way to spell it is *hunchha*, but I think for English-speaking readers it is better to write it like it sounds.

'Yeah, our first contact! Really exciting!' said one of the other riflemen.

'Amazing,' agreed Nagen. '*Achamma bhayo.*'

'But now we have to fight them,' said Gaaz. 'We should go after them, I reckon. Hey, *guruji*!' he went on. 'Why don't we go and find them? They must be out there somewhere. We should volunteer to go on patrol at first light.'

We spoke in low voices, but there was a lot of laughter and sometimes I had to tell the *gurujis* and *bhais* to keep their

53

voices down. There was no need, really – the enemy knew exactly where we were – but it's standard procedure to keep noise to a minimum at night. When we laughed – and, it's true, Gurkhas are always laughing – I told the *bhai*s it had to be tactical laughter. Soundless, in other words.

The talk turned to our equipment. Gaaz was desperate to fire the .50-cal.

'Reckon I could take out any of these buildings with the Browning, *guruji*.'

I wasn't so sure. I'd been in Afghanistan before and knew how much punishment these mud walls could take.

'So what do you think, *guruji*?' he went on. 'Do think we'll see some Talibs tomorrow? Do you think we'll get to kill some?'

He was just so enthusiastic, Gaaz. He was really disappointed not to have been able to do anything during the contact in the HLS. If he'd had his way, we would have put in an immediate section attack. But as we had learned, if you can't see the enemy, you can't engage them.

The talk turned to Osprey, the new body armour we had just been issued. It was heavy and quite uncomfortable, but although not nearly as good as the stuff we have nowadays, it was a huge advance in personal protection, and the *bhai*s and *guruji*s were convinced it was going to make them indestructible.

'You need to make sure you present it to the enemy, though,' said someone. 'It's not going to save you if he can get a shot behind it.'

We all agreed to this, though I wondered if it would really be any more effective than the talisman my mother had given me when I was last on leave in Nepal – a simple one-*paise* coin with a hole in it, minted in India in 1947. She'd had it blessed by one of our priests to deflect any bullets that came my way.

We were still pretty keyed up from having been shot at on arrival, but it all seemed quiet enough now. We carried on chatting for a while as we finished eating, mainly wondering about when the enemy was going to attack next. I suppose by the standards of a good restaurant, our food that night wasn't up to much, but I have to say it was one of the best meals I have ever eaten in my life.

Soon after we'd finished, I was called to another O-group. The OC explained the latest developments in the general situation. It was beginning to look as though we were going to be in Now Zad longer than we had at first thought: the Para battlegroup on its way to relieve us had been held up by unexpectedly stiff resistance. So there were clearly a lot of Taliban in this part of Helmand. Even so, he reminded us that our main priority was hearts and minds and that we would have to be extremely disciplined regarding ROE (Rules of Engagement).

'What we must avoid at all costs is causing any civilian casualties,' he explained before reminding us that we were only to engage when we ourselves were engaged or in obvious danger.

'If someone's carrying a weapon, that's not sufficient reason. A lot of people carry weapons in this part of the world. It doesn't mean they're Taliban. Of course, if they're pointing it at you, that's another matter. But even so, unless you are actually under fire, you are to clear it with myself or the 2 i/c first. Is that clearly understood?'

Everyone present nodded in agreement.

'So you are going to need to impress this on your sections. They are to be vigilant at all times, but also disciplined at all times.'

Thinking about what the OC said as I left the CT, it really hit me for the first time how difficult our situation was. We were here to support the locals, but at the same time we had to be on the lookout for insurgents who had shown themselves very capable in battle. The hardest thing of all was going to be telling who was who. It wasn't as if the enemy wore a distinctive uniform or anything.

When I got back to the *bhais* and *gurujis*, I spent a lot of time checking over their equipment and making certain they fully understood both the ROE and all the drills if we did come under attack. I had given the order to those who hadn't already had the opportunity to do so to clean their *bunduk* – their weapons – while I was on the O-group. So now I made it my business to make sure they had done it properly. In these sandy conditions you had to be extra careful to make sure everything was in good order, with plenty of oil to protect the working parts. At the same time, because of the situation, we couldn't strip them down fully and lay the parts out for individual cleaning as we did normally. It would take too long to put everything back together if we suddenly got bumped. Instead we did battle cleaning. That is to say, we only cleaned one weapon at a time, just taking out each individual part, inspecting it and cleaning it then putting it straight back.

The situation was complicated by the fact that it was dark now, so the riflemen had to take it in turns to hold a torch while their buddy got to work.

Gaaz in particular wanted to show me how well he had done the GPMG.

'What do you think, *guruji*? Good job, *hunza*?'

'Yes, good job, Gaaz,' I said, shining the light on the gas plug.

'Just make sure you keep your oil handy. You could be firing a lot of rounds when those Talibs come back.'

'You think so, *guruji*? I hope you're right.'

After checking everybody's weapons on the ground, I went up into the sangar positions to check theirs too. Obviously it's harder to clean weapons when you are in a confined space, but in fact they'd done a good job.

'Well done, Lance Corporal Shree,' I said. 'Excellent work.'

I find it's better to encourage and inspire the *bhai*s and *guruji*s under my command. That is how we Gurkhas operate. It's hardly ever necessary to give a telling-off. Of course, if there's need, I know how to give a good bollocking, but Gurkhas respond best to inspiration and leadership. For this reason, I make it my business to know everything about each of the men under my command. If they have any problems at home, with their family or girlfriend or something, they need to be able to come to me and I will help them sort it. They should look on me as they would look on their own brother.

After satisfying myself that everyone's weapons were in good order, I went back down to check on the ammunition. Again I had to use my torch tactically, even though there was quite good ambient light that night. I'd told my *bhai*s and *guruji*s to make sure that everything was ready to go. We'd already got as much into the sangars as was practical, but we had to be ready to resupply at a moment's notice. That meant cutting the locking wire on each box, and in the case of the 7.62 for the GPMG, and the belts of Minimi machine gun ammo, looking inside to make sure the links were all in good order. What you don't want is a stoppage due to a link being in the wrong place, which sometimes happens during the packing process.

Another thing that was really important was water. We'd amalgamated the whole platoon's supply in one place where it was readily accessible – a corner of a room where we laid the bottles floor to ceiling. In fact, it turned out that there was a well in the compound, but the police told us it wasn't working. I knew that Major Rex had it as a priority to fix it. He hoped to avoid needing it for drinking purposes, but it would be good for morale if we could take a field shower occasionally. And you never knew, we might need it for drinking if the enemy landed a lucky shot on our stores or we couldn't get a resupply.

By now, the off-duty *bhai*s and *guruji*s had swept out our quarters, which were an L-shaped building built up against the eastern perimeter of the compound. The rooms themselves had no windows, so I decided earlier we would sleep in the corridor outside because of the heat. As I went over to my bedspace, I noticed my kit had been moved as far away as possible from where the others were sleeping. Gurkhas always like to make their bed space really nice, a little home away from home. But that wasn't the real reason for this rearrangement, I knew. The actual reason, I understood perfectly well, was because I am a really bad snorer. My *bhai*s and *guruji*s try never to sleep near me for that reason. Instead, they do their best to isolate me They can't say anything, of course, because I am the *guruji*, but I know this is the real reason.

I don't know why I snore so much. It runs in my family. My dad is a terrible snorer, as was my grandfather. Now my son is too. In a way, though, it is a good thing. For five years, I was in Recce Platoon. That means you are always up ahead of the main body of troops when you are out on exercise, or on operations. So my snoring was a real problem at first. Most of the time, I didn't dare to sleep in case I gave away our position. As a result, I learned to hardly sleep at all. I learned to go without. This was to prove a big advantage in Now Zad.

Before turning in myself, I climbed up into the sangars one last time to make sure the *bhais* were OK. I reminded them that they were to call me on the PRR the moment they saw anything suspicious, and I made sure that they understood exactly what their arcs of fire were.

'Remember, the Cyalumes aren't just decorations,' I said.

When I finally got to lay down on my camp bed at the end of that first day, I was exhausted, but at the same time I was still keyed up. I knew I wasn't going to get a lot of sleep but I was content just to lie there. It was really quiet, I remember. There was just the sound of a few dogs barking. One would start up and be answered by another. Occasionally too, I could hear the sound of a donkey braying in the distance. But apart from that, nothing. No vehicles, no people. It was a bit like being back in my village in Nepal.

And with this thought, I started thinking about my family back home, especially my wife and baby son. I prayed to God, asking him to look after them. Then I checked to make sure I hadn't lost Mum's lucky coin. Somehow I had a feeling I was going to need its good luck before we got out of this place.

Establishing the Routine

I was dreaming about tigers when I woke with a start.
    'Guruji! . . . Guruji!'

It was Rifleman Lal come to tell me it was my turn on duty.
I got up straight away and grabbed my rifle and helmet.

'Anything happening?' I demanded.

'Nothing, *guruji*. All quiet.'

I'd arranged to be called at 2.30 a.m., so it was still dark as
I made my way over to the sangar. A dog barked in the distance
and I paused in my stride. Dogs are a useful warning signal and
I waited to see if it was joined by others, but no, it wasn't. I
walked on.

It felt like I hadn't slept at all. Straight away, my head filled
with thoughts about what we needed to do. The fact is, you are
at your most vulnerable during the first twenty-four hours of
occupying a position, a bit like a batsman during his first over.

You need to be able to respond with massive force and not be caught off guard. If I wasn't on duty at the time, I'd need to be up and about to support the *bhais* and *gurujis* who were. I'd need to be able to get ammunition up to them, water, food. I'd need to be able to talk to them on the PRR, to encourage them and keep up with what was going on so I could report to the OC. And I'd need to be able to help if the worst came to the worst and we had a man down.

Now as I walked over to the sangar, just as in the helicopter on the way in, I kept going over in my mind all the IAs and SOPs. You need to have them so firmly fixed in your mind you know exactly what you have to do in any given situation without having to think about it. At the same time, you have to be ready to adapt. When the shooting starts, nothing ever goes exactly according to plan. But drills and immediate actions stay the same whatever is going on.

I thought too of the flight in, the dust clearing, the sound of the helicopter flying off, then the TAK TAK TAK, TUM TUM TUM of gunfire aimed right at us.

How was it they hadn't hit anyone? Maybe we were just out of range. I suppose the enemy were just as constrained by the lack of cover as we were. If they were in the open, they would have had to stay in their trench. If they were using a building for cover, they would have had to be careful not to be seen moving in and out. But where were they now? That's what I wanted to know. And what about these people in here, the Afghans? Could we trust them? Whose side were they really on? It wasn't a good feeling to think they might not even be on the same side as us.

Climbing the ladder to get up to the sangar, I felt very exposed. Luckily there was some cloud cover, so unless the

enemy were keeping the position covered with nightsights it
wasn't too dangerous, but I made a mental note to get some
camouflage netting up at the first opportunity.

'Gaaz, Nagen – you OK?'

'OK, *guruji*.'

'Yes, *guruji*.'

'Seen anything?'

'Nothing, *guruji*. Just a few dogs down that alleyway.
Nothing suspicious.'

'Well keep looking. We know they're out there. It's only a
matter of time.'

'Yes, *guruji*.'

'Let's hope so, *guruji*. I want my own back!' said Gaaz.

In a way it was good we'd been contacted. If we'd come in
and there'd been no trouble, after two or three days it would
have seemed like a normal exercise. Inevitably we would have
relaxed a bit. As it was, everyone was properly keyed up and
morale was high.

For the first hour I was with Nagen and Gaaz, for the second
with Gaaz and Nani *guruji*. I organised the rota so that Gaaz
was on duty at the same time as me. You want your best man
on at the same time as you in case you get bumped.

Inside the sangar, there wasn't a lot of room for the three of
us. It was no more than 3 metres by 2 metres and a metre and
a half high, and with all our equipment there was hardly any
room to move around. It was also stiflingly hot and only going
to get hotter.

Because it was still dark, the world was displayed to us in the
eerie green and white of our night devices. As section leader I
had the use of a CWS – common weapon sight – which could

either be attached to the SA80 or LSW – light support weapon – or, dismounted, like a pair of binoculars. This was in addition to the HMNVS – head-mounted night-vision sight – that we were all equipped with.

As there was nothing to see except the buildings surrounding us, our other senses became very finely tuned. You could clearly smell the desert up here, carried in on a slight sigh of wind every so often. And any sound carried for miles. As a result, when we heard the call of the muezzin for the first prayers of the day blare out of a loudspeaker, I almost jumped out of my skin.

'*Allaaahu akbar* . . . Allah is most great . . .'

I looked at my watch. It was 3.30 a.m.

A few moments later, this call was answered by another a bit further away.

'*Allaaahu akbar.*' Seconds later, this too was answered by the same words recited a short distance behind us.

'*Allaaahu akbar* . . . Allah is most great . . . I testify that there is no God but Allah . . . I testify that Muhammad is the prophet of Allah . . . Come to prayer. Come to salvation . . . *Allaaahu akbar* . . . There is no God but Allah.'

'So there must be three separate mosques in the town. *Hunza, guruji?*' said Gaaz in a low voice.

'*Hunza*,' I replied in agreement. It was as if they were calling to each other.

It was still dark and there was no one around. I wondered whether the muezzin's call could be being used as cover for an attack. It could easily happen that way. The hour before dawn is an optimum moment to launch an offensive.

'Do you think they could be moving into position?' Gaaz wanted to know.

'Exactly what I was thinking,' I replied, pressing the Transmit button on my PRR to talk to the *bhais* in the other sangar.

'*Guruji bhai haru*, did you hear that?'

Of course I knew they must have done, but I wanted to be sure they were fully alert.

'*Guruji?* You mean the mosque?'

'Just making sure. Have you got your ammo properly sorted? Your nightsights are working OK?'

'Yes, *guruji*. Nightsight works OK. Ammo is sorted. Have you seen anything?'

'No, nothing. But keep alert. Sunrise will be soon now and this is just the time they're going to hit us.'

'*Hasur, guruji*. But do you think they will?'

'I'm sure of it.'

'OK, *guruji*. We're ready.'

'Well I hope you're right, *guruji*,' said Gaaz when I finished talking on the PRR. 'It would be good to know what they look like.'

The more I saw of Gaaz, the better I liked him. He was young and inexperienced, but he was full of energy and keen to do the best job possible. Just a week or so back, he'd got a commendation from the OC for the briefing he gave a general who visited our position back at Bastion. Usually, these senior officers just walk round while the local commander gives them a brief, but on this occasion the VIP decided he wanted to see inside a sangar, so when he came in with the OC, I gave him an overview. I pointed out things like the main entrance to the camp and which weapons covered it. I told him how long our period of duty was and what was the procedure at changeover, all the basic stuff. The general then went forward and started looking through his binoculars while Gaaz stood behind. Because the sandbags came up to just below chest height, the general had to crouch down as Gaaz gave him the briefing to end all briefings.

'From this position, the arcs of fire are: left-hand arc, reference rock outcrop at approx two hundred metres, ten o'clock, post. Right of arc, reference burned-out vehicle at three hundred metres, two o'clock . . . ' He went on like this for about five minutes, very precisely.

Afterwards, the general told the OC that in his entire Army career, he had never heard a briefing from a rifleman like the one Gaaz gave. It was, he said, the sort of briefing he could expect from a corporal with fifteen years' service.

What the general did not realise was that when we took the position over, me and Gaaz had sat down and worked all these things out together. We then wrote them up in note form on small bits of paper that we stuck on the wooden frame above the letter box (the opening you look through). We then practised giving a briefing several times, just in case one of the *sahibs* asked for one. So when the general came, Gaaz just had to remember what we had practised and read out our notes! But even so, it was an excellent performance. Gaaz went to a private school back in Nepal and was very good in English. He had a particularly clear accent.

After reassuring myself that the *bhai*s in the other sangar were fully alert, we were silent for a while. I myself was tense and expectant, but the sound of the muezzin reminded me that I too should pray to God. You could say I am quite religious. In fact most Gurkhas are quite religious, whether we are Hindu or Buddhist, or whether we follow the Kirat religion as my family does.

I prayed for my wife and children back in Nepal. And I prayed that God would make us fierce warriors. Although it was true that our mission was to protect the local population and build up relations with them, I knew enough to realise that the Taliban didn't see things this way.

If they were praying to their God, I'd better pray to mine and let's see who was listening.

I was just thinking these thoughts when Gaaz reached over and pulled my sleeve. '*Guruji!*' he whispered, grabbing me by the shoulder. 'Look!'

There was a lone figure walking along the street towards us. My heart thumping, I trained my sights on the apparition. This could be the start of something.

'Nagen, you keep scanning the buildings while I take a closer look,' I said quietly. You don't want everyone focusing on just one person and missing the main event happening elsewhere. 'It could be a decoy.'

'Looks like a woman, *guruji*. What do you think?' said Gaaz after a few moments.

'Looks like, yes. But let's see.'

From the clothes, it did look like a woman – but that didn't mean anything. The trouble with what people wear in this part of the world is that, at a distance, they don't look too different.

I watched as the figure came towards us. About 10 metres away, it stopped. Now what? There was a fumbling and a flapping of cloth, and then it sank down against the perimeter wall.

'*Aare jatha!* It is a woman. And she's squatting outside our house!' said Gaaz, incredulous.

There was no denying that was exactly what she was doing.

And when she'd remained there for a full minute, we both realised at the same time exactly the extent of what she was doing.

'*No ramro keti!*' exclaimed Gaaz. The dirty woman.

'*Guruji?*' It was Lance Corporal Shree on the PRR. 'Can you see there's someone squatting down about ten metres beyond your position?'

'It's OK, seen thanks. She's just having a *disha.*'

'Roger.'

'The dirty *jatha!*' said Gaaz again as the woman stood up and adjusted her clothes. 'You come all the way from Nepal to Afghanistan to help these people and this is how they reward you!'

Unfortunately, he was right. A slight stirring of wind carried the smell up to us and we all looked at one another and pulled faces.

This was something I never got used to in Afghanistan. The Afghans just did their business where they felt like. I'd even noticed they did it right next to where they carried out their cooking. To us Gurkhas, this was disgusting. We like to keep the place we live as clean as possible. Sorting out a latrine was one of the first things we'd done on arrival.

'We'll use the end room in that block over there,' Corporal Ramesh had said. 'See if you can find a tin or something and you and the other section commanders can draw up a rota. Once a day, we'll take it out and burn it, OK?'

The room in question was a small cubicle in a block of rooms that we weren't using. Once a day, or whenever it started to get full, someone took the tin outside and poured fuel on the contents and burned it. Everybody hated doing this job, of course.

But it had to be done and we all took our turn. I even tried to get the Afghans to copy us, but they weren't interested.

By now, the sky was just beginning to brighten, and to our dismay, several other people appeared, women to start with, and then some men, to do the same thing.

This *disha* patrol turned out to be a part of our daily routine in Now Zad. I often wondered whether it was part of the local people's way of telling us we weren't welcome. I also wondered whether they realised we were staring through our sights at them as they did their business. But I told the *bhai*s they must watch closely. One of my big fears was that the enemy would use a suicide bomber to blow the entrance gate away as the start of a big attack. Even though we had the two WMIKs parked in the way, they wouldn't be much of an obstacle. And this was one way they might try to get close enough.

'Keep them in your sights,' I said to the *bhai*s. 'You never know which one has got the explosives strapped to them.'

At around 4.15 a.m., just before dawn, we stood-to. Without any signal, everyone in the compound turned out to man their designated stand-to position. Three men in each of the four main sangars, two in the other two temporary sangar positions, HQ personnel on the roof of the CT, the remainder – the QRF – mustered outside the accommodation block.

Everyone in the compound, that is, except for our Afghan counterparts. There was no sign of them.

During training we were told that the drill of standing-to just before dawn was something the British Army started to do during the First World War. Apparently, most attacks on the Western Front began at this time. These days it's just a basic SOP. It's how you start the day on operations.

After stand-to, which lasts no more than twenty minutes, it was straight into normal routine. Until further notice, that meant two hours on sangar duty, four hours off. In theory, that is. Actually, as section commander, you always end up doing a lot more than your riflemen. For me and Corporal Santos it was probably more like four hours on, two hours off – three at the most. And none at all when we were in contact.

The thing is, as section commander, when not on sangar duty you would be taking time to go up to the other sangar to make sure everything was OK up there. It might sound repetitive, but you keep having to make sure everyone's weapons are properly clean and prepared, that the ammunition is out of its boxes and ready, that everyone knows what's expected of them. You have to let the *bhai*s and *guruji*s know that you are around and thinking about them all the time. Like I said before, it's partly to satisfy yourself that they're on top of everything and partly to reassure them that you are on top of everything. What's more, as a junior commander you have to show you are a little bit better than the *bhai*s at everything – from filling sandbags to cleaning your weapons and keeping your kit tidy. In my own case, I realised right away that I had a bit of a problem on my hands.

Rifleman Gaaz was a really nice guy. Really intelligent, really keen, with plenty of humour. But I had realised straight off he was always going to be trying to get one up on me. He was the one to watch – not because he had any kind of grudge: there wasn't anything bad about him, not at all. Quite the opposite in fact. It was because he wanted to impress me and the other *guru-ji*s. I'm not saying the other *bhai*s were any different. They all wanted to shine.

But Gaaz – he was determined to be the best.

I came off duty about an hour after stand-to. Next on was Baren.

'Come up as quick as you can,' I said, covering him as he climbed up on the roof. My top priority this morning was to get some more hessian up so as to screen entry and exit to the sangar. Otherwise we were going to be vulnerable every time people went on and off duty. Hessian is also a useful defence against hand grenades. It meant the enemy would have to throw them up a lot higher in order to get them into the compound. Hopefully they wouldn't be able to reach.

'Did you manage to get some sleep OK?'

'A bit, thanks, *guruji*.'

'That's good. So have you got everything? Have you had breakfast?'

'Yes, *guruji*.'

'OK, good. Now do you remember your arcs of fire? Show me.'

Baren did as he was told.

'Well done. So just remember you're looking out for anything suspicious. If you see anyone going in to the building opposite, let me know, OK? We don't want anyone using it as an assembly point or fire position.'

'*Hasur, guruji*.'

Satisfied everyone knew their responsibilities, I climbed out of the position, trying to make myself as small a target as possible. As soon as I was down, I went to Sangar 1. Of the two main positions, this was probably the most vulnerable, because it was overlooked by the two-storey building we had been told was the old school house. We would be an easy target for any sniper in there.

I scanned the building carefully through my binos. It had already taken a beating – there were holes everywhere – but these holes made perfect fire positions for the enemy. The other really good thing from their point of view was the fact that it could easily be occupied without us knowing. Because of the surrounding buildings, it was almost impossible to see anyone going in. Besides, even if we did see people going in, how could we be sure they really were the enemy? We couldn't just open up without provocation.

'Right, *guruji bhai haru*, if you see any suspicious movement, you're to let me know. Understood?'

'OK, *guruji*. On the PRR.'

'That's right, on the PRR. And by the way, have you checked the field telephone recently?'

'Just now, *guruji*.'

'Good.'

The field telephone is a vital piece of equipment. It's basically just a handset connected directly to Company Tac HQ by Don 10 wire. Because of this direct link, it doesn't suffer from the faults that radios are prone to when for some reason you just can't send or receive, even though you're less than 50 metres from the person you're trying to contact. It also has the advantage of being completely secure, because it doesn't use radio signals. You can only hack into it if you attach your own cable. It's vulnerable to a direct hit, of course, but then again so is anything. In contacts, we used it the whole time.

After reassuring myself that the *bhai*s in Sangar 1 fully understood what they had to do and were in good shape to do it, I went down to join the rest of the *bhai*s and *guruji*s off duty. The smell of cooking hung in the air, but first I wanted to check that everything was OK with everyone else. I walked over to the accommodation block. There were two or three men resting – having just come off duty – but most were up, excited to get on with the day, even if it did mean a lot more sandbag filling.

Next I went over to the ammo store. That all looked fine too, so I went and joined the rest of the off-duty group.

Breakfast that morning was the same as for all mornings: a cup of sweet tea and a few biscuits. For some reason Gurkhas don't worry too much about breakfast. We prefer to save up for a big meal later. If we're hungry, we'll eat whatever is lying around – leftovers from the night before usually. Some of the *bhai*s were smoking and there was already a lot of laughter. They were talking about their prospects of growing a beard.

During the first O-group, Rex *sahib* had declared a no-shave policy due to the water shortage. Everyone was very pleased about this. Although Gurkhas don't usually grow much beard, and me less than anyone, we liked the idea of looking as much like proper warriors as possible.

'After three days I'm gonna look like my grandad,' said someone. 'He fought in Malaya and he's got this photo of him in the jungle looking like a real *bahaduri*.'

The word *bahaduri* means 'warrior'.

'I bet my beard's going to be better than yours!' said Gaaz.

'OK, *guruji bhai haru*. We'd better get going now,' I said, looking at my watch.

Our first priority on that second day was to build up our defensive positions. We had to try to get as much done as possible before the sun got too hot. And even when it did get too

hot, we'd have to keep going, but the point was we were bound
to be more productive early on.

'Listen in, everyone,' I began. 'What we'll do is we'll have a
competition.'

'Oh no, not another one, *guruji*,' I heard someone groan
good-humouredly.

'We'll do twenty minutes on, twenty minutes off, and see
who can fill the most sandbags in that time. The winner gets a
bottle of Coke.'

We must have started around 7.30 a.m. As before, the work
was really hard because of the ground. We tried various different places to dig, but it was the same wherever we went. Again
there were calls for a party to go outside the compound walls,
but I had to remind the *bhai*s that although it was hard inside,
at least here we had some protection. Outside we'd be an easy
target.

As the morning went on, the Afghans gradually turned out
to watch us work. They weren't early risers, that was for sure. In
fact they were so relaxed it was hard to imagine they believed we
could be bumped at any moment. Maybe their intelligence was
better than ours. Maybe in fact they knew the threat was low.

As had happened yesterday, some of them came up and
patted us on the back.

'*Tik hai, dost?*' they asked. 'Are you fine, friend?'

'*Tik hai,*' we replied. 'Yes, fine.'

Gaaz always added a few very bad words in Gorkhali afterwards, calling them *jatha* and other things that I will not
mention.

Despite the friendliness, it was clear that while the ANP guys
were genuinely interested in us, the local police were basically

just pretending to encourage us. It occurred to me that the ANP probably were on our side because they came from else-where in the country. The locals, even if they didn't actually support the Taliban, were much more wary of us. The fact was, when we left, they would still be living here, so it was natural they wanted to play both sides.

'You look out,' said one of them, jokingly. 'If you put any more sandbags up there, the roof will come down.'

While this was a source of amusement to him, I was really wor-ried it was true. The buildings the sangars were built on top of would only take a certain amount of weight before they gave out.

'He's right, *guruji bhai haru*. We'll have to make sure we put the majority of the sandbags on the strongest parts, along the top of the wall. We can't put too many on the roof itself.'

All the riflemen nodded in agreement, with one or two making jokes themselves.

'You wouldn't want to fall through the floor just when you were about to fire the ILAW!' said one.

'Or worse still, go down just as the enemy were getting the ladders up!' said someone else.

Apart from this reminder, the Afghans did not contribute much. One or two of the ANP picked up a shovel from time to time, but although they were enthusiastic to begin with, they soon gave up. Then, as the morning wore on, some of them went out of the compound on patrol. They looked very unimpressive, with no uniform and nobody actually in charge by the look of things. It was also completely unclear what their intentions might be. The OC had mentioned that the ANP would be conducting their own patrols, which sounded like a good idea, but it was hard to feel encouraged by what we saw.

'Take a look at that lot!' exclaimed one of the riflemen as the gates opened to let them out.

'What do you think, *guruji*? Do you think they'd make it through selection?' said Gaaz.

He meant the Gurkha selection procedure, which recruits less than one man from every thousand who apply each year.

After the patrol had gone, the attitude of the remaining Afghans started to get a bit annoying. But although I knew the *bhai*s would have liked me to tell them to go away, I was determined to try to make friends with them. They could give us vital information.

'*Guruji*, can't we just tell them to go and *poraja jata*?' demanded Gaaz at one point. 'These guys should lend a hand or go away.'

I had to remind him and the other *bhai*s and *guruji*s that one advantage of not telling them to go away was that, as time went by, we might be able to work out which ones were likely to help us, and which were not. One or two in particular did seem sincerely friendly.

At the same time, it occurred to me they could be trying to get information from us just as much as we were trying to get information from them.

'Are there a lot of Taliban in this place?' I wanted to know while I waited my turn on the shovel.

'There are hundreds. All over the place,' said one of them.

'Not so very many,' replied another. 'They come and they go. We don't get too much trouble, thanks to Allah the Most Merciful.'

This was totally confusing and only made me more suspicious. I thought it more likely the first one was speaking the truth, however. We knew that 10 Platoon, who we had relieved yesterday, had suffered a big ambush when they launched a patrol in support of 3 PARA. It was a hazardous situation and they had only been able to extract with the help of Apache helicopter gunships, so we knew for sure there must be plenty of Taliban around, even if it did seem quiet today. What was more, they were well armed and highly motivated. They must have had good intelligence too or they wouldn't have been in position for our arrival. And their fire was accurate if not so disciplined. These were *chord ke dusman* – quite pro fighters. I found it impossible to believe that men like this would just disappear without having another go.

It could only be a matter of time.

The Afghans had lots of questions for us too. They asked whether we had been in England. Of course, we all had.

'What about America?' they demanded.

They seemed satisfied when we said no and started asking questions about Nepal. As it happened, there were one or two *hajira* among the ANP. These *hajira* are hill people from the northern part of the country. They looked a bit like Gurkhas but with beards, and they were really curious to know where we were from. I drew a map on the ground with a stick to show them.

'Same!' said one of them when he realised I had drawn the Himalayas. I showed him Taplejung district in the far east of Nepal where I come from, then he took the stick and showed me where he came from in the far west.

'Same!' he said again, hugging me like an old friend.

'If you shave your beard, you will look just like me!' I said.

'So how come in British Army?' this man wanted to know.

'Because in the British Army you get the chance to do a lot of fighting,' I said. All the Afghans listening laughed at this. Perhaps they didn't believe me. Well, they'd only have to try us to find out if I was joking or not.

It's hard to tell when a few grains of rice become a heap, and it's hard to say when all the sandbags we were filling started to look like they were making a difference to the sangar positions. But as the morning wore on, we began to notice we were making good progress. There were enough in place to start thinking about putting protection round them. There were some rolls of barbed wire brought in by 10 Platoon and Corporal Santos ordered us to use as much as we could, so I told Nagen and Nani, who had recently come off duty, to get to work unrolling it.

Meanwhile, the Afghans kept pestering us. Mostly they just sat around on their haunches smoking and looking at us with lazy eyes, not saying much. But every so often they would strike up a new conversation.

At one point, they wanted to see our kukris. We took good care to explain that they were easily capable of chopping off a man's head.

'Really?' they wanted to know.

'Really,' I said.

Then I told them a story about when Gurkhas were last in this part of the world, during the 1930s when the British were defending the North-West Frontier against the Pashtun tribesmen. There was a time when some of these tribesmen captured a British soldier and decapitated him and put his head on display, so the British *sahib* gave the order to his Gurkhas to capture a tribesman and cut off *his* head. They did that, and then the *sahib* invited the local villagers to watch a football match. When they got there, they saw it wasn't really a football at all, but their fellow tribesman's head. Then after the game, this *sahib* explained to the elders that if ever it happened again that one of his soldiers was attacked like this, he would order the Gurkhas to go out with their kukris and cut the heads off every single male over the age of fourteen.

The Afghans listened to this story in silence. Of course, we weren't allowed to do that sort of thing any more, but they didn't need to know that. I wanted them to be frightened of us.

'So the blade's very sharp?' one of the Afghans asked after some time.

'Gaaz will tell you another story,' I said.

'Oh yes,' said Gaaz, getting my meaning. He could also speak some Urdu. 'There was once a Gurkha cornered without any weapon except his kukri. The enemy was standing with a gun, ready to fire. The Gurkha slashed at him with his kukri.'

Gaaz made a slashing movement. The Afghans nodded.

'Ha! Missed!' Gaaz went on, imitating the enemy.

He now pretended to take aim with his gun before going on. 'But then the Gurkha said, "Now shake your head."'

There was a pause as the meaning of the story sunk in. Gaaz laughed and again there was a lot of nodding.

All the Gurkhas were looking at the Afghans at this point. Everyone wanted to see what their reaction was, but they didn't give much away. I liked to think these stories had a good effect, but I couldn't be sure.

It was at that moment I noticed one of the local police who

had just joined us was carrying a rocket-propelled grenade launcher concealed within his clothes.

'What's that for?' I demanded. It seemed strange for him to be walking around with an RPG hidden like this.

'When the enemy comes, I will fire,' he replied.

He's lying, I thought to myself. As soon as the enemy comes there's every chance he's going to use that thing against us.

It was a really bad feeling to have, but I couldn't shake off the idea that the people who were supposed to be supporting us weren't really on our side at all. But there was nothing we could do about it except remain vigilant.

By lunchtime, the sangars were beginning to look much more secure, though a lot of work still needed to be done. Now that the sandbags were up to a height of six or seven courses, we could start stretching the barbed wire round the outside. This was potentially dangerous work, as when you aren't inside your sangar, you are an easy target for snipers.

'Make sure you concentrate on what's going on around you, not what's going on with the wire,' I told the riflemen on duty in the sangar. 'You've got to keep them covered at all times, OK? Is that understood?'

The reason for putting out barbed wire was to present a further obstacle to any assault party that managed to get close enough to put a ladder up against the position. It wouldn't delay them for very long, as they would see it there and bring gloves, but even thirty seconds in a combat situation can make a big difference. Enough to swap magazines or pull the pin out of a grenade, for example.

Our other big priority was to put up proper arc markers. Last night, I had put out infrared Cyalumes round each sangar, but today I wanted solid posts in each position, like the ones we had in the sangars at Bastion. I had serious worries about people swinging round in the heat of battle and accidentally taking out one of our own side.

'What happens if they get right on top of us, *guruji*? Do we still have to observe arcs then?' asked one of the *bhai*s.

'You have to observe them at all times, yes,' I replied. 'Obviously, if they get into the sangar with you, you're going to need to do whatever it takes. But still you need to be aware of what you're doing.'

I was pleased the riflemen were asking questions like this. It showed they were thinking things through.

Having got the hessian, the barbed wire and the arc markers in place, we covered the whole structure with cam (camouflage) netting. This was particularly important in Sangar 3, as there were actually two parts to the position. The main part which had all-round protection was no more than about two and a half metres wide, two metres deep and a metre and a half high. But outside, at the front, there was a small platform where I instructed the *bhai*s and *guruji*s to put some sandbags as well.

'Just build it up three bags high, OK? It doesn't look like the walls are going to take any more.'

'OK, *guruji*. What about the sides?'

'You can leave the sides. It's just to give us another layer of protection at the front.'

As it turned out, during contacts I would often go forward to this part of the position, as you could get better situational awareness out there. And it wasn't long before we put sandbags round the sides too.

As soon as they got the chance to take a break after sandbag filling, the *bhai*s and *guruji*s turned their attention to our accommodation. They swept it out again, more thoroughly than they'd been able to last evening, and they also cleared the rest of the rubbish out of the rooms. Then they started to make it feel a bit more like home by drawing kukris on the walls and putting up 2 RGR signs.

As I said, the basic duty rota was two hours on, four hours off. But even during rest periods, there was lots to do. A big priority throughout our time in Afghanistan was preparation of ammunition. For the SA80s, we charged up all the available magazines. For the machine guns, we laid the belts out and checked through all the linkages again and again, taking special care when we fitted the belts together. We took it up to the sangars in this ready state and spent quite a lot of time deciding where the best places were to store it. This was critical because of the lack of space.

'OK, *bhai haru*, make sure you put it somewhere you aren't going to kick it with your feet,' I said. 'Put the field telephone on top of the back wall and you can pile the grenades there. The jimpy belts can go along the side wall.'

'What about here?' Nagen wanted to know, pointing to the front wall. 'I reckon it would be better here.'

'OK, if that's what you think, we can try that.'

I was particularly concerned to have a good number of grenades ready, as I had already decided that if the enemy got really close, these would be our best defence.

'More,' I told Gaaz. 'I want at least fifteen. Twenty if there's room.'

'OK, *guruji*.'

My simple plan in the case of the enemy actually getting ladders up against the walls beneath us was to drop grenades on them.

The standard fuse setting was three seconds. The ideal would be that the grenade exploded before actually hitting the ground – that way you would catch anyone climbing up – but even if it hit the ground before exploding it should take care of the ladders.

As things started to come together in the compound, I had a new concern. I was worried that the *bhai*s would simply get fed up with staring at the same buildings for hours on end. The fact is, it's almost impossible to keep 100 per cent focused the whole time. I reminded them it was essential to keep in the forefront of their mind what it had felt like to be shot at.

'And remember to use your sights, OK?' I said to the *bhai*s when I went to check on them. 'You're looking for possible enemy positions, any suspicious movements. It's tiring on the eyes, I know, but the people who bumped us yesterday are still out there. They haven't gone away, you know.'

One very important thing was to make sure that the duty rota moved people around. You don't want people ending up in the same place every time, as you need to avoid boredom. When you are bored you don't pay attention, and it's when you're not paying attention that you are at your most vulnerable. Even worse, when you're bored, you can fall asleep.

We continued to build our defences all day, with the result that, as evening approached without any further sign of the enemy, we began to feel a little bit more secure, though because of what had happened on the way in, and because of what we knew about 10 Platoon's experience during the last week, you couldn't exactly relax – not if you really thought about it.

Of course that wasn't what I told Sumitra when I called home later on that second evening. Because of our new baby, I was first on the list to be able to use the satellite telephone. I told her everything was fine.

I could tell that she didn't really believe me, but I had to do my best not to worry her. I didn't mention anything about the contact yesterday. Nor did I say I was certain there were going to be more contacts.

'It's really quiet here,' I said. 'There's nothing going on at all. We're guarding this police station and there's a bazaar outside. Lots of people shopping. It's just like home!'

We got twenty minutes of free telephone calls home every week. Every time I spoke to my wife at this time, I had to promise her that I would soon come back for her and our two children.

'Don't worry,' I said, 'I'll be back soon, then I'll bring you home to England.'

That pleased her. Of course, you never knew with operations, but we were due in Cyprus in early August. I would be going on leave immediately afterwards so, if all went to plan, I would arrive back at our place in Nepal soon after. They were staying with Sumitra's mother at the time, but my plan was to take them back to the UK.

'Do you think the weather will be fine when we get there?' she asked, changing the subject quickly. 'I've heard it rains a lot in England.'

'Oh, it should still be quite fine and sunny,' I said.

Of course, I had no idea. For my own part, I was just glad we had a son now – and so were Sumitra and her parents. Our first child was a girl, Alisa, now almost three years old. The reason for wanting a son so badly is that in our culture, it is the boys who look after the elders. A girl will marry and go out of the family, so if someone has only girl children, there is a chance they will have no one to look after them when they are old.

That was not my reason for wanting a boy, however. I wanted a boy because I wanted him to join the Gurkhas. Of course, I didn't tell my wife this either, but she knew already, I'm sure.

'Say hello to your mum and dad for me, and give a big hug to Alisa,' I said.

Walking back towards the lines after my phone call, I noticed that the Afghan police were all looking quite relaxed. Several of the local policemen were sitting next to a small fire, and one of them was taking something out of his pocket which he put on a small piece of metal. I stopped to watch as he ignited it and inhaled deeply. As he did so, he immediately started sneezing, and I could see water glistening under his eyes. This was obviously some of the opium that the Helmand region is so famous for.

'*Tik hai?*' I asked him. 'Are you OK?'

'*Tik hai, dost.*' Completely fine, friend.

Actually, he sounded completely drunk.

Later that night, Rex *sahib* called another O-group. As well as giving news of the progress of other friendly callsigns he brought us up to date with details of the general situation – where the enemy were believed to be and in what strength – and also what air support we could expect. On the subject of the ANP and the local police he told us he was sure there were bound to be some spies among them.

'So we need to show them we're ready for action. They should be in no doubt that if they take us on, we'll hit them back harder than they've ever been hit before. Is that clearly understood?' he said, looking round the room in the glow of our lanterns.

When I went back and briefed the *bhai*s and *guruji*s, they were all angry to think that there could be enemy right here in the compound with us, so I reminded them that our main role out here was in fact to win hearts and minds.

'We're just going to have to show them we're on the same side. We aren't looking for trouble after all. We'd be happy not to have to use our weapons at all.'

The *bhai*s nodded in agreement, but I wasn't sure they were completely convinced. I cannot say that I was either. With 10 Platoon's experience, plus the reception we met on the way in, it didn't look likely we were going to get out without some kind of a fight. And really, we were all quite looking forward to it.

In the meantime, things were definitely better in terms of protection up in the sangars. But I had one big anxiety. Earlier in the day, Mathers *sahib* had told us the OC wanted a .50-cal up in Sangar 3. It was now in place, but we had discovered that its arcs of fire were limited and at short range – anything under about 30 metres – it was going to be useless. Because of the design of the mounting, it was not possible to tilt the gun forward to fire downwards. In most situations this would not matter, but for us it could be disastrous. The enemy could easily get that close just by using the cover of the buildings nearby. All he needed to do was get into the building next door and he could get within 10 metres. Still, having our best weapon in one of the sangars was quite reassuring. It is a fantastic piece of equipment, accurate and very powerful. I had the feeling that, as well as needing the blessings of my lucky charm, we were going to be needing the blessings of the .50-cal too.

6

Goat Curry and a Contact

So the picture by day three was of a platoon plus of Gurkhas now well sorted, with defences much improved and morale high. We had even got a chess league going. Although we probably aren't brilliant players by international standards, chess is a big favourite among the *bhai*s and *guruji*s back in barracks, and as soon as we deploy anywhere, someone is bound to get a competition running. In Now Zad, you'd always find at least two people huddled over a board somewhere in the compound.

Easily the best player in our section was my 2 i/c, Lance Corporal Shree. In fact he was one of the two best players in the platoon, and he took it very seriously. It was he who organised the competition and updated all the results on the wall of the accommodation block. Gaaz was also quite a good player, although I could generally beat him and we could both beat Nagen. In my own case, I learned to play in my village by watching two of the teachers at my school who used to play using a bit of painted cardboard.

I think practically everyone in Now Zad was part of the league. Out in Afghanistan the currency in use by all the allies was American dollars, and it cost five to join. Altogether the prize pot was therefore well over a hundred, although one of the younger *bhai*s, thinking this wasn't enough, drew a huge cartoon cheque showing a million. Most of the games were played outside the accommodation block, usually with an audience of a few Afghans. We tried to get them to play too, though they never did. But everyone else joined in, even Rex *sahib*. He was knocked out quite early on, or so I heard – at around the same time as me, in fact. And as well as the games outside, there were games going on in the CT too. In fact I heard later that when the competition got really tense, there were some occasions when the riflemen would carry on even during the most serious contacts.

Another big pastime among Gurkhas is *bagh chal*, 'the tiger game'. This is a strategy game a bit like draughts, and is supposed to have been invented by a mythical Indian princess called Mandodari, daughter of the King of the Demons and wife of Ravana, a warrior prince. According to the Hindu *Ramayana*, Ravana misbehaved by kidnapping and making a mistress of the wife of the god Rama. As a result, Mandodari, who was very religious, was forced to spend a lot of time alone in their palace, and it was then that she created the game. One person plays as goats, the other plays as tigers. There are four tigers and up to twenty goats. The tigers win when they have captured five goats, which they do by jumping over them on the board. The goats win when they have blocked the tigers so they can't move. One really good thing about the game is that the board itself is very simple. You can of course get highly decorated boards with scenes from the life of Mandodari painted round the edge, but you can also draw it out on the ground using just a stick. And unlike chess, you don't need complicated pieces: just stones or pebbles will do.

It's a game we play out in Nepal where there's no time pressure. When I was younger we played a lot at school and at home, and quite often fights would break out afterwards. Two really well matched players will take several hours over each game. You take it in turns to be the tigers or the goats. Some people are particularly good at being one or the other. Gaaz was really clever at playing goats – it was so frustrating to play against him sometimes, though I did mostly beat him in the end. Another good thing about it is that, like chess, you can leave off playing at any stage and go back to it later, so long as the pieces aren't disturbed. Again, we tried to get the Afghans interested. They sometimes watched, but they never wanted to join in.

By this time, we had begun to realise there was a big divide between the two groups of Afghans. The ANP were much more friendly than the local police, and the interpreter – the *torjeman* – also seemed like a good guy. It was he who, at our request, went out and bought a goat for our evening meal that day.

Goat curry is something Gurkhas really enjoy, and it is a tradition with us to get hold of a live animal whenever we can. The person who held the record for most sandbags filled had the honour of slaughtering it – with a kukri of course. Those of us not on duty at the time all gathered round, together with some of the Afghans, and watched as the rifleman decapitated it. The hardest part of the operation is getting the goat to stand still, but on this occasion it was no trouble. Everyone stood round in a circle while the *bhai* steadied it. Standing slightly behind, he brought his blade down in a single stroke, and the head shot forward at least six feet, to a great cheer from the assembled company.

'Best meal I've had in a month,' said one of the riflemen when the curry was served.

'Best since I was last home,' said another.

'He seems OK, this *torjeman*,' said someone else. 'Let's hope he can get us some more.'

'Hey, did you see the look on the Afghans' faces when the head came off?' demanded Gaaz. 'I don't think they liked it at all. They didn't cheer, that's for sure.'

I noticed the same thing. In fact, they all looked rather uncomfortable. Of course, according to their way of thinking, any animal being slaughtered must have its throat cut and be allowed to bleed to death. That seems cruel to us. But they were clearly impressed seeing a kukri in action.

Later that evening, we had a bit of disappointing news. We wouldn't be going home as soon as we'd hoped.

'The Three Para Battlegroup is meeting heavier than expected resistance up country, so I'm afraid we're likely to be here for quite a bit longer than just a week,' Rex *sahib* announced during the evening O-group. The thing was, our deployment was really just a stopgap. Now Zad was one of several towns occupied by the battlegroup. Two others were Sangin and Musa Qala. As things turned out, instead of being able to fight the battle for hearts and minds, the Paras found themselves in a series of real battles and had called for reinforcements. Our occupation of Now Zad, which was supposed to be just temporary, would remain until those reinforcements – in the form of the Royal Regiment of Fusiliers – could be brought in.

'I'm in no hurry to get back to Bastion,' said Gaaz when I told my section the news. 'At least there's a chance of seeing some action out here. And the food's better.'

'Yeah, give me Now Zad any day,' said another.

'Careful what you ask for, *guruji bhai haru*,' I countered. 'We're very vulnerable out here if things turn nasty.'

All the same, that night I had what was probably the best sleep I would have during the whole of our time in Now Zad. We were now in good shape in terms of our defences, and at least it looked as though we had identified a supplier of good fresh food in the form of Afghan goat. If it wasn't for the fact that we knew that 10 Platoon had had such a hard time of it just before we got here, plus that contact we had on landing, you'd have said it wasn't such a bad posting at all. And yet I had an uneasy feeling this could be the calm before the storm.

The next day began like all the others. The *disha* patrol, followed by the call to prayer, then an hour until breakfast. But although we were still really keyed up and fully alert, you couldn't spend the whole time on duty just doing the same thing over and over. That would be impossible. As section commander, the moment I got up into the sangars I was busy checking all the equipment and making sure the *bhai*s and *guruji*s were doing their job properly. But then of course we started to chat a bit, especially in those early days when there wasn't anything much going on.

One thing the riflemen were all desperate to know about was

my previous experience in Afghanistan. I'd been one of a few of our people chosen for a tour back in 2003. On that occasion our mission was the reconstruction of the northern provinces. Among other things, this involved going round and searching for weapons and ammo dumps. The idea was that, after identifying them, noting their location and doing a survey of all they contained, the information was relayed back to HQ and the dumps would then be taken under allied control. With this as our aim, we had deployed in teams of six men, with two Land Cruisers per team, for several weeks at a time.

'So you mean you could travel around quite freely?' demanded Gaaz. 'You never got shot up, *guruji*?'

'Actually no. Our biggest worry was landmines. It was really different in those days. The Taliban were on the run and most of the places we went were in the hands of the warlords of the Northern Alliance.'

'Warlords! What do you mean?'

'These were the leaders of the Northern Alliance, which was the main group back in those days. They were on friendly terms with us, so we didn't have much trouble.'

'But did you ever meet any of them?' Gaaz was really excited at the thought of there being warlords. I think he secretly liked the idea of being one himself.

'There were two I met several times. General Dostum and Atta Muhammad.'

'Go on, what were they like?'

'Dostum was a real tough guy. But Atta – he was more like a movie star. You know, sunglasses, good clothes, all that.'

'Cool.'

'But it was General Dostum I saw the most. In fact I got to

92

know him quite well. We met five or six times altogether. One time we even stayed in his house.'

'You did?'

'Yes, and I'm telling you, it was like a palace!'

Gaaz stared at me as if he couldn't imagine such a thing as a palace in Afghanistan.

'You wouldn't think there could be places like that, but it was just like being in a millionaire's house anywhere in the West.'

Not that I'd ever been in a millionaire's house in the West. But I'd seen plenty on TV.

'It looked like an ordinary compound on the outside. A bit like this one. We'd been driving across the desert for hours without seeing anything, then we came to this place in the middle of nowhere. Just like here, there were a few small houses on the outskirts, flat-roofed and made with mud walls. The centre of town was just a street lined with some tumbledown shops on either side. And then you could see larger compounds with high perimeter walls and gates that opened onto a court-yard with buildings inside. The compound itself looked like any other, and we drove in. The main house looked quite ordinary too. But when you stepped inside, wow!'

The *bhai*s and *guruji*s looked at me, disbelieving.

'I'm telling you, it could have been anywhere in the West. I was completely shocked. There were people all around living in terrible conditions, with dust and dirt everywhere, while behind the wall was this incredible luxury! Even the bathrooms. You went into the guest toilet and you were completely surrounded by mirrors. It was really something.'

Of course, in Nepal we also have some very rich people who live lives of unimaginable luxury compared with the poor people of the country. On the other hand, my impression was that an ordinary Nepalese family lived better than the equivalent Afghan family. No one ever heard of a person dying of starvation in Nepal, whereas I believe that in Afghanistan people do occasionally die from lack of food. I think part of the difference is that Nepalese are harder workers. Certainly as far as the hill people are concerned, we have to rely entirely on agriculture, without any vehicles or machinery, and because of this we have to be completely self-sufficient, so that could be one reason. The Afghans have their agriculture too, but it was hard to understand how they survived, as the only crops I ever saw were watermelons and poppies and some potatoes. Also I had the impression that the Nepalese family system is closer than it is in Afghanistan. People look after each other more.

'And what about the general?' one of the other riflemen wanted to know. 'What was he like?'

I told them about the first time I'd seen him, surrounded by heavily armed bodyguards carrying a huge assortment of weapons from AK-47s through PKMs to RPGs. You immediately knew who was the boss round those parts. He was rather red, but with a very smiley face, and he wore a small black waistcoat to match his bushy black beard. Unlike most of the people you met in Afghanistan, his clothes were clean. In short, he really looked the part, strongly built and tough, even if he was a bit overweight. His manner was also very forceful. I remember him going straight up to Major Bevan, our team leader, and slapping him firmly on the back. He looked and behaved just like a warrior king of olden times.

'How arrrre *you*?' he said, rolling his r's in a way that we Gurkhas cannot, and emphasising the last word.

I distrusted him at once.

'And so did our *torjeman*,' I said. 'I could tell he was really scared to meet the general. Very proud to, but also very afraid. I suppose he knew that if it wasn't for us being there, things would have been very different. He told us afterwards that if the general didn't like a person, he would hit them. It didn't matter who they were. He told us that Dostum had killed a lot of people in fights.'

'Wow!' said Gaaz. 'I wish I could have met him!'

From talking to our interpreter later, I gathered that the general had two wives, an older one and a younger one. In Afghanistan, there seems to be nothing to stop a man taking even a young girl as his wife, no matter how old he is.

Over the course of several weeks, I met the general quite a few times in different places. It was always the same. There would be a huge house, with a big sitting room and lots of good food.

Apart from his looks and his manner, one thing that really impressed me about Dostum was the fact that he had risen to such a position despite being not very well educated, so far as I could tell, and despite not even being Afghan. Surprisingly enough, he was actually an Uzbek from Tajikistan.

The other surprising thing about the general was that although he had no formal military background, he had managed to acquire so much equipment – a huge armoury in fact. There were tanks, artillery, small arms and even, I heard, a helicopter for his own personal use. The Russians had left behind a vast amount of kit when they pulled out in 1989, and I suppose it must have been easy for the local leaders to take it over. Mind you, by the time we got there, the Americans had already destroyed a lot of the ammunition. Maybe that's why the general was so cooperative. All that equipment was no good to him if he didn't have the ammo for it. I wonder if he calculated that by making an alliance with the Americans he could get stuff from them.

I also heard that some of the warlords, whenever they went to one of their houses would call all the local girls to come and dance for them. Then they would choose one and keep her for as long as they were there.

By the time we got to Now Zad in 2006, however, General Dostum was completely out of the picture. I heard he had gone into exile in Turkey, though at the time of writing he is back in Afghanistan as Vice President. Meanwhile the Taliban had made a big comeback as an insurgency movement determined to expel the British and their allies from the country. So after hearing about my adventures on that first tour, the *bhai*s and *guruji*s wanted to hear everything I knew about them. Unfortunately, it wasn't much.

'Did you actually see any Taliban, *guruji*?'

'None at all. But don't forget, we were right up in the north. They never got that far. Besides, you'd never know if you did see one. They look just like everyone else. They don't wear uniform or anything.'

That was what made looking at the local Now Zad people so disconcerting. You had no idea whose side they might be on. As a result, we spent a lot of time up in the sangars speculating who the bad guys could be.

'Is that what you think, *guruji*? Do you reckon those *jatha* who hit us could be right outside in the street? Don't you reckon they've gone somewhere else?' Gaaz wanted to know.

'No idea. All I can tell you is that they're out there somewhere. And sooner or later, they'll be back.'

'What about their weapons, *guruji*? Do we know what weapons they've got?'

'Well, according to all the reports I've heard, it's still mainly Russian small arms.'

'So you didn't manage to get them all when you were here back in '03!'

'Definitely not.'

'But even so, you might have thought they'd all be broken by now. They don't exactly look after their weapons, do they?'

'That's true. But don't forget, these guys are getting stuff in from other places all the time, places like Iran and Syria.'

It wasn't until day four or five that we came under attack again. It's hard to be sure of the exact timings of the smaller contacts, as I didn't keep a diary and I don't know of anyone who did, though the OC kept a log of the most serious actions later on. I am also sure my memory of some things is a bit confused, as we were under such pressure at the time, and people will remember the same events differently. But as I recall, that first attack came sometime around mid-morning. I was off duty when the sound of automatic small-arms fire made us all look up.

'WOW! What was that?'

'Where's it coming from?'

'Did you hear that?'

Everybody spoke at once, instantly alert.

A moment later, Corporal Santos's voice rang out round the compound.

'STAND-TO! STAND-TO!'

I grabbed my weapon and my helmet. From listening on the PRR I understood that Sangar 6 was being engaged by medium machine-gun fire. At that moment, they were looking for clues as to where it was coming from.

'Possible fire position in treeline five to six hundred metres west.'

'Roger. Observe and return fire as soon as you get a PID.'

Pressing the Transmit button, I called the *bhai*s and *guruji*s in sangars 1 and 3.

'Everything OK, *guruji bhai haru*? Can you see anything?'

'All OK,' came the reply. 'Observing. Baren saw some smoke, but it turned out it was just some people cooking.'

'Roger. I'm coming up anyway.'

The sound of Sangar 6 followed by the CT both opening fire with GPMG filled the air as I climbed up into Sangar 1. They'd spotted muzzle flash in the treeline. There followed an exchange of fire that lasted about five or ten minutes. In the meantime, I told my guys they mustn't make the mistake of focusing only on the woodline.

'This could be the start of something big, you just don't know,' I said. 'We've got to keep an eye out all round. Don't get drawn into just looking at the one position. There could be raiders moving in nearby.'

'There's still quite a lot of traffic, *guruji*,' observed Baren. 'Do you think the enemy would want to risk getting mixed up in it?'

'They could be using it as cover,' I replied.

Just then a motorcycle drove slowly past. I could have sworn that the *jatha* on the back wasn't just looking up at us out of innocent curiosity. I pointed my weapon at him, pinning the cross-hairs to his head.

'That one's a spy for sure,' I said as the bike rode off. 'They're looking to see how we are reacting, I'm sure of it.'

'Yes, and I'm sure he had a weapon hidden under his clothes. Did you see the way he was sitting on the bike, *guruji*?'

'That's just what I was thinking. Could have been an AK, could even have been an RPG.'

I picked up the field telephone.

'Zero, this is Sangar One. Motorcyclist heading in southerly direction along main road. Possibly armed. Looks like he was gathering intelligence.'

'Zero, roger. Can you still see him?'

'No, he's disappeared in the crowd.'

'Roger. Any sign of the shops opening yet?'

I looked up and down the street. Some were, some were not.

'A few. But not all,' I replied.

'Roger. Keep observing and let me know if you see anything else that looks suspicious.'

'Roger out.'

Even though it was possible the enemy was using the traffic as cover, one thing that made a quick attack unlikely was the fact that life in the centre of town seemed to be going on just as normal. Although some of the shops were still shut, there were a lot of people around, buying and selling. I moved to the other side of the sangar and scanned with my binoculars. Somehow it didn't feel like there was a big attack coming, not today anyway. The enemy was just checking us out. They wanted to know how good our reactions were and what we knew about their fire positions.

We were stood down about two hours after the initial contact. By then it was late morning and the sun was beating down on us. I'd never been so hot in my life. It was just as well we were expecting a resupply soon, as our water stocks were going down at an alarming rate. We were each drinking at least ten litres a day.

For the rest of the morning and into the afternoon, everyone was on edge. Even so, we went on with our normal routine. This meant, among other things, carrying on with the various board games and football that had been going on round the compound.

I'd been playing Gaaz at *bagh chal* when the contact started, and we went back to it that evening.

'You're a good player, Gaaz,' I said, as I got him into a losing position. 'But not quite good enough!'

He smiled.

'I'll get you next time, *guruji*. You wait. I'll play goats and then you'll see.'

But I have to admit, despite the humour, I was starting to feel very nervous. That contact reminded me just how vulnerable we were.

After the game, I went up to check on the men in the sangars and gave them a good pep talk.

'OK, *guruji haru, bhai haru*? So now we know for sure they're still out there. They could be back any time. And when they do come back, it could be a full-scale attack. So you're gonna have to stay alert at all times, all right?'

'Yes, *guruji*.'

'Main thing is, don't get fixated on what's right in front of you. You've got to keep a full three-sixty lookout. Look ahead, yes, but also to the side. Even behind. You just don't know, they could sneak a man inside and come up when you're least expecting.'

'Do you really think so, *guruji*?'

'Definitely. Could be one of those local police guys.'

The *bhais* looked at each other and nodded.

'I don't trust any of those *jatha*,' said Baren.

'So you need to keep switched on at all times,' I continued. 'You've got to check, check, check. Could be they'll try and get a ladder up against the side when you're not looking. Could be they'll do something to distract you and then climb up and post a grenade inside.'

It wasn't hard to convince the riflemen of the need to be vigilant, but still it was worth reminding them. You can't repeat yourself too often, especially about basic SOPs.

'You're gonna be tired,' I added. 'Could be the attacks are going to last all night. So that's when you need to be able to do things without even thinking. That's why they're called Standard Operating Procedures. You should be able to do them automatically.'

'Yes, *guruji*.'

'All right, so you know where I am. If you have even a small suspicion about anything you see, just call me, OK? And don't forget to check your comms. Every five minutes, no longer.'

'*Hasur, guruji*.'

After briefing my section like this, I went back down into the compound to get some rest. I slept even less than usual, but there were no further incidents and we had a quiet night.

In the morning I was back on duty in Sangar 3, with Gaaz and Nagen as usual.

'Seen anything?'

'No, *guruji.*'

'What about anyone else? Have you been listening out on the PRR?'

'Nothing out of the ordinary, *guruji.*'

It was the same this morning as it had been every morning. Quiet except for the occasional bark of a dog, and yet I had this strange feeling that something was different. Maybe I was just imagining it, but I had the feeling that things were about to get a lot more serious.

For the first half-hour of my duty, I spent the whole time checking everything over and over, and I made sure that everything was stowed exactly where I wanted it. The field telephone out of the way, but within reach. A good supply of grenades out of their boxes and ready to throw. Belts of ammo laid out neatly. Map, binos, chinagraph close at hand. Field dressings – where were the field dressings? You never knew when you were going to need them.

'Over here, *guruji.*'

'OK, fine.'

What about water? Yes, there was plenty of water too.

'Anyone want a biscuit?' I always used to take up a packet or two of biscuits with me. Good for morale.

'Looks like another day at the office, *guruji,*' said Gaaz after some time.

It did feel a bit like that in a way. Here we were, back doing the same thing as the day before and the day before and the day before that. Except that in most offices you don't expect to be blown up at any moment.

There was the usual checking of comms between the CT and

the other sangars, and I spoke regularly to the *bhai*s and *guru-jis* in Sangar 1, just to make sure they were fully alert too. Eventually, though, as the morning wore on, the talk in the sangar turned to thoughts of home. It's something we Gurkhas never tire of talking about. Wherever we are in the world, we never forget where we come from and it's never long before the subject comes up. Gaaz in particular was always asking me about my place, as we were from opposite ends of the country and he wanted to know what life was like where I came from. I think it was partly that, and also partly the fact that he was trying to work out what made me tick. He wanted to know every detail of my early life, and then all about my time in basic training. Although I was only six or seven years older than him, he really looked up to me. Gurkhas have a very high regard for people in authority, so this wasn't as much a personal thing as him wanting to understand what it took to start climbing through the ranks. It was almost like he was doing a reconnaissance, so that when the time came, he would know the lie of the land.

'So, *guruji*,' he would always begin. 'Tell us some stories. When did you first hear about the Gurkhas?'

'From my grandfather. He was a Gurkha in India,' I replied.

As well as serving in the British Army, we have a long tradition of serving in the Indian Army. Of course, it's the British Gurkha regiments that people really want to join, but in my grandfather's day it made no difference, as the Indian Gurkha regiments were all part of the British system. India was still part of the British Empire until 1947.

'And what made you want to join, *guruji*?'

'My grandfather again. He said it was the way to prove you were a real man.'

'My dad said the same,' said Gaaz, and Nagen nodded in agreement.

'But in my own case, I think the thing that really inspired me more than anything else was my grandfather's gun.'

'Your grandfather's gun? How come? Tell us about it, *guruji*.'

That old rifle is one of my earliest memories. It was stuck through a hole in the wall of the house, pointing outwards so it could be fired at an intruder. Of course it never was, but as a kid I was completely fascinated by that gun and longed to play with it. But my grandfather was very strict and I was never allowed to even touch it. It wasn't until I was eight or nine years old that he finally let me have a proper look while he explained how it worked.

One memorable day not long after that, my grandfather took the gun down off the wall and announced we would go out and fire it. I was beside myself with excitement. My grandfather was an excellent shot, and he brought down a bird at the first attempt. I remember that when it went off, the noise was incredible. After that, I was always asking him to take me shooting, and in fact several times he did take me for *shikar* – that is to say, hunting.

Shikar became my favourite pastime. But because there was no question of my grandfather actually giving me his gun, when I was about eleven years old I decided to build one of my own.

'No way, *guruji*,' said Gaaz, not quite believing me.

'I did.'

'Wow, *guruji*. That's insane.'

Actually, Gaaz was right. It was a very risky thing to do. I started off by talking to as many people as I could about what made guns work. I learned all about the charge and how you needed to have a seal between the shot and the barrel so the explosion would force the shot along it. And I learned about how the trigger worked – how it made a spark that ignited the charge which in turn propelled the round up the barrel. Then I looked very carefully at my grandfather's gun to see how all these things fitted together.

I could see that the big difficulty would be to obtain a suitable barrel, but then I hit on the idea of using an old umbrella. Its hollow metal shaft would be ideal. So, having got hold of one, I closed up one end by banging it with a hammer and then I began to drill a small hole for the charge. I remember some of my cousins gathering round as I worked.

'What are you doing, Kailash?'

'I'm making a gun, of course.'

'A gun?'

'Yes, a gun.'

I could tell that none of them believed I could possibly succeed but, after making the hole for the charge, I took a long nail and fashioned it into a striker by bending it. This I attached to the shaft with several plastic bands. I was determined to prove them wrong.

Making the stock was the easiest part. I got hold of a piece of wood and shaped it with my kukri. I then tied the barrel to the stock using some wire I had.

For ammunition, I used the remains of an old metal pot that had been thrown away. Smashing it with a hammer, I used the fragments as pellets, hitting them until they were round. These I wrapped in paper so they wouldn't be loose in the barrel. From talking to various adults, I'd learned that there should be as little gas escaping round the ammunition as possible.

The next thing I needed was a charge. It would be difficult and expensive to get hold of gunpowder, but I had the thought of using the phosphorus on the tips of a box of matches. Six boxes cost one rupee, and I reckoned I needed at least two per shot. My biggest problem was how to get hold of some money. I knew from experience my mother wouldn't give me any, as I had often asked her in the past and she invariably refused. Luckily for me, I knew where she kept it, all rolled up very tightly and tied with a bit of cotton. One day, when no one was in the house – by this time we had moved into our own home, so fortunately there were times when it was empty – I stole two rupees. In those days, there were around seventy rupees to the pound, so this was the equivalent of about three pence – enough to buy thirty juicy oranges in the bazaar. I was absolutely determined to have a gun of my own and, feeling very guilty, I took the stolen loot and bought twelve boxes of matches. Luckily my mum hardly ever counted her money, so she couldn't be certain whether any had gone missing. There were a few times when she asked me if I had taken anything, but I'm sorry to say I denied all knowledge. In fact it was only very recently that I confessed the crime. My dear mother was really surprised, and she laughed and laughed when I told her.

'Well I never,' she said between chuckles. 'Who'd have thought it!'

After I had got the matches, I called my friends Mauta and Dhan and Hom over. These were three of my closest companions. Mauta was a near neighbour of ours, and a classmate of mine, even though he was a bit older than me. Mauta wasn't his real name – it actually means 'Fatso' – but that's what me and his family always called him. It was a bit unfair, as he wasn't really fat at all. You didn't see fat people in Khebang. He was just a bit chubby, that was all. Chubby, and quite serious. He could be aggressive too – a good man to have on your side.

Dhan was very different. He was one of those boys who quite fancy themselves. He had long hair and always carried a comb in his back pocket. But he was a good guy and full of laughter – the complete opposite of Hom, who was a man of few words. Maybe this had something to do with the fact that he came from a huge family. Hom had twelve brothers and two or three sisters as well. Although child marriage didn't happen much any more, his parents had been put together when very young. I think his father had been about nine, and his mother twelve at the time, so I suppose it wasn't too surprising they had so many children of their own.

'I'm going to fire my gun,' I announced.

'What gun?' they demanded.

'The one I've made,' I said proudly.

'You've made a gun?'

'I don't believe you.'

'You're lying.'

'Come with me,' I said, 'and I'll show you.'

They were completely astounded when I brought it out.

Taking it off into the jungle, I used my kukri to carefully scrape the phosphorus onto a piece of paper.

'What's that for?' Mauta wanted to know.

'It's the explosive,' I replied mysteriously.

When I had what I thought would be enough, I poured it carefully down the barrel, tapping the sides to make sure it all went to the end. The next thing was to carefully load one of my paper-wrapped pellets and push it right down to the bottom with a stick so that it compacted the charge. Finally, using some of the leftover powder, I poured a little of it round the hole I had made at the base of the barrel.

The other boys were really impatient.

'Come on, Kailash. Hurry up!'

'It can't be that difficult, can it? When are you actually going to fire it?'

'This is taking too long.'

But I took my time, as I wanted to be sure everything was done properly.

Eventually, the great moment arrived and I was all set. I'll never forget the good feeling I had bringing the stock into my shoulder. It was a bit awkward pulling the nail back to fire but it went off with a fantastic bang.

'WOW!' said Mauta.

'WOW!' I said.

'WOW!' said Dhan.

'WOW!' said Hom.

For ages I just sat there beaming while the others begged and begged me to let them have a go.

'Oh please, Kailash!' said Mauta. 'I'll be your best friend for life.'

'Me first, me first,' said Dhan. 'Remember I gave you some curd the other day.'

'What about me?' said Hom. 'Aren't we best buddies?'

But I said I needed to conserve ammunition. Maybe they could have a go another time.

Unfortunately, when my dad found out about the gun he wasn't at all pleased, so in the end, I probably only fired it fifteen or twenty times. Dad made me show it to him and then proceeded to explain that I was very lucky it hadn't exploded. I could see the sense in what he was saying even then, and today of course I realise it could have caused me serious injury. But I don't regret the experience. It was enough to convince me that when I was older I would have a proper gun. Not only that, one day I would be a soldier, a Gurkha in fact.

'Wow, *guruji*! You're a top man!' said Gaaz after I'd finished telling the story. 'I never did anything that exciting when I was a kid. I did have a catapult and a kukri, though,' he added.

There can't be many Nepalese country boys who don't have a catapult and a kukri. In my own case, I used the catapult for killing birds, and my kukri for skinning them. Killing birds with a catapult is quite easy if you have a good aim and so long as you have the right kind of ammunition. I used to spend hours looking for suitable stones and pebbles. It wasn't often you could find something exactly right, so I used a hammer and chisel to make them as smooth as possible. Then I would go out, often alone, in the hope of bringing something home to eat. Sometimes I succeeded, and I enjoyed cooking my kill, though I have to admit that none of the birds I took from the forest ever tasted very good. Actually, as I got older, I started to lose interest in the sport and in fact began to feel bad about my hunting expeditions and the nest-raiding I also used to do, even if at the time it felt like the best thing in the world.

The other thing I enjoyed doing in those days was taking my catapult and firing it at the monkeys in the jungle. They would let out a great squeal if you managed to hit them, but I now feel a bit bad about this too.

The kukri was a different matter. I was given my first one

when I was about four years old and I never left home without it. The first one I had was only quite small, so when I was about nine or ten, I told my parents I needed a full-sized one. After a lot of pestering on my part, my father eventually agreed and called the *kami* to the house. As a blacksmith, this person was from a lower caste, and he was not allowed inside, but he brought a blade which I sharpened and then made a handle and a scabbard for, both out of carved wood. As with any proper kukri, it came with two much smaller blades. These are called *chakmak* and are for sharpening.

Here I just want to say something about caste. It's something I've never really understood. The tradition of caste discrimination is not very strong among the Limbu people, but in parts of Nepal it matters a lot. The idea that you can or can't do certain things just because you happen to have been born into one kind of family rather than another makes no sense to me. People from lower castes can perform exactly the same tasks as other people. They can do exactly the same job. It's just a question of schooling. Yet in Nepal, because the great majority of positions in government are held by the upper caste, it's almost impossible for those from the lower castes to get in a position where they can give their children a good education. Because of this too, it is very frustrating for people of lower caste whenever they try to get something done that requires any sort of official sanction. It isn't unusual for such people to be met with shouting and outright rudeness when making even simple requests. Often they get blocked for no other reason than caste. The only thing that makes a difference is payment of money. Occasionally I discussed the subject with Gaaz, and he strongly agreed with me.

'It's just not fair,' he said. 'Anyway, who made these rules? Where did the idea come from? Why should one person be allowed to enter a house and not another? They're all human, aren't they?'

Gaaz had a very thoughtful side to him, and I really liked him for it – though he had a good sense of humour too. Probably more than me in fact. I especially remember how he used to make me laugh first thing every morning when I went on duty.

'*Namaste, guruji*,' he used to say. 'You're just in time for the *disha* patrol.'

Sure enough, not long afterwards came the first slow-stepping figures in the pre-dawn dark.

'I'll cover the one on the left, *guruji*. You can have the old lady on the right,' he said, bringing his rifle up to his shoulder. 'Always assuming it's not a suicide bomber ... I mean it could be, couldn't it? This could be the start of a big attack. They blow the gate in and follow on with a full-scale assault. For all we know, the alleyways could be full of fighters.'

'Well, that would certainly be a good tactic,' I replied.

'Except I don't think she is a suicide bomber,' whispered Gaaz a few minutes later. 'More like a stink bomber!'

It's amazing how a bad smell carries in the cool of the early morning.

'Oh please, *guruji*!' he went on. 'Couldn't I just put down one or two rounds? Not too close, you understand. Just to make them remember their manners. What do you think?'

Of course I knew Gaaz wasn't being serious, but I have to admit the thought did appeal to me. Couldn't they do their business somewhere else?

Soon after the *disha* patrol appeared in the pre-dawn half-light, the muezzin's call broke out in several places around town. In the early days of our occupation of the safe house, we mostly used to listen in silence. Sometimes Gaaz or one of the other riflemen would make a rude comment, but it was just a fact of life in Afghanistan, and it wasn't until later that we started to wonder what role the mosques were playing in the Taliban's operations.

This was one of our last quiet mornings and, as the sun, and with it the temperature, began to rise, there still wasn't much going on – apart from the men following the women to do their early-morning business. This brought more rude comments from the riflemen before again the chat drifted into talk about home, about wives and girlfriends, and Gaaz questioning me about my early life.

'This time of day reminds me of taking the cows up to the pastures in the summer. Did you ever look after your family's cattle, *guruji*?' he asked on one occasion.

Up until I went to school aged seven, my life revolved around the family farm. We had two fields next to the house, and several more further up the valley. As well as the main crops of rice and maize, we grew various other crops. There were also three or four goats and two bullocks.

'Taking them to the jungle was one of my favourite jobs,' I replied. 'And best of all was the fighting.'

'Fighting?'

The thing was, I sometimes got Mauta and Dhan and Hom to come along and we would stage bullock fights.

'It was the best fun,' I nodded. 'Especially as mine usually won.' I made a point of looking after them really well for that very reason.

'Hey, *guruji*, you're a hard man,' exclaimed Gaaz. 'But didn't you get into trouble for it?'

'Well of course we kept it a secret. Once, though, I nearly did get caught out.'

After a fight, it was our habit to let the bullocks graze in the jungle while we played in a nearby pond. On this occasion, me and my friends were so busy that it was quite late before we called the cattle and set off home. Unfortunately, in my case, the cattle did not come.

'SINDUREH! ... MALEH!'

I called and called, but there was no sign of either of them.

'Sorry, Kailash, but I need to get going,' said first Hom, then Dhan and finally Mauta, until I was all alone in the fading light of the dusk.

'SINDUREH! ... MALEH! ... Please come! I will give you extra hay ... Please ... '

They were nowhere to be seen.

In the end, I had no option but to set off home myself, as it was almost pitch black by now. I was desperate. My dad was going to kill me and I wouldn't be able to do anything about it. I'd neglected my duty.

'SINDUREH! ... MALEH!' I called one last time before setting off forlornly back down the hill.

If only Bhagawan would send them back to me.

It was so dark when I got back to the house that I could only just see its outline against the sky. For a few moments I stood outside, trying to summon the courage to enter. I was just about to go in and confess when, to my astonishment, I heard the familiar sound of hoofs brushing through the grass behind me.

'Thank God! Maleh! You're back! Sindureh! You're here and you're OK!'

I could have cried with relief.

'Kailash? Is that you?'

It was my father's voice.

'Yes, Dad.'

'Where have you been?' he said crossly as he stormed out of the house.

'Nowhere. I just wanted to give the cattle some extra grass. We're ploughing tomorrow, aren't we?'

'Hmmm. I wish I could believe that was the real reason. Well, hurry up and put them away. Your mother was getting worried.'

'So did he ever find out, *guruji*?' demanded Gaaz.

'No, but I'm sure he suspected something,' I replied. 'Because for a long time after that he didn't let me take them out alone.'

7

A Traitor in the Compound

Later that same morning, the OC called in the section leaders and told us there would shortly be a resupp coming in by Chinook from Bastion. He expected it to be some time around 1200 hours local, but he would give us five minutes' notice to move when he had exact timings. Mathers *sahib* would command from one WMIK. Me, Gaaz and Nani *guruji* would take the other and one of the *bhai*s from Corporal Santos's section would drive the quad bike. The 2 i/c would give a separate briefing after this one, but so far as everyone else was concerned, it was vital not to give any indication of our intentions to the Afghans.

'Just in case any of them feels like telling their friends in the neighbourhood . . .' said Rex *sahib* with a wry smile.

We all knew exactly what he meant. He didn't want anyone in the compound tipping people off outside. We didn't know for certain if this was going on, but we were reasonably sure of it. The local police in particular were always going in and out. It seemed likely they were telling people exactly what was going on with us, so it was vital they had no advance warning of what we were doing.

After talking with the OC, we went carefully over the route out and back with Mathers *sahib* – exactly the one we had followed on our way in – and rehearsed the various drills: course of action in the event of a contact, comms failure, vehicle breakdown, and so on. It was an SOP to start the vehicles every morning to make sure they were in good order, so we were confident in our equipment. All we would have to do was jump in, start up and go the moment the signal was given. There was no need for further discussion, though I would need to brief my *bhai*s and *guruji*s in detail. Speed was the key. The HLS was not exactly the same as the one we came in on, but at around eight or nine hundred metres away, it was about the same distance. The whole exercise should take not much more than fifteen to twenty minutes if we did it properly – a target we all agreed was feasible, especially since on this occasion there was nothing to go back on the heli. We were just collecting.

Having informed Gaaz and Nagen about the resupp, I was just heading towards the accommodation block when I was stopped in my tracks. One of the local policemen was walking across the compound with an RPG over his shoulder. That was enough to make me worried, and I was about to ask him where he was going with it when to my horror he raised the weapon and, taking no very careful aim, fired randomly in an easterly direction. The grenade blasted through the air and exploded a few seconds later somewhere harmlessly in the desert.

'WHAT ARE YOU DOING?' I demanded. Several other Gurkhas who had seen it came running over.

'What's going on?'

'What's he up to?' they all wanted to know.

'They will hear the noise,' the policeman said grandly. 'That will make them afraid.'

'Stupid idiot,' said one of the riflemen.

It certainly was stupid. The point is, every round wasted is one round less you have in your magazine when you really need it. But there was no point saying anything, so I let it go and went back in search of Nani *guruji*.

In fact there were several other occasions in Now Zad when something of this sort happened. I remember one time when one of the local militiamen actually came up into Sangar 1 with an RPG. We had been in contact, but at that moment it was completely quiet.

'What are you doing?' I demanded. 'Why have you got that thing?'

'I'm going to shoot it,' he replied.

'Where?'

'*Uddar, uddar.* Over there, over there.'

Although I tried to stop him, he just took aim at the building opposite and fired. I remember me and Gaaz and the other *bhais* looking at each other in complete disbelief. The building in question was clearly empty and in no possible way a legitimate target in the circumstances. It was the sort of thing I might have done as a ten-year-old boy. But in a way, it was completely in character. Whenever there was a contact, the Afghans would blaze away at random. Their shooting was completely without discipline in terms of adopting proper fire positions and conserving ammunition. On several occasions, I saw them actually firing one-handed from the hip. This is completely pointless. It's impossible to hit a target like that. Your rounds will just go all over the place.

I can't say the Afghans weren't brave in a way, however. They certainly weren't afraid to kill human beings. That takes some courage, to be sure. It was just that they didn't seem to care very much who they killed! It eventually got to the point when, if there was a sudden burst of fire, the *bhai*s would joke with one another.

'It's just the ANP firing,' they would say, or:

'ANP again.'

– to which the reply was:

'*Hunza*. ANP again. Nothing to worry about.'

On this occasion, we just watched in stunned silence as the policeman exited the sangar position without saying a word more and made his way back to his accommodation block as if he had no cares in the world.

'Oh my days,' said Gaaz very slowly and deliberately. 'What was that all about, *guruji*?'

I could think of nothing to say.

The sun was at its highest when the order for the resupp eventually came over the PRR.

'Reference the detail discussed earlier, five minutes' notice to move, OK?'

'Roger. Five minutes.'

'Five minutes,' agreed Corporal Santos.

This was exactly the right moment to be going out of the compound. The heat was so bad that even the locals were indoors. Nobody in their right mind would go out in this.

'Listen in, *guruji bhai haru*. The resupp is on,' I said to Gaaz and Nani. 'We move in five minutes, OK?'

'I'm ready, Kailash *bhai*,' said Nani, picking up his helmet.

'Me too,' said Gaaz, turning to the other riflemen sitting outside the accommodation block. 'Hey guys, this is just what I like. A resupp means there's a chance of a letter from my girlfriend AND the possibility of firing the Browning. It doesn't get much better than that.'

'Just make sure you aren't trying to fire it at the same time as you're reading the letter,' said one of the riflemen as Gaaz stood up. 'You might find you've got too much elevation!'

We all had a good laugh at this, including Gaaz.

'You're just jealous!'

Even now, because of the security considerations already mentioned, we had to make sure we didn't draw attention to ourselves as we prepared to leave the compound. The Afghans weren't much in evidence. Quite a few had gone out into the bazaar earlier. But it would only take a phone call from one of them to the right person and life could suddenly become very difficult for us. We did our best to appear as unconcerned as possible.

One last time, I was going over drills with Gaaz and Nani *guruji* outside the CT when Mathers *sahib* came out.

'OK, everyone, let's go! The chopper is on the approach.'

Straight away, we mounted up. Within thirty seconds of his order, the crews of both WMIKs were in place and the engines running. We did a quick radio check.

'Zero, Two One Charlie, radio check, over.'

'Two One Charlie, OK out.'

He then gave the order to move.

'Charlie Charlie One. Move now.'

At thirty-five seconds, the gate was open and our wheels were spinning.

We were very vulnerable going out like this, and the thought of someone lobbing a grenade or firing an RPG made me very nervous. At the same time, it was a good feeling to be getting out of the compound after almost a week inside, good too to get a close look at our surroundings from a different perspective. On the way in, there'd been too much to take in to offer a really good grasp of the layout of the town. Now, I was able to see up alleyways and through windows as we passed, and I made a mental note of several places I could see would make good fire positions for the enemy. I'd mark them on a chart to make sure we got fire down there next time we came under attack.

'Charlie Charlie One, this is Sunray. Chinook inbound. Will be on HLS in figures two. Out.'

That was the 2 i/c.

If the helicopter was that close, we should be able to see it. I looked in the distance and there it was, at no more than a hundred feet now, the familiar – and comforting – sight of the twin-propped workhorse. The Chinook was the mainstay of troop movements in and around Afghanistan, and my heart always lifted when I saw one – though I have to say it lifted even more when I saw its escort. There was an American A-10 high above, providing air-to-ground support in case of difficulty. Although originally designed as a tank-buster, the A-10's Gatling gun had proved very effective against ground troops as well.

'Good news, *guruji bhai haru*,' I said. 'There's an A-10 up there too.'

'So long as it doesn't mistake us for the enemy!' said Gaaz. He was referring to an unfortunate incident a few weeks back when the pilot had accidentally engaged friendly forces – luckily with no harm done. The air liaison officer had immediately spotted what was going on.

Our timings were coordinated so that we would reach the site just a minute or two before the helicopter arrived. You didn't want to get there much sooner, as you didn't want the enemy alerted. Our first action on arrival was to clear the ground out to 5 metres from the centre, using a metal detector to check for mines and unexploded munitions. If we were satisfied it was safe out to 5 metres, we would then go out to a distance of 20 metres, again sweeping with the metal detector, before dropping down and taking up a defensive position. The idea was to spend as little time static as possible. In our case, there was both small-arms and indirect fire to think about.

There was a great roar of its engine and a beating of blades as the bird touched down, completely enveloped in its protective dust cloud. Then sixty seconds. That was the maximum time the pilot would ever stay on the ground. If he could get away in less, he would. On this occasion, I'd say it was no more than twenty seconds before the engine note changed to a whine as the pilot opened the throttle wide and took off again. The helicopter was already 200 feet up and starting to manoeuvre by the time I'd finished loading the first crate of ammo. Moments later he had disappeared into the distance, a dark shape swallowed up in the shimmering heat of the desert.

Because of the need to work as fast as possible, we had put just two riflemen out in a defensive cordon around the vehicles while the rest of us got everything loaded up at top speed.

As me and Nagen were busy piling the supplies into the back of the WMIK, Nani revved the engine while Gaaz swung the Browning round through 360 degrees on the lookout for enemy. Because we knew they must be somewhere close by, I was expecting us to be engaged at any moment. Even if they only had a few minutes' notice, it seemed highly likely they could at least get a machine gun or two in place.

I don't know exactly how long it took to get everything on board, but definitely not more than five minutes. We'd agreed beforehand that as soon as our vehicle was fully loaded, Nagen and I would go and load the quad-bike trailer. Or if Mathers *sahib* and his crew finished first, they would go. It was whoever finished first.

'OK, Nagen,' I shouted when we were done. 'You come with me.'

We ran over just in time to help the quad-bike driver heave the last few crates of water on board the trailer. If we'd been in the mood for talking, we might have said something about how heavy they were. But the fact is, when you're straining with every nerve in fear of the TAKTAKTAK that tells you you're under fire, you forget the weight of water.

'OK, *guruji haru, bhai haru*, well done. That's everything. Let's get going before anyone decides to have a pop at us,' said the 2 i/c, taking one last look round.

We ran back to our vehicle 20 metres away and scrambled on board. A second later, I heard Mathers *sahib* come up on the PRR.

'Ready, Zero Charlie?'

'Yes ready,' I replied.

'OK, go!'

And with that I gave Nani the thumbs up. He released the clutch, the wheels spun and we raced off back towards Now Zad. Less than five minutes later, we were back at the compound. The QRF were out in the street covering us and the gates were open as we roared inside. The whole sortie could hardly have taken more than fifteen minutes from start to finish. Nothing bad had happened. Maybe in reality the Taliban were busy preparing for the campaign of the following weeks.

Back inside, we quickly got the stores unloaded and distributed. In strict order of priority, we dealt with the ammo first, then the water, then the food. Things like spares for the radios, an extra nightsight or two and the mail came after. And while we did so, the Afghans stood looking on – enviously, I thought – and holding hands.

This was one of the strangest things we had noticed about the Afghans. They seemed to be very friendly with each other. What was more, on Thursdays – which was their day off – they put on make-up. Most surprising of all was that leaders of both the ANP and the local police had young boys – teenagers or less – known as tea boys, who they took with them everywhere, even into their rooms at night. The first time I saw one of these boys, I was amazed to see his fingernails were painted red. Later I heard that because of the huge cost of getting married in Afghanistan, there are a lot of men who never do so. To pay the dowry costs a minimum of ten to fifteen thousand dollars, which many are never able to earn in their whole life. So it seems they take satisfaction in other ways. We found this very shocking. In our villages, if boys were good friends, they would sometimes walk round with their arms over each other's shoulders. But sex between men was completely unheard of.

'It's just as well we got more water in,' I remarked to the platoon sergeant, as we both stood surveying the small room it was stored in. 'At the rate we're going that's not going to last more than two or three days at most.'

'At least the well's working again if we need it,' replied Corporal Santos.

'Is it? That's good. I hadn't realised. Mind you, we want to avoid using it if we don't have to. We don't want to start going down sick with stomach problems.'

'That's right. That would be a big setback,' he agreed.

With the resupp out of the way, the afternoon dragged slowly on into the evening. It was another blisteringly hot day and we couldn't wait for the sun to go down – even if it did mean we were liable to come under attack again.

The one thing that did cheer everyone up was Gaaz's letter from his girlfriend.

'So, Gaaz, what does she say? Is she gonna marry you?'

'C'mon guys. It's not like that. I'm only nineteen, you know. And she's only eighteen.'

'Well if it isn't like that, what is it like? You tell us!' said one of the other riflemen.

'We're just friends, that's all.'

'Just friends? What's the point of that? So what do you do when you're together? Walk round holding hands like the ANP?'

There was a burst of laughter from all present.

'Well if you really want to know, the last time I saw her I got such a bad back I couldn't walk for three days.'

'You mean you were practising the *kama sutras*?'

'No, I was trying to climb up into her bedroom window when the gutter gave way and I fell down!'

This was one of the things I liked best about Gaaz. He could tell a joke about himself. We all had a good laugh at this.

In fact I think this really is one of the reasons we Gurkhas make such good warriors. Even when the going is really tough, we keep our sense of humour. Except when we were in contact or performing a specific task, a lot of the conversation was based on humour. Whenever I walked past the *bhai*s off duty there would always be someone making a joke.

I don't know how much later it was, but not long before sundown the air was suddenly torn apart by the sound of a sustained burst of fire from an automatic weapon.

'STAND-TO! STAND-TO!' the platoon sergeant's voice rang out a moment later as those of us not already wearing their helmets grabbed them.

'SANGAR THREE CONTACT!' Lance Corporal Shree's voice came up over the PRR. 'OBSERVING!'

The 2 i/c's voice replying was drowned by the answering sound of machine-gun fire from the CT.

Grabbing my rifle, I burst out of the accommodation block and, taking a quick look round, ran over to the sangar, ready to climb up. As I did so, I was surprised to see one of the Afghans standing outside their block talking on a mobile phone. Each time there had been gunfire before, the Afghans had been nowhere to be seen.

'*Guruji bhai haru!* Are you OK in there?' I shouted up. 'Any idea where it's coming from?'

'Not sure, but it could be Smuggler's House.' This was the name we'd given to the old two-storey school building.

The bloody school building. I always knew it was going to

give us trouble. Not that I blamed the enemy. It was exactly where I would put my weapons if I was in their position.

The exchange continued for about five minutes, not more. Lance Corporal Shree and the rest of the section joined with the *bhai*s on the roof of the CT in returning fire. But then it stopped.

I pressed the Send button on my PRR.

'Seen anything?'

'Nothing, *guruji*.'

'OK, I'm coming up.'

Before I did so, however, I looked back towards the CT and was just in time to see the OC emerging from the hatch on top of the CT roof. What you had to do was climb through this and then crawl or dash the short distance to the sandbags that had been put up to provide cover. But no sooner had the OC appeared than there was another long burst of enemy fire. They must have seen him! Maybe they'd even planned this. They'd engage the CT and then stop in the hope that he would come out to see what was going on, then try to hit him as he climbed up!

And it was at that moment I realised what was going on. Looking back towards the Afghan accommodation block, the same person was still standing there with his mobile phone held to his ear. The dirty *jatha*! He was directing the enemy fire! He had to be. I wanted to kill him there and then, but by this time the OC was safe behind the protection of the sandbags. Meanwhile, with my heart full of murder, I climbed into the sangar.

'Seen anything?' I demanded.

'Nothing, *guruji*.'

This made me even more frustrated, so after spending a few

minutes straining my eyes scanning possible fire positions, I told the *bhais* what I'd just seen. They all erupted at once.

'What! What are you gonna do, *guruji*?'

'Kill the *jatha*!'

'Where is he now?'

Looking down into the compound I could see that the local policeman had now disappeared inside. He obviously thought there was nothing more he could do.

'Well I'm not going to say anything over the radio. You don't know who's listening. But I'll tell the OC in person, as soon as I get the chance.'

After about an hour, we were stood down, and I went straight over to the CT to speak to Mathers *sahib*.

'Are you completely sure?' he wanted to know, when I finished telling him all I'd seen.

'Absolutely sure, sir. Not a question.'

'Right, well I think I'd better have a word with the *torjeman*. We'll see whether we can't confiscate the man's phone if that's what he's up to. I had an idea something like that was going on. He's the head man of the local police.'

'Confiscate his phone!' I put my hand on my kukri. Didn't he want me to kill him?

The 2 i/c must have seen how angry I was.

'It's all right, Kailash. Let me deal with this.'

I left the CT feeling bad for Rex *sahib*. He had enough on his plate without traitors in the house. I knew it was wrong, but in my heart I would have liked to put the little *jatha*'s head on a stick right outside the police quarters. Instead, all that happened was the OC persuaded him on some pretext to hand over his phone.

Of course, I now see that what the OC did was exactly right. If he'd given the order to kill, there's a good chance the Afghans would have turned against us completely. By taking the man's phone, Major Rex got the result he needed without loss of life and without causing a rebellion. But I must say that even now I would like to have killed that man for doing what he did. And I wouldn't be losing any sleep if I had.

8

A Change of Atmosphere

At that night's O-group, the OC announced that he was concerned about the safety of people getting on and off the sangars during daytime.

'It's quite clear that our friends in here are talking to their friends out there,' he began. 'We've now had several contacts clearly aimed at people going on and off their position. If this carries on, someone's going to get hit.'

We all nodded in agreement.

'So from now on,' he continued, 'I only want duties to change after dark – with all that that implies, I'm afraid. What is more, we are going to have to change duties at different times. We don't want a set pattern, OK?'

I looked at Corporal Santos. This was a serious development, but the OC was definitely right. They had obviously cottoned on to our movements, and even if one mobile phone could be confiscated, there was nothing to stop them acquiring another. They were still able to go in and out of the compound quite freely. But this meant that life was going to get considerably harder from now on. We would have to take rations up with us. We would have to organise ourselves so that we got rest while up in the sangar. And of course we would have to be careful not to need to defecate during the day, if we could help it.

The OC's change of tactics coincided with a change in the enemy's tactics too. The next morning, having gone on duty just before first light, I was up in Sangar 3 when a sound caught my ears that had me instantly on full alert. An explosion, maybe half a kilometre away, close to the base of ANP Hill, where there was a small graveyard.

'WOW! Did you hear that, *guruji*?'

What was going on? It was quite far away – too far to be dangerous – but it couldn't be friendly fire.

'It came from over there!' said Nagen, pointing.

'What do you think it was, *guruji*?'

I was busy looking through my binoculars for tell-tale signs of smoke when there was another crump – this time considerably closer.

A moment later a shout went up from Sangar 6 and the PRR crackled into life.

'IDF! I-D-F!'

Another voice joined in.

'TAKE COVERRRR!'

Mortars! A moment later there was a third explosion, this time less than 100 metres away. IDF, by the way, stands for indirect fire. The enemy was clearly creeping rounds onto us.

Another shout came over the radio. It was the section up on ANP Hill.

'CONTACT! SUSPECTED BASE PLATE IN REGION OF AOI SEVEN!' This was followed a second later by the sound of ANP Hill's sustained fire, their GPMG and Minimi being fired in anger. But it didn't come quite soon enough to prevent the enemy firing a fourth round, followed quickly by a fifth – both of which landed right inside the compound. I turned to see where they impacted. The damage was not great and it occurred to me that you would have to be very unlucky to get taken out by mortar fire. It's not very accurate. On the other hand, it's an excellent way of forcing people under cover while you launch an assault. And with that thought, I redoubled my efforts with my binoculars.

'Keep a good lookout, *bhai haru*. Could be this is the start of something.'

But that was it. The fire from ANP Hill must have been accurate enough to put the enemy off his aim, because the base plate went quiet, though we remained on a state of high alert.

A short while later, the OC came on the PRR to announce the imminent arrival of air support.

'B-52 will be delivering ordance onto suspected mortar position in figures five,' he announced. I immediately relayed his message to the rest of my section.

'*Guruji bhai haru*, be advised that air support will be hitting suspected mortar base plate in next few minutes.'

It turned out that by fantastic luck a passing aircraft had spotted a suspicious heat source and relayed the information to the bomber.

'Roger out.'

'If it's a B-52, do you think we're even going to see it, *guruji*?' demanded Gaaz. 'He won't come below about thirty thousand feet, will he?'

That was almost certainly correct.

'The plus point is that if we don't see him, the enemy won't either,' I replied.

'Yeah, the first thing he's going to know about it is when he's got thirty-six virgins come to take him away,' said Gaaz happily.

In fact, we did just catch a glimpse of the aircraft, but not before it had dropped two laser-guided 500-pounders on the position.

'HURRAH!' we all cried as they erupted in giant plumes of smoke.

'That'll teach them a lesson they won't forget!'

'Well done, everyone! Well spotted and good shooting!' The OC sounded really pleased. As this was our first successful engagement with the enemy, I guess that was hardly surprising, even though it was really the pilots who had done the job.

When we'd settled back down, I impressed on the *bhai*s that it was really important not to let anything go unreported. 'They're testing us for sure,' I told my section. 'Checking our reaction times, checking our arcs. No question about it. And they'll have noticed how long it took to get air support. A minute's a long time in battle. So if you see anything suspicious, anything at all, you must inform the CT immediately, OK? And if we do get given clearance to fire, don't mess about. We've got to show them we mean business.'

The enemy needed to be in no doubt about how the Gurkhas would fight if they decided to take us on.

It was strange looking out of the sangar later that morning.

Despite the contact, life in the town continued just as before. Most of the shops were open as usual and there were people milling about as if nothing had happened. The Afghans inside the compound behaved no differently. They appeared long after we'd been stood down and spent most of their time sitting in the shade talking or sleeping. There was no weapon cleaning or anything like that. In fact, the only thing they did with their weapons was to sometimes stick a flower in the barrel. Quite often you would see an AK-47 propped up against a wall with a marigold poking out the end.

Towards afternoon, however, we did begin to notice a change. There was a lot of extra traffic on one of the roads leading out of town.

'Take a look at this, *guruji*,' said Gaaz. 'Looks to me as if people don't like this place so much any more. Reference the road approx three kilometres.'

He was right. When I looked through my binoculars I saw a long stream of people – probably several hundred, including a lot of women and children – heading out of town in an easterly direction. Many were pushing small carts with their belongings piled high. Others drove donkeys laden with goods. Some of the kids, I noticed, were carrying chickens in their arms, while others were pulling goats along on leads. It was clear there was a major exodus under way.

I picked up the field telephone.

'Zero, this is Sangar One.'

'Zero. Go ahead, over.'

'Reference road running east–west approx three kilometres. Large movement of civilians. Looks like they're leaving town.'

'Zero, roger. Wait out.'

As all of my military readers will know, *Wait out* is the response you give when you need time to reply – in this case, Mathers *sahib* would probably be plotting this movement on his map, or perhaps speaking to someone else. Although the field telephone was secure, we more or less kept to standard radio procedure, partly out of habit and partly because it kept speech disciplined. When you are using a radio, what you don't do, for security reasons, is hold down the transmit button while you are undertaking some other activity. If you do, there is a strong danger that you give the enemy the chance to intercept the transmission and then follow the rest of the conversation. The idea is to keep all radio transmissions as short as possible. In our situation, it wasn't likely that the enemy had sophisticated equipment to break into our radio net, but he would know roughly on which frequency bandwidth we operated. By simply scanning this using an ordinary cheap scanner of the kind you can easily get on the internet, he might be lucky and intercept a transmission – especially if it was a long one. Then he'd be able to listen in until such time as you changed the frequency. In our case, that would mean until the end of the day – unless of course we became aware he was eavesdropping and changed sooner.

The telephone rang.

'Sangar One, this is Zero.' It was the 2 i/c again. 'OK, understood. I think you're probably right. Sounds like people could be moving away. Keep an eye out and let me know any developments.'

'Roger, out.'

'So what do you reckon, *guruji*?' Gaaz wanted to know, his curiosity aroused. 'Do you think they're abandoning the whole place to the Talibs? Maybe there's a really big attack coming and they know it?'

'Could be,' I replied. 'Could be the women and children are being moved out, and the elderly. In which case, yes, the Talibs might be taking over.'

'*Hunza, guruji.*'

In the event, though, the day wore on with no further sign of trouble. We were still pretty pumped up from the morning and passed the time in a state of high alert. Our tension was heightened by the fact that the traffic on the road out of town was heavy throughout the day. But after a while, we began to calm down, and soon Gaaz began asking me questions again.

'What about your school days, *guruji?*' he wanted to know. 'I bet you were a star pupil.'

Actually I wasn't, at least not to begin with.

In fact, during my first year, I was an extremely lazy pupil. The only thing that really interested me about school was the opportunity it gave for fighting. I was always challenging other boys, and one time I remember asking six or seven of them to take me on at once. They refused. The trouble for them was I was the tallest by far, taller than some of the kids five years older than me.

Best of all was when there were *lathi* fights between whole year groups. *Lathi* as we played it was a kind of kick-boxing. On these occasions, you would get thirty or forty people in a great bundle. Every so often, a few got hurt, but on the whole it was just really good exercise.

The other good thing about school was the opportunity for sport. We played football and volleyball, and when we weren't playing either of those, we would make our own balls out of discarded rags and plastic wrapped inside an old sock, which we proceeded to throw at each other as hard as we could.

But the learning side of things did not interest me one bit. The result of this was that when we sat an exam at the end of year one, I failed. I remember my uncle telling me the news.

'Kailash, you'd better look out. Your parents have just had your school report. You're in big trouble.'

I remember I was so ashamed that I ran to the top of the house and cried. It was at that moment I made up my mind that I wanted to be at the top of the class and not the bottom. As it turned out, it took me most of the second year to catch up, but by the end I finished in first place and after that, by working hard, I never lost my place.

'So you were a star pupil after all, *guruji*!' exclaimed Gaaz.

'Well, I suppose you could say that. But it didn't mean I stopped fighting and I was still always getting into trouble.'

Luckily for me the teachers usually let me off punishment. I put this down to my good performance in class and also in sport. I had quickly become quite a good volleyball player.

'Wow! I wish I could have been your friend back then, *guruji*,' said Gaaz. 'I suppose everyone knew you were planning to be a Gurkha one day, did they?'

Actually, that wasn't exactly right either. Although I'd started out with that wish, something happened to make me change my mind. When I was in Class 4 my mother gave birth to a little girl. I remember the first time I saw her, she seemed so small and beautiful. I nicknamed her Gudiya, meaning 'doll', because that was how she looked to me. I still call her that, even though she is now a teacher in a primary school. Unfortunately, it was a difficult birth and my mother became very ill. To make matters worse, this was the time that my father went to work in the Gulf. As a result, I had to start helping out in the house a lot. My grandparents kept an eye on us, and sometimes one of my aunties came to help out. But even so, I had to do all the cooking, as well as working in the fields both before and after school. The result was that for a long time, it became hard to keep my place at the top of the class. What was more, when I was actually in class I found it very hard to concentrate, as I spent the whole day worrying about my mother. Did she have enough food and water to see her through and how would she be when I got home? At the end of class, I used to run home even though it was uphill all the way.

'How are you, Mum?' was always the first thing I said as I went through the door, and always the answer was the same.

'I'm feeling a little better.'

But I knew it wasn't true. It wasn't until almost a whole year had passed that, eventually, she did start to improve. For a month at a time, she would be well, and then for the next month she would fall ill again. It alternated like that for a long period. But when she still didn't fully recover even after several years, I remember having a big argument with her. I told her she should go to the hospital in Jhapa district and see a proper doctor. Her sister would look after my sister.

'It's a waste of time seeing doctors,' she said. 'They just take your money and you don't get better. If you want, you can call the priest back.'

She said it was better to rely on the priests, as they had more power over the gods.

'After all, it is the gods who will decide whether I get better or not.'

Eventually, though, I managed to persuade her that, as she was not getting fully better with the priests, she should at least give modern medicine a try, and when she was having one of her good spells I took her down to the nearest bus stop. It was a real struggle for her. She could only manage a few minutes at a time before she had to take a rest. But she never complained. Altogether it took almost three whole days to get there, even though normally you can do it in just over twenty-four hours. In the end it was worth it. The doctors diagnosed some kind of heart problem and prescribed some pills. After that she made a good recovery.

But because of my mother's illness, for a long time I gave up my dream of joining the Army. I was determined to become a doctor instead. I really wanted to help her, and people like her. Instead of guns and ammunition, I became interested in biology and chemistry, both of which I excelled at. In fact, after passing my School Leaving Certificate aged seventeen, I enrolled for a science course at Hattisar College, the nearest place of higher education.

'So you nearly became a doctor, *guruji*!' exclaimed Gaaz. 'That's incredible. I can't imagine you with a stethoscope round your neck. So what made you change your mind again?'

'My grandfather.'

When I told him my plans, he said it was good if I became a doctor. 'But there's no harm in having a try at Gurkha selection,' he said. 'If you pass, you'll have a choice. If you don't – well, you have a college place.'

'That was good advice,' said Gaaz.

It certainly was, and I've never regretted taking it and putting myself forward for selection. But I must admit that there were moments in Now Zad when I might have thought different.

*

That evening, I remember me and Gaaz noticing the town was more or less deserted.

'What do you reckon, *guruji*? Do you think the Taliban are going to come visiting tonight?' demanded Gaaz.

'They could be back any time,' I replied.

In the event, the evening was quiet, and so was the night. Back on duty in Sangar 1 at first light with Gaaz and Nagen, we talked about what might be in store for us that day.

'They're bound to be back, aren't they, *guruji*?' said Nagen.

'Well even if it's not this morning, we've got to be ready for them,' I replied.

'I hope they do come back today,' said Gaaz. 'It would be good for them to see how Gurkhas fight. It would be a shame to go home without having the chance to show them.'

'Like I said, be careful what you wish for,' I replied. 'Ten Platoon were lucky not to take any casualties.'

As things turned out, we didn't have much longer to wait before the pace of life changed dramatically. But for one last day, we had plenty of time to talk. As usual, Gaaz steered the conversation back to my early life. He wanted to know about my experiences during selection.

'How many people were at your first selection, *guruji*?' Gaaz wanted to know. 'Did you get thousands like we did in Pokhara?'

'No, maybe six hundred,' I replied.

'Tell us about it, then, *guruji*. What happened? Were you nervous at all?'

'Of course! Everybody is a bit nervous, aren't they?'

'Well yes. But you're lucky with your height.'

At five feet seven, I am two or three inches taller than the average Gurkha, although I have noticed that recruits are getting bigger and bigger every year. It must be something to do with improved diet.

'Well it wasn't just that. I'd passed top out of my school, so as well as my School Leaving Certificate, I had a good report. That must have helped.'

Basically, every Gurkha's selection is exactly the same, so Gaaz's experience wouldn't have been much different from my own.

I was one of 32,000 hopefuls back in 1999 when I joined up. In those days, the Brigade was considerably larger than it is today, and there were approximately 250 places on offer. These days it's around 200. Then as now, the units making up the Brigade are two front-line infantry battalions of The Royal Gurkha Rifles, The Queen's Own Gurkha Logistics Regiment, Queen's Gurkha Signals, The Queen's Gurkha Engineers, Gurkha Staff and Personnel Support Company and The Band of The Brigade of Gurkhas. In all we are 2600 men at the time of writing. But, for example, during the Second World War, there were ten battalions and more than 250,000 Gurkha soldiers serving the British crown. So we are already a fraction of the numbers we used to be. On the other hand, there are approximately 100,000 Gurkha soldiers serving in the present-day Indian Army, plus maybe 2000 in the Singapore police. There are also some others elsewhere, such as in His Majesty the Sultan of Brunei's security forces.

But it is the British Army everyone wants to join. In the British Army Gurkha units, the standards are higher, the tradition is longer and the history is the best. In two hundred years of service to the British crown, Gurkha soldiers have won a total of thirteen Victoria Crosses and fought bravely all over the world.

9

The Brigade of Gurkhas

According to the history books, the first time British soldiers came into contact with Gurkha warriors was during the siege of Kalunga in 1814. On that occasion, just 650 Gurkhas defended a hill fort against a British force of 4000. It is said that as the battle was raging, a single Gurkha soldier appeared behind the British lines. He was holding his jaw, which had been shattered by a bullet, and indicated he wanted it bandaging up. No sooner had the bandage been tied in place than the soldier requested to be permitted to return to his own side to continue the fight.

This is the Gurkha way.

Today, one of the most famous names in Nepal is that of Captain (QGO) Rambahadur Limbu. He is the most recent Gurkha winner of the Victoria Cross, and the only one still alive. Not long ago, I visited his house to pay my respects but unfortunately he was not at home at the time. I had wanted to tell him that his action in Malaysia in 1965 had personally inspired me throughout my Army career. It was not until the end of 2014 that I finally got to meet him. What a great man.

The rank of QGO (Queen's Gurkha Officer) no longer exists, but it used to refer to someone who had joined up as a regular rifleman and worked his way through the ranks to become an officer. Nowadays, Gurkhas who come up through the ranks are treated exactly the same as regular British soldiers who become officers. At that time the highest-ranking QGO in the Brigade was the Gurkha Major, although there have since been more senior Gurkhas. Some years back, one of the battalions was actually commanded by an ex-QGO.

In any case, Captain Rambahadur Limbu won his VC back in 1965 in Malaya during a fire fight when two members of his section were wounded. The situation seemed hopeless and it looked as though the two injured would have to be left to die, as the enemy was only a short distance away. Rambahadur Limbu tried crawling to his comrades' position in the hope of getting them back to safety, only to be forced back by the weight of automatic fire. After some time, he tried again, with the same result. In the end, he realised the only way he could save the two men was by exposing himself completely and running across open ground in full view of the enemy – which he did, not once but twice. He then went back to the position a third time, and used the machine gun the two wounded men had been manning to inflict four confirmed casualties of his own.

As his citation says, Rambahadur Limbu's 'outstanding personal bravery, selfless conduct, complete contempt of the enemy and determination to save the lives of the men of his fire group set an incomparable example and inspired all who saw him'.

It was a great honour for me to be able to tell him personally that not only did his bravery inspire his own comrades, but it continues to inspire people to this day, myself included. I told him that the thought of his heroism, and the heroism of all those warriors of earlier times, is exactly what kept us going in the darkest moments of our time in Now Zad.

To us Gurkhas, our history is very important. It is how we keep our tradition alive. We remember and honour the great deeds of our ancestors, the men who have gone before us. When, today, a Gurkha does something heroic, he does not do it for himself, but for his comrades and in honour of these ancestors. For us, there is nothing greater a man can do than act courageously in battle, and we take enormous pride when one of our number is commended for bravery. For example, when Lachhiman Gurung was invested with the VC by the Viceroy of India in 1945, family members actually carried his disabled father for eleven whole days over the hills until he got to a road where he could take public transport down to Delhi.

The number of battle honours won by Gurkhas fighting alongside the British is too large to put them all down here. It is enough to say that there have been Gurkha regiments involved in all parts of the world the British have fought in during the last two centuries. These include the Indian Mutiny, Afghanistan (several times), the First World War – where they served both on the Western Front and in places like Gallipoli and the Middle East – and then the Second World War, again both in Europe and in the East, notably Burma. More recently, there have been further honours won in Malaysia, Borneo and the Falkland Islands.

A big change came about after the Second World War when in 1947 India became independent. By then there were ten Gurkha regiments, and it was decided that six would be absorbed into the Indian Army while four would remain under British command. But while the British Gurkhas have been cut still further, the numbers in India have continued to grow. There are now seven Gurkha regiments with a total of 39 battalions serving in the Indian Army.

To become a British Gurkha, you will be one in a thousand who succeeds in passing three selection boards in a process that the successful recruit will never forget. The first board is the local one. In my case, this was at Telog, a few hours' walk from Khebang village. I went down with two or three other guys from Khebang, people I knew but not close friends. I did talk to Mauta and Hom before going and they did consider putting themselves forward, but in the end they decided against it. I found that I was one of about six hundred candidates competing for just twenty places to go forward to the next stage. At first I was a bit nervous, but as I looked left and right I became more confident. Gaaz was right. I was taller and, judging from what I could see, fitter than most of the other guys. I also had my good School Leaving Certificate result. I felt confident that even if I wasn't at the top academically, I must be somewhere near.

We waited in a crowd, sitting or standing, until eventually the recruiting officer, or *galla*, came out and addressed us.

'RIGHT, LISTEN IN, EVERYONE!'

To start with he struggled to make his voice heard above the noise of six hundred eager young men chattering away.

'All right. ALL RIGHT. Q-U-I-E-T! If you want to be

Gurkhas you will have to learn to do as you're told, now QUIET!'

Eventually he established order.

'OK THANK YOU!' he began. 'So what's going to happen is that you will file in one by one in order of arrival. You will give your name, your village, your caste and your age. Then you will have one minute exactly to do some sit-ups. Then another minute to do some pull-ups. After that, there will be a health check, some running and finally an educational assessment. After that you will come back out here until the results are called at the end of the day.'

After the recruiting officer had finished speaking, everyone started excitedly talking again.

'How many sit-ups and pull-ups do you reckon you can do?'

'At least twenty of each.'

'Bet you can't do more than ten.'

'It's not as easy as it looks, you know.'

'I heard the record is fifty sit-ups and forty pull-ups.'

'That's impossible!'

'No it isn't.'

'Yes it is!'

Actually, the pass mark was twenty-five sit-ups and twelve pull-ups.

One by one, we were called forward into the building where the *galla* sat at his desk.

'Name?'

'Kailash.'

'Village?'

'Khebang.'

'Caste?'

'Limbu.'

'You said Limbu?'

'Yes sir. Limbu.'

'Right, go and wait over there. NEXT!'

We stood nervously watching the other potential recruits being put through their paces. The recruiting officer's assistant held a stopwatch and clipboard and had a slightly bored look on his face.

'All right, go!'

I recall that I achieved twenty-five sit-ups, just as required.

'Not bad. OK, do you see that bar over there?'

A thick length of bamboo was supported on a frame.

'What I want you to do is reach up and hang from it. Get your feet up off the floor. That's it. Feet off the floor, I said! OK, now you have sixty seconds. Go!'

Because of my height, I could actually touch the floor with my toes, so I had to bend my legs as I heaved.

'Right, go outside and wait.'

The whole thing couldn't have taken more than about five minutes, but now there was a long wait while the rest of the candidates filed in. In the meantime, some of the others asked me how I got on.

'How many did you manage, *guruji*?' Gaaz wanted to know.

'Twenty-five sit-ups and twelve pull-ups.'

'Seriously?'

'Yes. Why?'

'I managed twenty-six and thirteen!' he said proudly.

As things turned out, after the running and educational assessment, it became apparent that I'd done pretty well. In fact I don't think anyone had done more, so when I finally heard that I had passed, I was more relieved than excited. But when I got back home at the end of that week, my dad and my grandfather were completely delighted.

'Kailash! You have brought honour to the family! Now you must go to the final selection and pass that too,' said my grandfather.

'If you do, then you will have the respect of everyone in the whole of Limbuwan!' said my dad.

I later found out that I was the first person from Khebang village to have got through the first round for eighteen years – since my uncle, in fact.

My mother was not so pleased, unfortunately. She really wanted me to stay at home. My grandmother wasn't too enthusiastic either. But this didn't matter too much to me, as when I went to work in the fields the next day, everybody was talking about it. I remember playing volleyball in the afternoon with the other boys from the village, and they looked at me almost like I was a different person. Then afterwards several of the girls came up and tried to talk to me. Unfortunately, I was so shy, I didn't know what to say.

'You shy, *guruji*?' said Gaaz, interrupting. 'I don't believe it.'

But it was true, I was.

10

Ambushed

That night before going back on sangar duty, I did manage to get a bit of sleep, but it was only fitful. I kept waking with a start. I had this feeling we were under attack from inside the compound. Sitting up, I listened carefully, only to lie back down and drift off for another few minutes before it happened again.

Suddenly, I was fully alert. Why, I didn't know. There was no sound apart from the quiet snoring of the rifleman in a cot two or three bedspaces away from mine. Somehow I realised something was really wrong. My heart thumped in my chest and I readied myself to spring up in an instant. But while instinct was telling me to call out, an even more powerful force made me stay silent.

Concentrating with my whole being, I strained my ears. The rifleman's snoring had turned into heavy breathing while the intermittent crackle of radio traffic came from a helmet right nearby: someone had left their PRR switched on. But apart from that, there was no noise other than the barking of a dog in the distance.

Yet still I was sure something wasn't right.

As I mentioned, although some of the soldiers slept inside the building, my own section slept outside the accommodation block along the corridor that ran underneath its overhanging roof. My bedspace stood right in the corner of two adjoining walls and there were three or four other beds to each side of me.

Now as I lay on my back looking into the compound, I saw that the sky was quite cloudy and there was not much ambient light. Enough to make out shapes, but not enough to see detail.

Turning my head first to the left and then to the right, I scanned along each row. As usual, less than half were occupied. At this stage, we were sleeping with our boots off, but still fully clothed, with our helmets, our rifles and our webbing close at hand. I kept my rifle on my bed with me and, instinctively, I closed my hand round it as I squinted into the darkness.

But there was nothing.

I shut my eyes and relaxed my grip.

I must have drifted off for a few seconds – maybe even a few minutes – when, coming to yet again, I detected movement out of the corner of my eye. Not a hurried movement, just the soundless arrival of a darker shape close by. For just a second longer, I paused.

At first I assumed it must be one of the riflemen coming to wake the next person on duty. There was someone quite clearly squatting down next to the sleeping rifleman just two bedspaces away from mine. But, as I listened, the shape made no sound.

It just remained motionless. Only when it moved almost imperceptibly did I sit up – just in time to see a dull glint of metal.

All at once, I realised what I was looking at. A MAN WITH A KNIFE IN HIS HAND.

With a surge of adrenalin, I threw myself out of bed.

'*Ayee! What are you doing?*' I screamed as I leaped up, reaching not for my rifle but for my kukri.

The figure stood and hesitated, unsure whether to meet my attack or run. By this time I had drawn my blade and raised my arm. I could see enough now to judge where the head was and I grabbed a fistful of hair from under its turban and, twisting the head round, I brought my kukri down hard with a loud cry—

'*Guruji? Guruji?*'

For several seconds, I was too stunned to answer.

Only then did I realise I must have been dreaming.

'What time is it?' I asked at last

'Two thirty. You're on duty now, *guruji*.'

'OK thanks,' I replied, noticing that I was dripping with cold sweat. 'Just a moment.'

I took a long pull on my water bottle as I brought myself back into the real world.

'Anything happening?' I wanted to know.

'All quiet, *guruji*.'

Despite his reassurance, I still felt anxious as I crossed the compound and climbed up into the sangar. I realised that my nerves were starting to get to me but it was important not to let on to the *bhai*s that I was feeling any stress so I took a few deep breaths before speaking.

'Seen anything, *bhai haru*?' I asked quietly.

'Nothing, *guruji*. Nothing unless you count those dogs over there. Looks like they've caught something.'

As soon as I was in position, I pulled my HMNVS, my helmet-mounted night-vision sight device, down and squinted through it.

'Where?'

'Over there,' said Gaaz, zapping them with his laser. Later, we would use our lasers like this to indicate targets for the air assets, but on this occasion I was just looking at three or four animals tugging on what looked like a small carcass.

'Maybe it's a desert fox!' said Gaaz.

He was referring to the time back at Bastion, when one night out on patrol in the WMIK we had seen a desert fox. It was only just over a week ago, but it already seemed like five years. Nani was driving and I'd ordered him to give chase. I thought it would be fun if we could catch it and take it back with us. It could be our mascot. But as we discovered, the desert fox is nothing like the foxes that raid the dustbins around Shorncliffe, the Gurkha barracks in England. They look similar, but the desert fox is a lot, lot quicker. And it can change direction like a hare. We set off after it, bucketing over the sand, weaving this way and that to try and keep it in our lights. But no sooner did we think we'd run it to ground exhausted than it got up and started running again. We must have chased it for at least twenty minutes at speeds up to thirty miles an hour before we eventually lost it. The thought that these mangy dogs could have caught one didn't seem likely at all.

'Whatever it is, I doubt it's a desert fox!' I replied.

'I don't think so either, *guruji*,' Gaaz admitted. 'More likely a diseased goat or something.'

'Hey, *guruji*!' said Nagen a few minutes later. 'Looks like we've got the early-morning patrol coming again.'

Sure enough, there was a figure moving quite slowly along the road towards us.

'She must have eaten something bad,' said Gaaz. 'It's not even three thirty.'

'Zero, this is Sangar Three. One civilian moving along road in a southerly direction. Looks female. Am observing.'

'Zero, roger.'

Within the next half-hour, another one or two women appeared, followed not long after by some men, though there were notably fewer than before.

'Hold your nose. Here come the rest of them,' said Gaaz, pointing. Not long after they had finished, the sound of the muezzin calling people to prayer broke the silence.

'OK, *bhai guruji haru*, same detail as yesterday,' I said. 'Be vigilant in case they're using the sound for cover.'

I turned to Gaaz.

'By the way, Gaaz, how are you doing? How's your back?'

He had been working out the evening before and had unfortunately tipped off our makeshift sit-up equipment. I was worried he'd pulled a muscle.

'It's OK, *guruji*. No problem.'

'You're not just saying that, I hope?'

I'd told him he might as well go and see one of the medics in the morning if it gave him any trouble. They might be glad of something to do that wasn't serious.

'Honest, *guruji*, I'm fine.'

After that, we were all silent with our own thoughts. Later that morning, however, we noticed that again there were a lot of people heading out of town. It was an uncomfortable feeling looking out from our position, knowing that most of the local population was on the move. Apart from the main street, where there was some buying and selling still going on, the town was beginning to take on an abandoned air. There was hardly any movement among the buildings within our arcs of fire. The hospital clinic next door lay empty and the compounds beyond showed no signs of life. Occasionally you might see someone walking into or out of a building, but that was all.

'It reminds me of those FIBUA (Fighting In a Built Up Area) exercises we did at Shorncliffe,' said one of the riflemen. 'The place looks completely empty, but you know the enemy is lurking in there somewhere.'

I agreed. It did look a lot like that.

'With one big difference,' said Gaaz. 'These *jatha* have got live ammo.'

The big event of the day was a *shura* that Rex *sahib* had called for the early evening. A *shura* is a meeting of elders – the important people of the town – and we were all looking forward to seeing who would turn up. We have similar meetings back home in Khebang when there is important local business to discuss, or if there is some dispute in the community. But this was likely to be a gathering with a difference. As the OC had said, there were bound to be some spies among them. This made it exciting in a way, to think that we might be being visited by the very people who had been attacking us. But it was an uncomfortable thought in other ways. Who was to say they wouldn't turn up with a suicide bomber and try to hit us at the meeting?

'What are we going to do if a suicide bomber comes in with

the elders for this *shura?*' demanded Gaaz, as if reading my thoughts.

'These guys are brave. But I doubt they'd want to kill all the elders. Not that you can ever know with these people.'

'What happens if they try to take one of us hostage?' demanded one of the other riflemen.

Both of these scenarios were possible, and neither of them was easy to think through. The visitors would be searched on arrival, but of course that did not help very much if one of them was carrying a suicide bomb. We would still be taking casualties. But as for hostage taking, that was less likely – although we had heard of a recent incident when some Canadians were attacked by someone who had managed to smuggle a machete into a similar meeting. But we would search them thoroughly and we would have men standing guard while the *shura* was going on. Plus we were going to cover the proceedings from up in the sangars. But still, there was danger, and it was very difficult to predict all the possible scenarios.

'It's a pity we don't have some cardboard cut-outs we could post around the place to make them think we were more than just a platoon plus in strength,' said Gaaz as we waited for them to arrive.

'They'll already know our numbers, you can be sure of that,' I replied. 'Their friends in the local police will have told them.'

For myself, I particularly wanted to try and work out which were the ones who had been attacking us. I really wanted to see what they looked like, to see who it was who had been trying to kill me. I wanted to look them in the eye. And the reason for that was, I wanted to kill them.

'You know what, *guruji*? If it had been me, I'd find some way of bugging those *jatha*. The younger ones I mean,' said Gaaz later on. 'I mean, if you could find out where they are living, you could send a fighting patrol to take them out.'

But the fact of the matter was there just weren't enough of us to launch any kind of offensive. To send out a fighting patrol, you'd need a minimum of twelve men, plus another six on stand-by in reserve. If you had a man hit, you'd then have to have an extraction party to come and get him out. And all the time, you'd have to keep the sangars at full strength in case they launched a counter-attack before you had a chance to get back in. The numbers just didn't add up. Besides, there were the ROE to think about. We couldn't go out taking people on just because we didn't like the look of them.

'Make sure you look really fierce when they get here, OK?' I told the riflemen. 'We want to make sure they understand we are capable of hitting them ten times harder than they can hit us.'

Everyone agreed.

When the elders eventually came, there must have been about fifteen or twenty of them. Most were old, a few were very old, but some were a lot younger, and it was fairly obvious these younger ones were sizing us up. As the men came through the gate, the *bhai*s all pulled themselves up to their full height and made a big thing of showing their weapons off. Every so often they would put their rifles to the shoulder as if reassuring themselves there was nothing obstructing their sights.

The *shura* went on for about two hours, and during that time, Major Rex did his best to convince the elders that we were there to help and not to harm people. But I was told you could sense they were all very suspicious of his words as the *torjeman* translated them.

At the evening O-group Major Rex confirmed that the *shura* had had mixed results. He told us that on the whole, the elders were not very forthcoming. They certainly didn't welcome our presence. On the other hand, they didn't seem too keen on the Taliban either. They just wanted to be left in peace, they said. About the only serious thing that came out of the meeting was a request that from now on, the ANP wear uniform when they went out on patrol. The elders complained that they didn't know who was who, and at least if the ANP wore uniform, they would know they weren't the Taliban. This seemed reasonable to the OC, so he had asked the ANP commander whether they had any uniform. Apparently they did, but they didn't like wearing it as it was so hot. In that case, he said, they must wear it from now on whenever they went out of the compound, but they didn't need to wear it inside. So that was agreed.

It was early morning the next day that we saw the real results of the *shura*. The ANP decided that it would be a good idea to make a show of strength to the local people – or what was left of them. At the unusually early hour of 6.30 a.m., a group of about eight or ten armed men assembled at the gate. They didn't look exactly threatening. In fact it looked more like they were going on a sightseeing trip than on an armed exercise. Maybe what they really wanted to do was to demonstrate goodwill by showing off their uniforms. All of them were wearing a sort of light blue jacket which, although not very military-looking, did at least identify them as belonging to the ANP.

There was a certain amount of arguing before they set off, then the gate opened and out they went. It can't have been more than ten minutes later when we heard shots in the distance, followed by a pause, then more shots – single rounds first, then machine-gun fire.

At once, I could hear Corporal Santos yelling.

'STAND-TO! EVERYBODY STAND-TO!'

Already I could see the QRF mustering at the gate, tightening their helmets, adjusting their body armour and readying their weapons.

'Zero, this is Two Two Charlie, ready to deploy now.' That was Corporal Santos, who was leading it.

'Roger. Sangars One and Three, make sure you keep them covered at all times.'

'Sangar One, roger out.'

'Sangar Three, roger out.'

I was on maximum alert, my heart racing. Looking down into the town, I scanned with my binoculars. There was nothing to see for the moment. Inside the compound, the gate was being opened to let the QRF out and the ANP back in.

'OK, *bhai haru*, we need to be careful here. There's a good chance the enemy will follow. Gaaz, you keep Smuggler's covered. Nagen, you cover the gate. I'll keep the alleyway covered.'

Just then I saw some people running along the alleyway towards us. From their pale blue uniforms, I could see that they were ANP. A few moments later, another group appeared, half-carrying, half-dragging a wounded man. Every so often he gave a cry of agony. I pressed the Send button on the PRR.

'Zero, this is Sangar One. Patrol returning. Looks like one man wounded. Covering,' I said.

'Roger. Just one casualty?'

'Looks like.'

'OK, keep them covered. If you see any targets, you are to engage, but only if they are definitely hostile. Be very careful with your shot selection. Controlled bursts only. And look out for civilians.'

'Roger.' Actually I hadn't seen a civvie since the *disha* patrol.

'OK, *bhai haru*,' I shouted. 'This is it. If you see the enemy, you are to engage. But short bursts only. Did you get that? And only if you get a PID.'

'Yes, *guruji*.'

'OK, *guruji*.'

'And watch out for any civvies,' I added. It was true, you can't be too careful in situations like this. 'Gaaz, Nagen, did you get that? We don't want blue on blue. And no more than three rounds at a time. Is that quite clear?'

Looking down, I could see the QRF had not deployed and were instead helping with the casualty. There was shouting as the rest of the ANP men came through the gate.

Inside the compound, the two medics were ready and waiting and the casualty was immediately taken into the CT for treatment. He had been hit in the leg, but nothing worse, luckily for him.

'Charlie Charlie One, this is Zero. The patrol is now back inside the compound. All sangar positions are to remain vigilant. Report any suspicious movement. Over.'

'Sangar One. Roger. Out.'

'Sangar Two. Roger. Out.'

'Sangar Three. Roger. Out.'

Each of the callsigns working the PRR acknowledged the order in turn.

Here perhaps I should explain some radio procedure. The word 'over' as a question means 'Have you got that?' As a response 'roger' shows that you have understood what has been said, while just 'out' signals the end of the message with no response expected or required. The phrase 'Charlie Charlie' is used by the commander to alert all radio callsigns on the net. It means he is speaking to all subordinate commanders. Otherwise, he uses individual callsigns, such as Two One Alpha, Two One Bravo, Two One Charlie and so on. My own callsign was Two One Charlie. 'Sunray' is the name used by the senior commander working the net.

Having satisfied myself there was no enemy pursuing the retreating ANP patrol, I turned to the *bhais*.

'OK, listen in, *bhai haru*. The OC hasn't stood us down yet so we've got to stay focused. We know they're out there. They could be back any time.'

I remember looking down from the sangar into the DC a short while later and being just in time to see a burst of tracer streaming in the direction of Sangar 4. Suddenly someone in one of the other sangars shouted:

'R-P-G! . . . R-P-G!'

I heard a loud fizzing sound and watched as first one, then another round appeared, each an intense flash of white light, hurtling through the air.

Aare jatha!

Flying at just under 120 metres per second, I had no difficulty following the trajectory of the grenade – which was fortunately well wide of the intended target in both cases. They went right over the top of us and exploded harmlessly outside the compound.

But a moment later, a call went out over the PRR.

'ALL STATIONS, THIS IS ZERO. CONTACT! WAIT OUT.'

Mathers sahib's voice came over the headset loud and clear.

'Nagen! Gaaz! Can you see anything?'

'Can't see anything at the moment, *guruji*. But I think I know where they are,' replied Nagen.

'OK, keep it covered,' I said.

'*Guruji bhai haru* in Sangar Three, can you see anything?' I shouted into the PRR.

'Nothing seen from Sangar Three,' came the reply.

Hardly had I registered this when there was a burst of small-arms fire, quickly joined by another, and another.

I realised it was us who were under attack.

'Get your heads down, *bhai haru*!'

You couldn't see anything but you could hear rounds flying through the air.

It was the same sound we'd heard on landing.

TAKTAKTAK ... TUMTUMTUM TAKTAKTAK ... TUMTUMTUM ...

The only difference was that you could hear an occasional thud against the sandbags where a round struck the position. And every so often there would be a small explosion of sand as a tear opened up.

It took maybe a second or two to understand the seriousness of the situation, but in that time my heart rate must have tripled. The sangar that a moment before had been like a miniature home was transformed into a zone of imminent death.

Khebang, looking
down the valley
from our house.
(Author photo)

My home. We
moved here when I
was five years old.
I paid for the new
tin roof on my first
leave after joining
the Gurkhas.
(Author photo)

Aged twelve, with
my classmates. I
am wearing the
white hat. (Author photo)

Aged fifteen, with my sister Gudiya. (Author photo)

From the left, my great uncle, my father's father Nainabahadur, my maternal grandfather and my maternal grandmother. (Author photo)

At the Gurkha Museum during my recruit training.

(Author photo)

Digging a trench during recruit training, Church Crookham. (Author photo)

On a local commander's horse, 2003 tour of Afghanistan. (Author photo)

D 'Tamandu' Company that deployed to Afghanistan on Op Herrick 4, 2006. (Gurkha Brigade Association (GBA))

Now Zad: Looking at the CT from Sangar 3. The cam net on the right screens the OC's external command and control point. (GBA)

ANP quarters with Sangar 1 on the right. Smuggler's House is the two-storey building in the middle distance – shown here before it was destroyed in an air strike. (GBA)

This shows Sangar 2 and the main gate. All traffic passed through here. (GBA)

Myself with Rifleman Nabin about to engage the enemy's rocket position with the .50 cal. (GBA)

Sangar 3 is on top of the building. The local police were accommodated below on the right-hand side. The roof of the clinic can be seen just the other side of the perimeter wall. (GBA)

Sangar 3 under attack. (GBA)

In Sangar 3, seen here in real time during a day contact, sending a sitrep over the field telephone. (GBA)

Riflemen Mahesh, Gaj (Gaaz) and Lukesh seen here on the roof of the CT. Sometimes when not on duty on the sangars, they gave support to the command section. (GBA)

A10 strike seen from ANP Hill. (GBA)

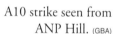

Local police going out on patrol. We were never quite sure whose side they were on. (GBA)

After a contact. I am on the left, standing with some of the *bhai*s from Corporal Ramesh's section. I'm smiling mainly for the benefit of the riflemen. (GBA)

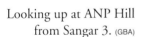

Major Rex (centre) seen here on deployment on Op Herrick 4. (GBA)

Looking up at ANP Hill from Sangar 3. (GBA)

From left to right, Riflemen Gaj (Gaaz), Mahesh and Sanjiv sharing some food during a resupply of ANP Hill. (GBA)

I am third from left. Rifleman Gaj (Gaaz) is on the far right kneeling, Rifleman Lal is standing behind him on the extreme right, Rifleman Baren is in the front centre wearing a helmet. Behind him, Rifleman Nagen is leaning forward. Lieutenant Mathers is on the back row, centre. Lance Corporal Shree, my section 2 i/c, is seen on the right of Mathers *sahib*. (GBA)

With VC Rambahadur Limbu on his visit to Sir John Moore barracks in 2014. (Author photo)

With my family, my parents and children seated, in Brunei, 2011. (Author photo)

Looking out now was like looking into an abyss we were perched on the edge of. One stroke of luck for the enemy and we were dead and buried.

'OK, *bhai haru*. We need to work out where it's coming from!' I yelled, throwing myself from one side of the sangar to the other to quickly scan with my binos before picking up the field telephone.

'Zero, this is Sangar One, CONTACT! We're under heavy fire. Observing!'

A second later, I heard Lance Corporal Shree in Sangar 3 give exactly the same contact report.

'Zero, this is Sangar Three, CONTACT! Heavy fire. Observing.'

'Zero, roger. We're under fire too.' Mathers *sahib*'s voice came up over the PRR sounding as calm as if he was watching a sunset. 'Observe and engage any fire positions you can iden-tify. Any idea where it's coming from?'

That was exactly what I wanted to know.

'Can't you see anything, Gaaz, Nagen?'

'Still nothing, *guruji*.'

'Nothing at all, *guruji*.'

For a few seconds at a time, no more, we put our heads above sandbag level, trying desperately to get an idea of where the fire was coming from. And when we did, the sound got even worse. As well as the TAK TAK TAK TUM TUM TUM of the rounds in the air all around, and the thumping sound as they hit the sandbags, every so often there was a loud click as a bullet hit a wooden roof support or one of the arc markers. This was accurate fire, and a lot of it. Must be ten weapons or more.

It was like being in a shepherd's hut on the mountainside underneath an avalanche of rocks. It's no good running out because your skull will be smashed to pieces by falling rocks. It felt very lonely suddenly, like we were a thousand miles from the rest of the DC.

The *bhai*s were using their weapon sights to scan, but I had binoculars as well. These offer a slightly better magnification than the SA80 sight and are generally better for target acquisition. Having poked my head up for a few seconds to look down into the main street and make sure there was no sign of an imminent assault, I began to look further out.

It was just a question of ignoring the danger. You know it's there, all around you. But you just have to get on with things.

One obvious place for the enemy to occupy was the treeline to the north-west of our position, but at more than 300 metres range, it was going to be hard to get a positive fix on any position dug in there. But as I looked, I saw some flashes of tracer which made me think that was where they were.

'Gaaz,' I yelled. 'I want you to target the AOI in the treeline, OK? Get some rounds down. We've got to try to get the initiative away from them.'

Although I couldn't be sure that was where they were, at least this would force them to get their heads down should they be.

'OK, *guruji.*'

'But controlled bursts, all right? I don't want you to just spray it about.'

I hardly needed to say this, but on the other hand you can't repeat basic SOPs too often. They have to become so ingrained that they are second nature, and one way of making this happen is by constant reminder.

If I'd had time to think about it, I might have been glad that at last we were getting to fire our weapons, but what I was really focusing on was trying to identify the enemy positions. So while Gaaz engaged the treeline – which we had nicknamed Kathmandu – and Nagen covered east and south over the town, I began to concentrate on Smuggler's House, the two-storey old school building, which stood about 300 metres to the north. That was one place where I would be if I were the enemy. But although I looked and looked, I couldn't see anything.

Still the rounds kept pouring in on us.

Grabbing the field telephone, I sent a brief sitrep.

'Sunray, this is Sangar One.'

'Go ahead.'

'Am engaging AOI to the north and observing within arcs. Nothing seen yet, but Smuggler's House looks a big possibility.'

'Roger. By the way, can you see any civilians around the place?'

'No. Everywhere is completely empty.'

Until then I hadn't thought about civilians. I was just concentrating on the situation. But of course, that told you they were keeping out of the way. It told you this wasn't just a few isolated gunmen. This was a concerted effort to blow us to bits.

Somehow, we had to find their positions and get on to them.

'Roger. Keep looking. We have air assets en route. Expected in figures three five.'

That was good to know. Aircraft were just over half an hour away.

'Roger. Out.'

I replaced the receiver and crawled back over next to Gaaz. There was still a blizzard of rounds flying up at us.

TAK TAK TAK TAK. SMACK! TUM TUM TUM . . .

I'm not saying you get used to it, but it is true that after a while, it becomes easier to think straight. At least there was no more RPG. Thank God. I put the thought of any more to the back of my mind as I peered out at Smuggler's House.

'Seen anything yet, Nagen?'

'No. Nothing, *guruji*. It's just coming in from everywhere,' he shouted.

I redoubled my efforts with my binos. All I needed was some smoke . . . just a puff of smoke. Or a line of tracer. Or some muzzle flash . . . Just one movement would be enough. I scanned and scanned, looking at every building, every window, every crack and crevice.

'*BHAI HARU!*' I shouted after a few moments. 'I think I've got something. Reference Smuggler's House . . .'

Something had caught my eye.

'Where is it? Where is it?' shouted Gaaz. 'Let me get at him.'

'Wait a moment. Just wait.'

I stared hard, crouched on my haunches, my elbows tucked in. Yes. YES!

Or was I imagining things? Three hundred metres is quite a distance when you're looking for something as momentary as muzzle flash, even when you've got six times magnification.

But yes, I was sure I'd seen something. I can't say it was anything very clear. It was more like an idea of something. My eye kept being drawn back to two spots, one on the extreme right of the building, and one just to the front and left of it: a low shed about 20 metres from the main school building.

'OK, Gaaz! Let me have the jimpy for a second.'

He rolled out of the way.

'Reference Smuggler's. Front, far right. Small aperture. Watch my tracer,' I said as, steadying the butt with my left hand and squinting through the iron sight, I took a couple of deep breaths and fired a short burst.

I watched carefully as the rounds rammed into the building, slightly left of and below the position I was aiming for.

'Wait a moment,' I said, adjusting my aim and firing another burst. 'OK, that's it. Target! Did you see that, Gaaz?'

'Seen, *guruji*!'

'OK, I'm going to indicate the other position now.'

I took aim at the smaller structure. Again the rounds went slightly to one side. I made a mental note to re-zero the weapon at the first opportunity.

'Hold on. That's not quite it. Rounds are falling just below and left. You'll need to aim off a bit.'

I fired again, this time directly hitting the small hole that I took to be the enemy fire position.

'TARGET! Gaaz, did you get that?'

'Yes got it, *guruji*!'

'OK, you take over,' I said, handing him the weapon. 'But again, keep it short and controlled.'

The reason for using the GPMG, rather than my personal weapon, to indicate the target for Gaaz was that with the jimpy you could actually see the rounds landing. The 7.62 ammo is heavy enough that it kicks up a bit of dust on impact. It's much harder to see the SA80's lighter 5.56 mm round hit.

Gaaz said nothing as he scrambled into position. The enemy fire was still smacking into the sangar. Every so often a cloud of sand erupted from one of the sandbags overhead, adding to the difficulty of seeing anything.

I kept my eye on the targets as Gaaz took aim. Unlike the SA80 and the Minimi, the jimpy doesn't have a telescopic sight. But in spite of this, and in spite of the fact the design is more than fifty years old, it is the infantryman's weapon of choice.

With his first burst, Gaaz was on target.

'TARGET!'

'OK. Now go for the shed.'

It took him no more than two bursts to get onto it.

'TARGET!' I shouted when he had fixed it accurately.

'OK, Nagen, have you seen anything yet?' I said, leaving Gaaz to it.

'Still nothing, *guruji*.'

'OK, keep looking. I'll send a sitrep, then I'll come over.'

I picked up the field telephone.

'Zero, this is Sangar One. Engaging targets to north-east. Old school building and low shed in front.'

'Zero, roger. Seen. That's good work.'

A moment later, I heard a burst of .50-cal and watched as its trace thudded into the school building. Scrambling back over to the street side of the sangar, I scanned up and down with my binos. There were just so many places to look, but I couldn't see anything.

'OK, Nagen,' I said, 'you take the bunker in front of Smuggler's. Gaaz can keep on at the main building and I'll cover this side.'

It made sense to have our heavy weapons hitting the two definite positions while I looked out and covered the bazaar and beyond with my SA80.

The big problem we had now was that it was almost impossible to decide whether our actions were having any positive effect. What you want to see is positions destroyed and dead bodies lying around. To show you've done your job. But it wasn't like that. It was hardly ever like that in Now Zad. Instead it was all about returning fire and suppressing the enemy. Keep him under cover. Curtail his movement. Prevent an assault. It was a question of stopping him from gaining the initiative. But with very little to show for it.

Taking care to keep his head down as he dismounted the weapon, Nagen repositioned the Minimi next to Gaaz.

The enemy onslaught was still intense, and the air inside the sangar was thick with gunsmoke, cold sweat and dust, but when Gaaz was firing the jimpy and Nagen had the Minimi going, I got the impression there weren't as many rounds coming towards us. It was hard to be sure, but it seemed our efforts were having some effect.

I was wrong. A call over the PRR made me realise that the enemy had turned their heaviest weapons on the CT. They were trying to take out the .50-cal. As it turned out, Rifleman Nabin – who was manning it – was actually struck on the helmet, though luckily only a glancing blow. Stunned, he took time out to smoke a cigarette before getting back to work. Sangar 3's .50-cal was also taking a lot of very accurate fire. So even though our position might be under a bit less pressure, the other *bhai*s were really struggling.

I grabbed the field telephone to give another quick sitrep – it's vital to keep the commander updated even if nothing has actually changed. He needs to know you are OK and still doing whatever you said you were doing.

'Sunray, Sangar One. Sitrep. Still concentrating fire on Smuggler's House. Engaging with GPMG and Minimi.'

'Roger. Let me know if you see anyone breaking cover.'

'Roger, out'

'And be advised that both .50-cals are being pinned down.'

'Roger.'

It was a good tactic. If they could disable these, they would greatly reduce our capability.

A moment later, there was a call on the PRR: 'Charlie Charlie One, air assets will be overhead in approximately fifteen minutes. I say again, air assets in figures one five.'

That was both good news and bad. Good news that they were getting closer – but bad news that we had no air support for at least that long. A lot can happen in fifteen minutes when you are under an attack as intense as this. The question now was, could we hold out that long?

I threw myself back to the front of the sangar and took another look at the old school building. Gaaz and Nagen were right on target, but their fire was just not having enough effect on the amount of fire coming back at us.

What about using the ILAW? I thought to myself. If I could land one in the right place, that might do it.

'Zero, this is Sangar One. Suggest I deploy ILAW on Smuggler's.'

'Do you think you can?'

'I'll give it a try.'

'Roger, out.'

What I was going to have to do was climb out onto the roof and just ignore the incoming fire. I turned to the *bhai*s.

'Give me maximum weight of fire when I say go!'

'You're a brave man, *guruji*,' Gaaz shouted.

To be honest, I didn't think so. I was just so frustrated, I'd have done anything to get a result.

I'd never actually fired a live ILAW before – somebody once told me they cost over a hundred thousand dollars each, so practice was out of the question – but I knew the drills very well. The weapon was already out of its box, so it was just a question of pulling the safety pins out and aiming carefully.

I put my SA80 down and crawled out onto the side of the roof and gave a quick call over the PRR.

'Charlie Charlie One. Rapid fire on Smuggler's. I'm going to fire the ILAW.'

I'm sure the enemy saw me and did their best to get me, but all I was thinking about was engaging them. I just wanted to hit them as hard as I possibly could. I wanted the *jatha* dead, simple as that.

Weighing about 7 kilos, the weapon is quite unwieldy, but once you get the shoulder strap on, it's easier to handle.

I brought the sight up and took aim. As I did so, to my heart-thumping delight, I caught a clear glimpse of several gun barrels poking out of the building wall. The enemy was in at least section strength in that one position. Well this is a present for you, I thought, as I squeezed the trigger.

BLAM!

The next thing I knew, I was sprawling on the floor, thrown down by the force, my head spinning. For a few seconds I just lay there, not knowing what was going on.

Looking back, my first thought was, Bloody hell! I didn't expect that!

The noise had been incredible and the shock of the missile leaving its canister had caused the whole building to move.

'Wow, *guruji*! I thought we'd been hit by mortar or RPG!' said Gaaz afterwards. 'The whole structure was swaying. I was certain the roof was going to collapse. Nagen thought we were under mortar fire.'

'*Guruji! Guruji!* Are you OK?' The two riflemen spoke at once, their voices full of concern.

'I'm OK. Hang on. Coming back inside. Give me cover. Rapid fire!'

Back inside, I grabbed my binos.

'Check that out, *bhai haru*!' I said as we watched the smoke billowing up in a huge, dirty cloud where the round had struck.

For me, though, the worst thing – leaving aside the noise – was the fact that as the smoke cleared and I surveyed the scene I saw that the round had struck the base of the building and done hardly any damage at all.

'*Aayo!* These Afghan walls. They're just so thick.'

'You'd better just wait for air support. A five-hundred-pounder will do it,' said Gaaz.

'No. I'm going to fire another one.'

'You're mad, *guruji*!'

I ignored him.

'Again I want rapid covering fire from all of you.'

Picking up the field telephone, I notified the OC of my intentions. 'Zero, this is Sangar One. Am going to have another go with ILAW.'

'OK, Kailash, if you're sure.'

The fact that Rex *sahib* used my name in clear speech showed the seriousness of the situation.

The only thing I wasn't sure about was what to do for ear-defenders. The truth was, I'd forgotten them first time, and now

I realised I didn't know where I'd put them. But I could be deaf for life if I fired another one without any sort of protection.

Looking round, I suddenly hit on the idea of using two spent 5.56 cases. I'd heard other people say they fitted perfectly and found that, sure enough, they did. Hurriedly inserting them, I went outside and took up my position. I don't know whether having ear-defenders had anything to do with it, but this time the missile was exactly on target. As the smoke dispersed, I saw that the window I was aiming at had been replaced by a gaping hole.

TARGET!

I grabbed the field telephone.

'Zero, this is Sangar One. TARGET!'

'Yes, I can see. Well done, Kailash. Very good work.'

But our joy was short-lived. It soon became clear that even if they had taken some casualties inside the school house, these *jatha* weren't giving up. Scanning the building with my binos, I saw that they'd simply made another opening further along and were now firing from that! They were brave, you had to give them that.

And the rounds continued to come, thudding into the sandbags and occasionally striking the roof supports. The enemy still wanted us dead, make no mistake. But the weight of fire was definitely less, so that was something.

With both the section ILAWs now expended, we carried on suppressing the building with machine-gun and SA80 fire for several minutes until Rex *sahib*'s voice came up over the PRR.

'All stations, this is Zero. Fast jet inbound, five minutes.'

'Good news, *guruji bhai haru*. The OC says air support is coming. Five minutes.'

'That's *so* good, *guruji*,' said Nagen. 'Did he say what?'

'A-10.'

'Wow! This should be good.'

'That's really great, *guruji*! Now we're going to get these *jatha*! Let's see how they like this!' exclaimed Gaaz.

We were all really excited. None of us had seen an A-10 in action before, but we'd heard a lot about them. People said they were really effective.

'But that doesn't mean we can just stop, *bhai haru*! Come on, we've got to keep at them. We don't just give up because the air force is on its way. There's still five minutes. We mustn't let the enemy seize the initiative. You never know what's going to happen. The aircraft could develop a fault at the last moment.'

With these words, I opened up again with my SA80.

This was something I found whenever the OC announced the imminent arrival of air support. The *bhai*s would relax a bit, and I'd have to remind them to keep going. The point was, if the enemy could actually close with us, air support wasn't going to be any use due to the danger of blue on blue.

So for the next few minutes, we carried on looking and engaging every time we saw the brief flicker of muzzle flash or a wisp of smoke, until at last the OC gave confirmation of the jet's arrival.

'Charlie Charlie One. Fast jet inbound, thirty seconds. He'll start by engaging Smuggler's House.'

We all looked up, straining our eyes and ears.

'There he is!'

'Where?'

'Over there! Circling!'

Both riflemen were shouting at once.

'Charlie Charlie One. A-10 will begin his run in twenty seconds.'

'Can you see him, *guruji*?'

'Yes I can.'

Still just a tiny glinting dot in the sky, I could see him circling overhead.

'Ten seconds. HEADS DOWN!'

'Take cover, *bhai haru*!' I yelled and Gaaz and Nagen got down, though I myself did not. I wanted to see it happen.

Now he was beginning his descent. My spirit soared. These *jatha* were about to get a big surprise!

'Five seconds.'

We were all excited, but I was a little bit frightened too, I have to admit. If they hit us by mistake, that was the end, no question. I'd heard about blue on blue contacts from the air in previous conflicts and realised how much we had to rely on the pilot's skill.

'Three.'

We could hear him now. There was a high-pitched sound—

'Two.'

—that turned to a scream.

'One.'

Then there was a deep BOOM! as he dropped his bomb – a 500-pounder – which was followed by a whine as he climbed away.

Immediately the *bhai*s got up to watch as clouds of smoke and dust leaped into the air – thirty, fifty, a hundred feet – and we all gave a great cheer.

'Wow, *guruji*! Fantastic! No one could survive that!' Gaaz looked at me with a big smile on his face.

'That's done for the *jatha*!' agreed Nagen, equally cheerful.

The smoke began to clear. Elation turned to astonishment.

'*Hernuhos, guruji!*' cried Gaaz. 'It's still standing!'

The pilot had hit the target all right, and one side of the building had collapsed. But the rest of it was still there. That meant it could still be used and, to our further amazement, we realised the enemy had resumed firing at us almost immediately.

'Unbelievable!' I exclaimed, scanning the building with my binos once more.

'So much for that,' agreed Gaaz. 'I guess we're just going to have to nuke it!'

All of a sudden, I saw a figure on the first floor of Smuggler's House run past the window from right to left.

'*Aye!* I just saw someone!' I shouted, putting my rifle down and reaching for the field telephone.

'Zero, this is Sangar One.'

'Go ahead.'

'Good strike on the target but have just seen enemy move from right to left on first floor of building. Engaging.'

'Zero, roger. I'll ask the pilot if he can do anything more.'

A few moments later, the OC came back up on the air.

'Charlie Charlie One, this is Sunray. Aircraft will engage same building with cannon. HEADS DOWN! HEADS DOWN!'

This time, the jet came in a lot lower and the first thing we heard was the deep burbling of the cannon.

BRRRRB BRRRRB BRRRRB

Then there was a roar and a whine as he climbed away steeply.

'BANG ON! BANG ON!' the *bhais* shouted, both relieved and happy to see some serious destruction.

That was more like it! There were now several gaping holes in the wall. OK, so the building could still be used, but for now that had to have done for the enemy. Thank God for our air assets.

The field telephone rang.

'Sangar One, have you got a good view of that?' It was the OC.

'Yes, that's a target,' I replied, scanning the wreckage with my binos as I spoke. 'First floor successfully destroyed.'

'Roger.'

I had just put the receiver down when to my amazement I saw muzzle flash coming from the ground floor. Immediately I called back.

'Enemy still engaging from ground floor!'

'Zero, roger. I'll see what else he can do.'

A second A-10 had just arrived overhead, and on his first run he attacked with missiles.

'TAKE THAT, *jatha haru!*' yelled Gaaz as the rockets streaked in.

But a second later, he was shaking his head in despair.

'Oh my God! They missed. How did that happen?'

He was right. The missiles had landed at least 150 metres to one side.

'I didn't think they *could* miss, *guruji!*'

'Hey listen,' I said. 'There's never going to be a perfect weapon system. Unless it's a kukri. You can't miss with that!'

'Yeah. That's true. If only we could take these *jatha* on in hand-to-hand combat. I'd like that a lot,' agreed Gaaz.

On his next run, the A-10 fired his cannon, but again they were wide of the mark, by about 50 metres.

'Why can't we have the first pilot back?' demanded Gaaz. 'This guy's obviously having an off day.'

Actually, although there were those two misses that afternoon, I don't remember seeing more than one or two others the whole time we were in Now Zad. Mostly the aircrafts' accuracy was incredible. This was hugely important. We were reliant on them not only for hitting targets and avoiding damage to ourselves, but for keeping collateral damage to an absolute minimum. That was vital. You don't win hearts and minds by hurting the civilian population.

I can only assume that there was a slight malfunction of the second aircraft's systems. Luckily, from listening in on the PRR, I understood that another aircraft was approaching and would drop another laser-guided bomb. Less than five minutes later, the munitions landed smack in the centre of the building.

When at last the smoke cleared, we were rewarded with the sight of a huge hole in the middle of Smuggler's House. You could see right into it now.

The enemy's automatic fire could still be heard when the sound of the jets subsided, but it was definitely much less, and there wasn't anything coming from Smuggler's House. But that didn't mean the enemy had given up. Shortly afterwards, the OC's voice came up over the PRR. It seemed that the ANP had picked up some enemy radio signals about bringing more troops in to reinforce their positions in the town.

'Charlie Charlie One, PID of enemy reinforcements gathering at the petrol station. Air assets are engaging. At least twenty pax reported seen.'

Wow! So the enemy was still there in force.

Because of their advanced sights, and because of their freedom of movement, the pilots were capable of seeing much more than we were in our fixed positions with only basic weapon sights. We knew where the petrol station was and could see vehicles arriving and leaving, but we didn't have a good view of what was going on there, so it was good that the OC was keeping us informed. It was even better when a few minutes later we saw another 500-pounder find its target. A pick-up truck suddenly rose 20, 30, 40 feet into the air.

'WOW! Did you see that, *guruji*?' yelled Gaaz. It was an incredible sight – one of the most satisfying things I've ever seen. The vehicle went up with tremendous force, seemed to hang in the air for a moment then came crashing down. It was so hot that we saw it smouldering for a week after.

'Got you, you *jatha*!'

By this time, it must have been about mid-morning. We'd been on the go for only about three hours, but it felt like half a lifetime. For quite a lot of the enemy, that morning had been their last, although how many kills there were we had no idea. Because we were unable to go out on patrol, there was no way to verify numbers. Besides, it was the habit of the Taliban to remove their dead, just as we do. But the casualty rate must have been enough to convince them they should leave us alone for now. The sound of gunfire had died away and the town was eerily silent. There was no one to be seen in the street outside. Even the dogs were quiet.

11

Target!

The rest of the day and the evening were quiet. We remained stood-to and spent the night in the sangar, taking it in turns to rest. Next morning, some time after first light, Major Rex came up into the sangar and shook each one of us by the hand.

'Well done, Kailash. Well done, Nagen. Well done, Gaaz. That was outstanding work.'

That was one of the things that made Rex *sahib* such a good officer. He took the time – and the risk – to come up and talk to us all personally after each action.

'You especially, Kailash. Firing the ILAW was definitely a turning point.'

I felt very proud to hear him say this. Of course, I was even prouder when, many weeks later, the OC called me to his office.

'Congratulations, Kailash,' he began. 'You've been Mentioned in Despatches.'

Apparently, the OC had written about my firing the ILAW in his report to higher command, and it had been picked up for special commendation. That was a big honour for me.

But of course I have never been more proud in my life as the moment when, a few days after that, I received a letter through the post. It was on very thick writing paper and, I realised straight away, obviously from someone extremely important.

'Dear Corporal Kailash,' it began, 'I was so pleased to hear the news of your award of MID for your efforts in Afghanistan and wanted to send you my warmest congratulations.'

The letter was signed by the Colonel in Chief of the regiment, Prince Charles himself.

Yet the strange thing is that, although now I can see that what I did was quite risky, actually at the time, it didn't seem such a special thing. Anyone else would have done the same in that situation. At least, any Gurkha would.

But all this lay in the future. Shortly after the OC's visit we were stood down and, after talking to some of the *bhais* in my section, I managed to get a few hours of proper sleep.

When I next went on duty, I found the riflemen in high spirits.

'Everything OK, *bhai haru*?' I said, climbing back onto the position.

'Well we haven't been having as good a time as you have, *guruji*,' said Gaaz.

'What do you mean?'

'I swear we could hear you earlier.'

179

'But I've been asleep.'

'Exactly, *guruji*. We could hear you sleeping.'

'You'd better mind what you're saying, Rifleman Gaaz,' I replied when I'd caught his meaning. He was implying they could hear me snoring. 'Or you might just find yourself doing an extra duty!'

I said this good-humouredly, as I don't mind a bit of joking around from the *bhais*. You want them to respect you, but not to be so frightened of their seniors that they can't have a laugh at your expense from time to time. That said, there were a few occasions when extra duties did get handed out. Once, one of the *bhais* was caught singing a song over the PRR – though that was early on, before the action started.

'So have you seen anything?'

'We saw some vehicles in the distance, that was all.'

'When?'

'About forty minutes back, *guruji*.'

'And did you report it to the CT?'

'Yes, *guruji*, of course.'

'Where were they heading?'

'Out of town, *guruji*.'

'I see. Anything else?'

'Nothing else.'

'OK, good.'

'Nothing except he thought he saw a ghost,' said Gaaz, nodding towards the rifleman next to him.

'What do you mean?' I demanded.

'It was nothing, *guruji*. It's just that we were talking about the jungle and Gaaz said he didn't believe all that stuff about Training Area C being haunted.'

Training Area C is one of the jungle warfare training areas in Brunei. Some of the riflemen say it's haunted by evil spirits.

'But you do,' said Gaaz.

'I said I did because one time I was out there the guy right next to me woke up screaming. He said he was being strangled.'

'And as you said it, you thought you saw someone trying to get into the sangar position from outside the compound. Except there was no one there.'

'It was just for one second, *guruji*.'

'Well, so long as you're both certain there really wasn't anything,' I said.

'Don't worry, *guruji*. We had a good look.'

After this, and after I had carefully scanned the area with my nightsight, we carried on the conversation.

'So what about you, *guruji*? What do you think? Do you believe in ghosts?' Gaaz wanted to know.

'Well I can't say I've ever seen one. On the other hand, I don't rule them out completely,' I replied.

'Seriously, *guruji*? You think there could be something?'

'Well I don't see why not. I mean, it could be like that. The world could be a world where there are ghosts.'

'Well I don't think so,' said Gaaz. 'I think it's just people hallucinating.'

'It could be that some people are hallucinating. But maybe one time in a hundred, or even one time in a thousand, they're not.'

'Well I suppose so . . .' His voice trailed off.

Gaaz was very practical. Unlike me, he didn't go in for religion at all, and he thought anything supernatural could be explained by science. At least, that was what he wanted to think. But I think a part of him did secretly believe.

The fact is, even today, belief in the supernatural is still very strong in the rural parts of Nepal. Most Gurkhas are brought up on stories about witches and ghosts and snakes with special powers. My mother, for example, is a great believer in ghosts and other mysterious beings. When I was young, she used to tell me stories of various things she'd heard about. I'd listen half excited and half scared. I remember her once talking about a particular kind of ghost called a *churel.*

'If you see one,' she said, wagging her finger at me, 'something bad is going to happen in your life. It might be that you are going to get ill or even die yourself soon after, or that someone in our family will. So you watch out.'

'But who are these *churel?*' I wanted to know.

'They are people who have died in bad circumstances. Murder and things like that.'

'And how will I know if I see one? What do they look like?'

'Just like ordinary people except for one thing,' she said, fixing me with her eye. 'The special thing about them is that they have a front, but no back. That is how you can tell. They will never turn round.'

I was really scared when I heard that, and I spent a lot of time wondering what a person with a front but no back could be like.

'And you should be careful of witches, too,' my mother would say. 'There are some, even near here,' and she mentioned the names of several women in the neighbourhood to avoid.

'It's not their fault,' she went on. 'It's something the gods bring about. But if a witch sees a child, that child will become ill. And that includes you. What's more, if you try to argue with such a person, something bad is going to happen, so you be very careful.'

As to whether I still believe these things, I am not too sure. On the one hand there is science, but on the other you have to ask yourself whether such a thing is even possible. If it is, then it would be surprising if absolutely everything you hear about them is a lie. Some things could be true. So while I have never seen a ghost, I must admit that if ever I go past a place that is said to be haunted, I do feel a bit uneasy, and I cannot say that I completely disbelieve those soldiers who say they have experienced things in the Brunei jungle warfare training area, down by the river.

There is also a story I heard some time back which I think could be true. There was a Gurkha soldier in Hong Kong, when the regiment was stationed there before the colony was returned to China, who for no reason became weaker and weaker. The doctors couldn't find anything wrong with him and couldn't offer any explanation. It was only when it had been going on a long time and he was in a really bad way that he finally told his *guruji* how he was being visited every night by a *churel* who made love to him, taking his strength bit by bit. It turned out she was a Chinese woman who had died in tragic circumstances and had selected him as her victim.

I have even heard some stories about officer *sahib*s who have had mysterious experiences. One young officer who went trekking in Nepal just a year or two back started having repeated, disturbing dreams about a girl he had known when he was younger. She had died very young. As he arrived in a remote village after several days' walking, a local holy man asked him about the girl following this young officer along the track.

'What girl?' the officer replied. 'There are no females travelling with us.'

The holy man then described very precisely the girl he had seen. It was the girl the officer had been dreaming about. The holy man subsequently conducted a ceremony to set her spirit free, after which the dreams stopped.

The sun was beginning to light the horizon now, and one important question we had was whether we were going to be seeing anyone appear on the usual morning *disha* patrol.

'Looks like they've taken their business elsewhere, *guruji*,' said Gaaz after some time. 'But is that a good thing?'

'Good in one way definitely,' I replied. 'But you're right – maybe not in another.'

As the sun rose and the muezzin's call came and went, it gradually became even more apparent that the town was more or less completely deserted. That meant the civilian population must be expecting more trouble. And if they were, so must we. That was one thing. The other was that, in the absence of any civilians, the enemy would have complete freedom of movement. There'd be nothing to stop him occupying any building at all. Another consideration was that having people and traffic in the street was a welcome distraction, even if it meant that you were always on your guard in case someone produced a weapon at close range. There was even less to look at now.

Still, we had enough to do to keep us occupied. As I mentioned, a big thing in desert conditions is cleanliness of the ammunition. Sand and dust get everywhere. Although the weapons can tolerate a certain amount of dirt, you need to make sure there isn't a build-up. It only takes one stoppage at a critical moment to make the difference between life and death. For this reason, we spent a lot of time brushing down the rounds, especially the belted rounds of the Minimi and the GPMG. First we would lay it out carefully on the ground, then we went over it with a soft brush, then we lightly oiled it with a cloth. This was harder to do up in the sangar positions, but still we made sure that we went over it at least twice a day. Ditto the firing mechanisms of our grenades. In fact in the sangar positions it was even more important to do this, because every time you moved, you couldn't help kicking up small clouds of dust.

The main event planned for today was the evacuation of the ANP casualty so that he could get his leg properly treated. As before, the OC did not give out specific details, other than to put those of us on the detail on fifteen minutes' notice to move. There would also be some supplies coming from Bastion, and this time we would be taking some stores up to ANP Hill as well.

It was quite a nerve-racking prospect. If the enemy had any idea of our plans, he'd shown himself capable of causing us real difficulties. An RPG strike on one of the WMIKs would be all it took. Follow this up with some accurate small-arms fire and we would be needing to airlift more than one casualty for sure. Realising this, I paid extra-close attention to Mathers *sahib*'s briefing.

'If we get hit less than halfway to the HLS, we'll fight our way back to the DC. If we get hit in the HLS, we'll have to call on air support as well as the section on ANP Hill,' he announced.

'So there will be other aircraft?'

'Yes, Apache will provide top cover.'

That was reassuring. Even so, when the moment came and we were mounted up, engines running, with the gates opening, it felt a bit like we were about to go out on a live firing range with ourselves as targets. We were all quite tense. Nani *guruji* had one hand on the steering wheel and his rifle in the other hand, safety catch off. Gaaz too had the safety catch of the .50 already off, and I did the same with my SA80. But although we had our rifles at the ready, we did not select automatic fire. Single shots are more accurate, even if the rate of fire is a lot lower.

As we set off, I glanced back at the DC and wondered whether I'd ever be seeing it again.

I don't recall the exact time of the casevac, nor anything much about the casualty actually getting onto the Chinook. But I well remember going up to the position on ANP Hill with Mathers *sahib* afterwards. It was a hard climb up to the top – about ten minutes of steady work completely exposed to the enemy. Although it wasn't much more than 100 metres high, it was too steep to get a vehicle up there, other than a tank, so all the resupps of the position had to be done on foot. With full body armour, ammo, water of my own, plus several belts and bottles for the men on the position, it was quite tough going, not to mention the heat. It made me very grateful to have had the experience of the hardship of Gurkha selection and to know something about how to keep going in difficult circumstances.

The men on the position were all in good spirits, as was the ANP contingent. Before I even had a chance to speak to the others, their leader came up to me.

'HEY!' he said. 'It's the danger man! Ve*rrr*y good! Ve*rrr*y good!'

Somehow he must have heard that it was me who had fired the ILAW the day before. He seemed genuinely impressed and patted me warmly on the back.

'Thank you,' I replied, but he kept on and on.

'Yes, you are the *rrr*eal danger man!' he exclaimed, rolling his r's.

I laughed and told him if ever he found himself in trouble he should just call me. Only then did he let me go so that I could hand out the rations we'd brought and speak to the others. Since our arrival, a half section of reinforcements from my own platoon, 12 Platoon, had been flown in to support the ANP on the position, along with a two-man mortar detachment from the RRF (the Royal Regiment of Fusiliers). They were under command of Captain Bedlabh *sahib*, our company ops (operations) officer and a senior QGO. It was great to see them all and to have the opportunity for a catch-up. As usual, I began with the serious stuff.

'OK, *bhai haru*, you listen to what Bedlabh *sahib* says. You're very vulnerable up here. The enemy's going to try and creep up on you one of these days for sure,' I told them. 'It's a good position, so they're going to want to take it off you. All it's going to take is a sniper getting close and your life is going to be really difficult.'

'Yes, *guruji*. We see that.'

'Or a few well-placed RPGs. And watch out for mortar too. You haven't got any overhead cover so you're really vulnerable.'

They all nodded in agreement. The trouble was, the ground up there was so hard it was impossible to dig a very deep trench and, although there were now plenty of sandbags around them, they had nothing at all in the way of overhead protection.

*

When at last I had the opportunity to actually talk to Captain Bedlabh, after his usual friendly greeting he told me how the enemy had recently fired an RPG at them which failed to explode. Immediately, he had begun to conduct the '4 C's' (Confirm, Clear, Cordon, Control), which is the SOP for dealing with unexploded munitions. But then, all of a sudden, one of the ANP men spotted where it lay, ran over and picked it up in his bare hands and threw it off the position.

'Well at least you can't say they're aren't brave, these people,' I said.

'Brave, or just ignorant?' he observed.

That was a good point. I think the truth was they just didn't really have a clue.

Captain Bedlabh is one of the Brigade's few Gurkha Christians – although whether he was raised as a Christian or became one subsequently, I don't know. But I have to say that, as well as being a very fine soldier, he is a very good man – very kind and completely straightforward – qualities that make him one of the most highly respected officers in the regiment. I would add that he was a very good advertisement for his religion, which he always enjoyed talking about, especially all the miracles Jesus performed.

'Kailash,' he would begin. 'Did I ever tell you the story about the loaves and the fishes?'

'I'm not sure.'

'Oh well, it happened like this ...' and off he would go. Sometimes I realised I was hearing the story for the second or third time, but I didn't like to say so. They were very nice stories and I genuinely did enjoy hearing them. He would tell me that it was a good idea for me to become a Christian too.

'It's going to make your life so much better,' he said.

I didn't mind that at all, though I do remember one particular occasion at Bastion when I didn't so much want to know. I was just back off duty and really tired. Captain Bedlabh was there, and after exchanging a few friendly words, he began.

'Kailash, did I ever tell the story about Jesus and the feeding of the five thousand?'

'I'm not sure.'

'Well it goes like this . . .' And he told me about how Jesus had fed five thousand people using just five loaves of bread and two fishes. Or maybe it was two loaves of bread and twelve fishes. I really liked the story, but I don't remember the details. When he had finished, he wanted to tell me a lot of other stories too. Of course I couldn't object as he is my *guruji*. But the truth was that at that moment what I most wanted was not to get to heaven but just to get some sleep!

On this occasion, as we shared a bottle or two of water I noticed that although I offered my bottle to the ANP men, they all refused. It turned out that the Afghans would only ever accept drinks from us if the bottles were unopened. In fact I almost think they would rather have died from thirst than share with us. Also, they would only accept rations – biscuits for example – after checking first to make sure they didn't contain pork. We Gurkhas also have some dietary rules, so I could sympathise to some extent about checking for pork. For us, it is wrong to eat beef, but nobody would have a problem if nothing else was available. But we had the impression the Afghans would rather starve to death than eat pig.

When we got back to the DC after the casevac and resupp of ANP Hill, the OC called an O-group. As well as telling us that we needed to be extra vigilant that night on account of the clear skies and good moon forecast, he updated us on 3 PARA's progress. It seemed they had again been held up by unexpectedly heavy resistance. For this reason, there would be a further delay. We should not expect to be relieved for at least another week, possibly longer.

'So how long do you think we're really going to be here, *guruji*?' the *bhai*s all wanted to know when I went back to brief them.

I had no idea. I could only tell them as much as I knew.

'Looks like our leave in Cyprus is going to have to be postponed at this rate,' said Gaaz later. 'So what about your family? Your *memsahib* is going to kill you, isn't she?'

I hardly needed reminding. Sumitra was going to be very disappointed if I didn't come and get her soon.

'True. But we've got a war to win. She understands that. So come on, let's get our weapons cleaned.'

'We're ahead of you there, *guruji*,' said Gaaz triumphantly. As a matter of fact, I don't think I ever had to remind the *bhai*s about weapon cleaning. They did it as a matter of course.

After I'd inspected their weapons, the riflemen started speculating about what was holding 3 PARA up. We knew that they were leading a full battlegroup.

'That means more than a thousand men!' said one of them. 'It says a lot for the Talibs if they can hold a whole battlegroup up.'

'Well if that ANP guy was telling the truth, there are hundreds of Talibs in this part of the world too,' said Gaaz. 'So just do the maths. How many Paras do you need to defeat ten Taliban?'

'But shouldn't it be the other way round?' came the reply. 'How many Talibs do you need to hold up ten Paras?'

'Well you hope the answer is one Para to ten or more Talibs, don't you?'

'That's what you thought. But maybe this is telling us something different.'

The conversation continued up in the sangar later in the evening. Nobody could quite understand what was taking the Paras so long. It wouldn't be until afterwards that it really came home to us that they were hugely overstretched with other commitments.

'Could be they're having trouble getting supplies in,' suggested someone.

'Maybe they've taken more casualties than they were expecting,' said another.

'What about sickness?' said Gaaz. 'Could be they've all gone down with a stomach bug.'

That didn't seem very likely.

All the time we were chatting like this, I was moving round inside the sangar, trying to get the best view of the buildings around us. I kept swapping between my nightsight, my binos and my personal weapon sight. There was a good moon that night and you could actually see quite well. Every so often, I'd call the *bhais* in Sangar 3 to make sure they were OK. And then about every half-hour I would send a sitrep to Platoon HQ. In fact there weren't too many minutes of quiet either over the field telephone or on the PRR, so all the chatting we did was in snatches.

From talking about 3 PARA, the riflemen started talking about the prospects of another quiet night.

'So what do you reckon, *guruji*? They gonna come back tonight?' Nagen wanted to know.

'There's a good chance,' I replied.

'I don't know why they'd bother,' said Gaaz. 'Just look at the state of this place. It's a dump.' He gestured towards the building opposite, its doorway blackened from yesterday's engagement. That was one shop that wasn't going to be open for business for quite some time.

The silence that followed was broken by Nagen, holding up a bottle.

'Anyone need a drink?'

'Thanks,' I said, swallowing half a litre.

Although it was still a lot warmer than room temperature, we prevented our water supplies from getting too hot by keeping them in a sock soaked in urine. This isn't something you would want to do at home, but it was a practical solution to the problem, and surprisingly effective.

At around ten thirty, Lance Corporal Shree in Sangar 3 came up over the PRR.

'Vehicle movements east and north-east, distance approximately three kilometres,' he announced breathlessly. 'Could be they're RV-ing.'

I snatched up my weapon sight. RV-ing means rendezvousing. It sounded like enemy troops were on their way, but I couldn't verify this as the view from Sangar 1 towards the east was partially obscured by the buildings in the way.

'Can you give a more accurate position?' I wanted to know.

'Looks like they're heading for AOI Three.'

'Roger, can you see anything else?'

'Nothing at the moment. Just a lot of vehicle lights.'

'Roger.'

I picked up the field telephone.

'Zero, this is Sangar One. Sangar Three reports increased vehicle movement near to AOI Three.'

'Roger. I'll give him a call.'

At once, we were on hyper-alert again. This could be the start of something big.

Not long after this sighting, we heard a rifle shot, followed by another and then another.

'ZERO –THIS IS SANGAR THREE. CONTACT – WAIT OUT!'

Lance Corporal Shree's voice was charged with tension.

For a few minutes we were silent – three men fully alert and watching for the slightest movement on the ground.

'So what do you think, *guruji*?' Gaaz demanded after some time. 'Are they coming d'you reckon? Or are they just pretending?'

'If it was me, I'd just be pretending,' said Nagen. 'I wouldn't want to be hit by A-10 again.'

You might be right, I thought. But on the other hand, it took a certain amount of time to get air support. The OC mentioned in one of his O-groups that unless there was an aircraft in the vicinity at the time of a shout it was going to take a minimum of thirty minutes before they could get to us. And thirty minutes was quite enough time for the enemy to make serious trouble for us.

While the other two kept lookout, I went carefully through everything in the sangar one more time. GPMG rounds? How many boxes and are they all open? Check. Minimi rounds, how many and are they all open? Check. Rifle magazines. I counted mine. Twelve.

'Nagen. Show me your magazines.'

'They're here, *guruji*.'

'OK good. What about yours, Gaaz?'

'Here, *guruji*.'

Next, grenades. I straightened the pile. Twenty grey-black canisters promising death to anyone who came close enough. Including ourselves if the enemy got lucky.

'How about water, *bhai haru*? Nagen, how many've you got left?'

'Four, *guruji*.'

'Gaaz?'

'Same.'

And I had four. Plus there were six spares. That should see us through the night. *Should*.

The minutes ticked slowly by. After the initial contact, there was no follow-up. So maybe it had been just a random gunman. Even so, I felt quite uneasy. Maybe it had to do with the town being so quiet. It felt like a graveyard. Now that it was dark, it seemed even more empty.

Gaaz suddenly called out in a loud whisper.

'*Guruji! Guruji!*'

'What is it?'

'Down there!' He was trying not to raise his voice above a whisper, but he was clearly agitated. I pulled down my night-vision sight and crawled over to where he was aiming his weapon, down into the alleyway a few metres to the left of the burned-out shop.

'Straight ahead! Thirty metres! I saw one of them, *guruji*. Leopard-crawling. Crossing between those two buildings!'

'Was he armed?'

'Yes. On his back. Looked like an AK.' Gaaz was having trouble keeping his voice down.

'Show me with your laser.'

The place he indicated was the T junction at the end of an alleyway. There was a building directly ahead and two more either side of the alleyway itself. So there must be a narrow passage running at ninety degrees to it.

I pulled out my map and shone my torch on it to check the exact location.

'Zero, this is Sangar One. Contact,' I said into the field telephone, covering the mouthpiece with my hand to minimise the sound of my voice, and talking hardly above a whisper. 'Gunman crossing alleyway south to north grid—' I gave the grid reference. 'Am observing, over.'

'Zero, roger. Keep me posted.' Mathers *sahib*'s voice was as cool and calm as ever.

I lay next to Gaaz, peering through my sight for several minutes. Because of the good moon, I could see very clearly, but it's impossible to concentrate on empty space indefinitely, so I put the sight up and took a rest.

'Could be just one guy,' I said quietly.

Gaaz said nothing.

'A sniper getting into position,' I went on.

'You think? But he's so close. They're coming to kill us, *guruji*!'

You could be right, I thought. It sounded more like he was making for an FUP, a forming-up place, from which they might launch an attack in section or platoon strength. This was a really bad thought, and for a moment I wondered what I was going to say to my *bhais*' families if one of them got hit. I felt completely responsible for them.

'Well if he's not a sniper, there should be more of them. Do you reckon there might have been others?'

'I think I'd have seen them, *guruji*.'

It's movement that gives you away before anything else. Sound can come from anywhere, and you'd be amazed how difficult it can be to see a static target even if it isn't well camouflaged. It was easy to believe what Gaaz was saying. He surely would have seen if there had been others. But then again, maybe those sniper shots earlier were designed to distract us. Maybe the others had crossed while we were looking elsewhere.

This was puzzling. If it was me and I was leading my section across an obstacle like that, I'd do the same – get down and crawl so as to present the least target possible. But I'd get my troops over at ten-second intervals, maximum twenty. I'd been watching the place Gaaz indicated for almost five minutes now, and hadn't seen anything. Chances were that if the one he had seen was one of a group, the others were already across.

'OK. We just wait,' I said.

I could tell that Gaaz was really nervous, and I pulled down my nightsight again to take another quick look at the crossing. I didn't expect to see anything, simply to try to figure out where the FUP might be when—

Contact!

I was just in time to see another one cross. Like Gaaz had said about the previous one, he had a rifle on his back and he was leopard-crawling between the two buildings. My pulse rocketed.

I picked up the field telephone.

'Hello Zero, this is Sangar One, contact! Another suspected enemy seen leopard-crawling between the two buildings at end of alleyway. Same location.' My breath was coming in short, sharp gasps and I had to make a conscious effort not to shout.

'Zero, roger.'

'Looks like they could be crossing at five-minute intervals. Will keep observing.'

'Roger. Sounds like they could be moving forward to occupy an FUP. And he was definitely armed?'

'Definitely.'

'Was he pointing his weapon?'

'No. But definitely posing a threat. No question from my point of view.'

'Roger. In that case you may engage if you see any more.'

'Roger out.'

I turned to the others.

'OK, so Gaaz, bring the jimpy over here. If we see any more, I'll use it to fire first. When I do, I want you to engage with your rifle. Nagen, you keep the main road covered.'

As I set the GPMG up, I caught the expression on Nagen's face in the moonlight. He looked a bit disappointed. Of course, he wanted to be in on the action. But it could be that the enemy were going to assault from his side first anyway.

The time ticked past agonisingly slowly. Because the GPMG doesn't have a nightsight, I was relying on the moonlight to see. It was a real strain, and even though I didn't want to take my eyes off the crossing point even for an instant, I found I had to look away for a few seconds every so often.

Suddenly, at what must have been five minutes exactly,

another gunman appeared. Without hesitation, I squeezed the trigger.

BABABA

I gave him a three-round burst while Gaaz followed up with another two.

TAK TAK

There was a loud scream and we saw the enemy roll over and over. But a moment later he was pulled out of sight by unseen hands.

'Zero. This is Sangar One. Target! Rifleman crossing alleyway hit. Has now been dragged off position.' I could still hear him screaming.

'Roger. Well done. So the others must still be there.'

'I don't think he could have got himself away, so yes. Must still be there.'

'Roger. Well you probably won't see any more, but keep an eye out all the same.'

'Roger, out.'

I suppose you will ask how I felt. The answer is, not much. We were in an extremely tense situation. We had had an engagement that had lasted on and off the whole of the previous day, followed by a respite of twelve hours during which none of us had managed more than three or four hours' sleep. And now we were facing the prospect of another serious engagement. For me at the time, he was just a target. Now, looking back – well, of course I can think about him as a human being. Someone's son, a brother perhaps, and maybe a father like myself.

But I have no regrets. On the contrary – I would not hesitate to pull the trigger again.

You see, we'd been out there two weeks at this point. We'd had a lot of quite small contacts. Then there was the big contact of the day before. Up until then our only sightings of the enemy had been fleeting glimpses. The guy with the RPG on his back. The muzzle smoke giving away a fire position. But that was about it, unless you counted those guys on the back of a motorcycle riding slowly past with insolent expressions on their faces. Or the scowls of the older men at the *shura*. What we really wanted was to do our job. We wanted to win the battle of hearts and minds and to protect the locals. But if people were going to attack us, what we wanted was a fair fight.

As for the guy in the alleyway, what I'd really like to have done was to go down and stand with my boot on his chest and just ask him:

Why?

Why are you doing this? Why are you trying to kill me? I didn't come here to kill you. I didn't fire a single shot at you, not before you tried to kill me. I'm not here because I wanted to kill you. I'm here because I was sent to help. To help you and your people. But you are here because you want to kill me. Tell me why.

And he could tell me. I'd have listened to everything he'd had to say. But then I would have killed him. I would have killed him because I knew that if I let him go, he would try to kill me. This man wanted me dead. This was war.

Maybe he'd have some excuse. Maybe he'd tell me about how his brother was killed, or his father or mother. Maybe he'd tell me that this was Holy War for him. That he was fighting for Allah. But I would still kill him because I want people to understand that you can't do this. You can't set out to kill and not expect a reaction from us. You don't take on the British Gurkhas and think we aren't going to hit back.

It's simple. If you try to kill us, we will try to kill you. And I know who will win. Give us the same weapons, we will win. Give us the same food, we will win. Give us exactly equal conditions, we will win. And if you won't give us a fair fight, we will take you down with us just the same. You need to understand this.

It could be like it was in Burma, at the siege of Imphal, where the Japanese were in total superiority as they tried to invade India during the Second World War. The Gurkhas were ordered to retake Mortar Bluff, and Subedar Netrabahadur Thapa – who won the VC – found himself and his section completely cut off by the enemy. When he radioed for reinforcements, they were all killed. But he managed to get the ammunition they'd brought and he and his section immediately renewed his attack on the Japanese with kukris and grenades. The enemy shot him in the mouth and then blew him up with an artillery shell, but when they recovered his body, they found a Japanese soldier next to him with his head cut in half by a kukri.

So if I could have spoken to that Talib in the alley, I'd have congratulated him. I'd have admitted his courage.

'You are not cowardly,' I would have said. 'You are courageous. You know our capabilities. You know our weapons. You have seen our air support. Yet still you come. That is brave and I respect you for that.' And then I would have added, 'But we are braver. Definitely braver. You need to understand this. We will fight harder than you. We will have more aggression than you. We will even have more laughter than you. In the end, we always win. We are Gurkhas.'

'They're not going to come again, are they, *guruji*?'

Nagen snapped me out of my thoughts. He was surely right. That was too much to expect. But, just in case, I kept the crossing in my sights. As you would a rat hole.

'They can't be that stupid,' Gaaz agreed.

'You just never know,' I replied. 'Same detail. Keep observing.'

Again the time dragged past so slowly that five minutes seemed like half a lifetime. Maybe because you're concentrating with your whole mind and your whole body, completely alert, time really does slow down. But then—

Another one!

BABABA!

TAK TAK!

Exactly five minutes after the last one!

Again there was a scream. And again the body was pulled away by unseen hands.

We looked at each other, astounded.

'WOW, *guruji*!' said Nagen, looking round over his shoulder.

'Bloody hell,' I said.

'They're crazy!' said Gaaz excitedly. 'Totally crazy!'

'Zero, this is Sangar One. Target! Another one! Same location.'

'Zero, roger. Well done. You'd better keep it in your sights. Maybe they've got a death wish.'

'Sangar One roger. Out.'

You would have thought that after two ambushes like that, the enemy would realise his route was completely compromised. But then again, you never know what's going to happen in a combat situation.

'All right,' I said to the *bhai*s. 'We keep watching.'

'OK, *guruji*. But do you really think . . . ?'

'I don't know. If it was me, I'd have changed my tactics by now. But maybe there's some reason why they can't use any other route.'

A dog barked in the distance. Then another and another. There was definitely still movement out there.

In the meantime, the seconds ticked slowly past. It just couldn't be that they would send anyone else. But maybe they'd try to pass some weapons over, or some ammo. That was a possibility. Still my heart was raging in my chest and I was taking some deep steadying breaths when—

BABABABA

TAK TAK

Another one! I didn't even pause to think this time. Again he rolled over several times before disappearing.

'That's it, *guruji*. Now we're going to get the whole lot of them,' said Gaaz excitedly. 'They obviously think it's Allah's plan they're gonna die tonight.'

'Zero, this is Sangar One. TARGET! Same location again!'

'Good work, Kailash. Just make sure you don't fixate on the one position. Keep looking elsewhere.'

'Roger. Will keep covering within arcs,' I replied.

It was beginning to feel a bit like we were on a firing range.

'There couldn't be more,' said Nagen disbelievingly. 'Not really there couldn't.'

'Well we've got about another four and a half minutes to wait before we find out.'

They passed in an agony of breathless tension.

Was it possible? Was it really, really possible? It was hard to believe. I couldn't even account for the three kills we'd already had, let alone a possible fourth. Surely they'd change tactics? What possible reason could there be for falling for the same mistake time after time?

The only thing I could think of was that maybe these were recruits new to the area. Maybe they didn't know the ground. Or maybe it really was fatalism. They actually thought that Allah had decided this was what they must do, and if it was his will they should die tonight, so be it.

Judging by what I had seen of the Afghans so far, this didn't seem completely impossible. And it did seem to fit with some other things I saw subsequently. I remember on a later tour of Afghanistan – Op Herrick 14 in 2011 – hearing about some Gurkhas coming across an Afghan position at night where every single one of the guys was asleep. I wasn't too surprised to hear that every single one of those same guys was found dead on their position a few days later. They just didn't seem to care.

The minutes came and went in another agony of anticipation. No, nothing. That must be it. But the question was, what was coming next? We realised something serious must be coming.

'All right, *bhai haru*. I don't think we're going to see any more,' I said.

Silence followed as we looked out over the empty roads and buildings, our nerves taut, every sinew straining.

'It's ten to one now,' said Gaaz after a while. 'Could be their start time was exactly half past midnight. Do you think the next phase will begin at zero one hundred hours?'

I liked the way Gaaz worked things out like that. He was going to make a very effective NCO one day, and it seemed quite likely he was right. There was no doubt something was about to happen. The fact that there were all those vehicle movements earlier, followed by the leopard-crawlers, meant that positions were definitely being occupied. It only remained to be seen what the enemy were going to do next.

We didn't have much longer to wait. A minute or two later, a call came in from Sangar 6 over the PRR.

'Zero, this is Sangar Six. Contact! Pax approaching from the west. Less than one hundred metres.'

'Zero, roger. Is he armed?'

'Not seen.'

'OK, just let him have a couple of warning shots. Make sure you don't hit him, all right?'

'Sangar Six, roger out.'

Immediately, two rifle shots rang out – followed less than ten seconds later by a loud explosion nearby.

Aye! What was that?

I just had time to realise that Sangar 6 had been hit when, in the next instant, all the fires of hell erupted round us.

12

All the Fires of Hell

'C-O-N-T-A-C-T! R-P-G! I SAY AGAIN RPG!'

The riflemen in Sangar 6 sounded seriously shaken up.

'Zero, roger. Are you OK in there? Any casualties?'

'No casualties . . . Am observing.'

'Zero, roger.'

A moment later, the sky itself seemed to short-circuit. Streams of fire crackled and spat through the air in bright, malevolent streaks, criss-crossing above and around us.

Aare! This was really serious.

We ducked down, too stunned to say anything at first. I think my heart didn't just miss one beat but ten. The noise was intense. The rounds thudding into the sangar position sounded like the drumming of Himalayan rains on a tin roof – you think the sky is falling all round you. Only this was louder, and worse. But it wasn't just the sound – you could feel the whole position vibrating with the weight of fire.

Coming to my senses, I grabbed the field telephone. 'ZEROSANGARONECONTACTWAITOUT!'

'Zero, roger. Are you OK in there?' Rex *sahib*'s voice was calm and controlled.

'All right for now. But fire is very heavy. We're keeping our heads down,' I replied, catching my breath.

'OK, as soon as you can, return fire.'

'Roger.'

Then I heard Sangar 3 come up on the PRR to me.

'SANGAR ONE, THIS IS SANGAR THREE. CONTACT! POSITION UNCERTAIN. OBSERVING!'

'Roger,' I replied. 'Which direction? Any idea?'

'Can't say.'

I could hear the tension in Lance Corporal Shree's voice.

'OK. Let me know as soon as you see anything. Get some rounds down as soon as you can. But remember your arcs.'

'Roger, out.'

I passed on the message from Sangar 3 to HQ, shouting to make my voice heard above the noise.

Now what? I had to take a look, no matter what the risk. There could be a raiding party.

Flicking my HMNVS down, I wriggled forward and raised my head for a few seconds to see if there was any movement. No, all I could see was an empty street. But as I did so, the weight of fire increased even more.

'*Ayo jatha!*' I shouted, dropping back down under cover. 'Bloody hell!'

I could just make out the features on Nagen and Gaaz's faces.

They were both looking at me wide-eyed. As soon as I'd shown my head above the sandbags, the thud of rounds hitting the position had multiplied still further.

The field telephone rang.

'Enemy fire position identified in treeline to north. Are you able to engage?' It was Mathers *sahib*.

'Will try,' I replied, then gave orders. 'OK, *bhai haru*. We're going to have to do something. Here, Gaaz, let me take the jimpy.'

Putting my SA80 down, I crawled over him to get to the GPMG and put my head up just enough to be able to take aim.

Pulling the stock into my shoulder and looking through my nightsight at the same time, I started to scan. But before I could identify the target, I gasped at a sudden flash of white light. There was a loud explosion, as the whole position shook and the sangar filled with smoke.

RPG!

For a second I was too stunned to move, my head spinning and my ears ringing. Another one of those and it felt like the sangar could be blown apart.

For the first time, I was truly afraid.

'*Guruji*,' said Gaaz quite quietly – his face only inches from mine – 'we're gonna die. We are, aren't we?'

He's right, I thought.

We probably are.

But then again—

what are we?

We are GURKHAS!

'*KAPHAR HUNNU BHANDA MARNU RAMRO!* I shouted.

'*KAPHAR HUNNU BHANDA MARNU RAMRO!* Nagen yelled in reply.

'*KAPHAR HUNNU BHANDA MARNU RAMRO!* Gaaz shouted at the top of his voice.

This is the Gurkha motto. 'It is better to die than be a coward.'

'So come on, *bhai haru*,' I said, 'it doesn't matter if we do. We need to get some rounds down. Then who knows? Maybe we won't die after all.'

Saying these words, I threw myself forward to the sandbags and again put my head up just enough to be able to take aim in the direction of the tracer climbing towards us. Squeezing the trigger, it felt good to be doing something about our situation.

A second later, Gaaz was up and firing the SA80 with the change lever set to automatic and Nagen, back in his position on the side looking out over the bazaar, began to lay down suppressive fire with the Minimi.

The enemy was on to us straight away and the incoming fire became even more intense. But we had to keep going. If we did not respond, there was nothing to stop them sending an assault party forward. They could be on top of us in less than a minute.

Ladders . . .

RPG at point-blank range . . .

Grenades through the letter box . . .

The thought made me all the more determined, and I got off several long bursts before again my eye was caught by a ball of intense white light spinning through the night sky towards us and my ears registered the pshhhhhhhhhhhhhhhhhhhhhh of another RPG round. Gaaz saw it too and ducked down at the same time as me, just before it hit the wall below.

'The *jatha*! I'm gonna get that bastard!' cried Gaaz.

Both of us had seen the direction the round had come from, not more than two to three hundred metres away, and together we began to engage the area.

We hadn't fired more than a few bursts before I became aware of the field telephone ringing. I let it ring a few more times. If I answered, it meant holding fire. On the other hand, I needed to let the OC know we were OK.

'Gaaz, you take over on the GPMG. I need to answer this.'

We swapped weapons and, moving to the back of the sangar, I picked up the phone and pushed back one of my earphones.

'SANGAR ONE?'

'Are you OK in there, Kailash?' The OC's voice was full of concern.

'YES OK. WE ARE ENGAGING TARGETS TO NORTH!' I shouted, registering only that the OC had heard me before slamming down the receiver. There would be time for a nice conversation later – or not. Either way, I needed to get back behind my weapon. I was just in time to see yet another burst of light hurtling towards us.

Aayo! This could be third time lucky for them.

Because of the RPG's low muzzle velocity, there's enough time to clock where the round is coming from and still be able to duck before impact. And time to realise this could be your last second alive.

Pshhhhhhhhhhhhhhhhhhhhh—

Fortunately this one went over the top of us, but how much longer before they got lucky? At anything less than 200 metres range, it is just about impossible to miss a target with this weapon. Maybe they weren't that close yet, but unless we hit

209

back, it wouldn't be long before they got one through the letter box.

'Come on, Gaaz, let's tell them we're still here,' I yelled as, scrambling back into position, I took aim.

But my words were wasted. He was already sending down successive short bursts of fire in the direction it came from.

'Reckon it definitely came from somewhere over there, *guruji*,' he said.

This time using the CWS, I looked carefully at where Gaaz's tracer was hitting. You can fit the Common Weapon Sight to the SA80, but generally I preferred to use it for scanning like a pair of binos. It's more usable that way. I saw that his rounds were falling just short of one of the AOIs in the treeline.

'You're off target!' I shouted. 'Go up a bit! Watch my tracer!'

So saying, I took careful aim with my SA80 and zapped it with the laser. This is visible using the nightsight as a thin bright beam, like a white pencil light.

'OK, got it, *guruji*!' he shouted.

It was impossible to be sure of the enemy's exact position. All you got looking through the sight were streams of bright dots heading towards you, but there was no point putting rounds down in the desert.

Leaving Gaaz to it, I went over to Nagen. The weight of fire coming in at us was still very heavy, but it was now clear most of it was coming from the north and the region of Smuggler's House.

'Anything seen down there?'

'Nothing, *guruji*.'

'In that case, come over next to Gaaz. I'll cover this side. We need to get some more rounds down on the treeline. He's definitely in there,' I said. The only good thing to be said about the situation was that there was no problem with ROE. When you're being shot at, there's nothing to stop you shooting back – and in this situation no civvies in the area to worry about either.

We had just swapped positions with Nagen settling down when, all of a sudden, Gaaz let out a yelp.

'*Guruji!*' he exclaimed. 'Look! Over there!'

I looked over. He was pointing in the direction of Smuggler's House.

'There must be twenty of them!' he went on excitedly as I scrambled back over with the CWS and looked in the direction he was pointing.

'*Aare jatha!*' He was right. No more than 200 metres away, I could clearly see a group of men in at least half-platoon strength. My heart-rate rocketed.

'ZERO, THIS IS SANGAR ONE. CONTACT! ENEMY IN AT LEAST HALF-PLATOON STRENGTH ADVANCING FROM THE NORTH. RANGE TWO HUNDRED METRES MAXIMUM.'

'Zero, roger. Are they armed?'

'Not clear. But they are definitely headed in this direction.'

'Roger. Over to you. Keep me informed.'

I slammed the field telephone down and got myself in position ready to fire as soon as I was sure they were armed. Meanwhile the *bhai*s were shouting at me.

'What did he say, *guruji?*'

'Can we fire?'

'No, hold on. Let them get a bit closer. We need to be able to see their weapons.' We needed to be absolutely certain we were engaging legitimate targets.

I pulled down my HMNVS again and looked in the direction of Smuggler's House.

Aare! Where were they? They had disappeared from view. *Disaster!* The *jathas* had completely vanished from sight!

'Gaaz! Where have they gone? Did you see where they went?'

'They were definitely heading for Smuggler's. I was just adjusting my HMNVS . . .'

I barely had time to report this development to the OC before there was a sudden massive increase in the weight of fire. Grabbing the field telephone, I yelled into it: 'ZERO, THIS IS SANGAR ONE. ENEMY HAVE GONE FROM VIEW. INTO SMUGGLER'S HOUSE, I THINK.'

That must be exactly what happened. In fact it's my opinion now that they had their weapons and ammunition all laid out ready for them in the ruins of the old school building. A clever tactic. They must have guessed we wouldn't engage them if we couldn't see them actually carrying weapons.

So now what?

'OK, *bhai haru,*' I shouted. 'We need to hit their position with everything we've got. When I give the word, we all go up at once. Nagen, you go in the middle, I'll stay on the end so that I can get over to the bazaar side if necessary.'

'Ready, *guruji,*' they both said together.

'All right, GO!' I shouted.

Without a moment's hesitation, Gaaz was up again and letting rip with the GPMG while Nagen got going with the LSW.

'Remember, controlled bursts!' I shouted. 'Go for the obvious. The windows, the doorways.'

For the next minute or two, we just concentrated on getting fire down onto the building. Every so often, I paused to scramble over to the bazaar side and quickly check down there to make sure there wasn't anyone in the area. If the enemy was going to assault us, that was the side he'd be forming up on, as he could get to within a few metres of our position without having to expose himself.

Just then, Sangar 3 came up on the PRR.

'Sangar One, this is Sangar Three. Enemy fire position identified approx one hundred and fifty metres north of your position. Muzzle flash and smoke.'

'Sangar One, roger. Is it within your arc?'

'Position is not within my arc. Also we are taking accurate fire on the .50-cal. They've got us fixed. Unable to use.'

'Roger. In that case concentrate on what you can do. Can you give an exact grid of that fire position?'

For a few tense moments, Lance Corporal Shree was silent while he worked out the position on the map. I kept looking.

'Sangar One, this is Sangar Three. Grid, over.'

'Go ahead.'

As my section 2 i/c gave me the grid reference, I plotted it directly on my map.

'Roger. Will engage as soon as identified.'

I then relayed the information to the OC.

'Zero, roger. Well done. Keep me posted.'

These exchanges look quite calm written down like this, but in reality they were mostly shouted and interrupted by the sound of gunfire. Only the OC's voice hardly changed from normal.

'OK, *bhai haru*!' I shouted, taking out my compass. 'We need to get onto that position ASAP.'

There was just enough ambient light to be able to take a bearing. First I looked at my map and marked the grid reference

Lance Corporal Shree had given. Then I worked out what the bearing of the position would be. Finally I checked it against my compass.

'It's just beyond that building over there!' I shouted at last, aiming my weapon at it and letting fly a short burst of tracer.

'OK seen,' said Gaaz. 'Shall I engage, *guruji*?'

'Fire at will,' I replied before continuing to Nagen. 'OK, *bhai*, bring the Minimi over this side and engage the same target. I'll keep on at Smuggler's House.'

The sound inside the sangar reached a crescendo as the second machine gun opened up and the smell of oil and cordite filled the air.

'Gaaz, how's your ammo?' I demanded.

'Still plenty,' he replied between bursts.

'Barrel?' I readied the spare as I was speaking.

'Good for another hundred rounds I'd say.'

'OK, let me know when you want to switch and I'll bring it over.'

In the meantime, I picked up the oil can we kept at the ready and poured a good amount over the firing mechanism.

'That should help too.'

Gaaz nodded. I turned to Nagen.

'OK, *bhai*?'

'OK, *guruji*.'

'Seen anything definite?'

Of course he hadn't, otherwise he'd have said something, but I asked all the same.

'Nothing, *guruji*,' he replied in between bursts.

'OK, I'm just going to take a look over here again with the nightsight,' I said.

The contact had been going on for probably around twenty minutes, and the sky was still deadly, with tracer criss-crossing above and around our position. Sangar 3 and the CT were also still taking a beating . But I began to get the impression that it was slightly less. Maybe not much, but a bit. This was good news if you read it that our fire was having some effect. But if it meant the enemy was now moving forward for an assault, then it was not a good sign.

I got myself in position next to Nagen and flicked my night-sight on. It was frustrating because this sangar, as well as being the most exposed, did not have a very good view close in. If I climbed out onto the platform in front, I'd get a better view.

'Nagen. I'm going forward. You cover me, OK?'

'OK, *guruji*. But you think it's a good idea?'

'There's only one way to find out,' I said, picking up my rifle and grabbing two grenades, just in case.

'Gaaz, I'm going forward,' I shouted above the noise.

'It's been nice knowing you, *guruji*,' he replied without turning round.

It certainly was dangerous. But tough – I'd just have to hope the Osprey body armour was as good as people said. And that the god's magic in my lucky coin would work.

Clambering out, I immediately found I had much better situational awareness. At this stage, there was just a low wall of sandbags to the front, with no overhead cover except for the camnet. The first thing I would do when we had an opportunity would be to get some more sandbags, because in terms of actual protection it offered none at all. Hopefully, though, the cam was enough to screen my movement. The main thing was I was in a much better position to indicate targets using either the infrared laser on my rifle or tracer. So I began to scan the road, paying particular attention to the alleyways leading off it. It was from there that the enemy assault would come.

Being out here alone was also quite strange, and for a few moments I watched transfixed as the little streaks of light came towards me. The thing was that if you didn't know they carried death and destruction with them, you would say these streams of tracer climbing through the sky were actually very beautiful. It would be nice to just sit there and watch it, like you watch a fireworks display. To make matters worse, the longer it went on and the longer I hadn't been hit, the stronger the temptation was to ignore it. I found I had to keep reminding myself that it was meant for me, that it would hurt very badly, that it was the kind of beauty that kills. It was better to be a bit frightened.

Suddenly, out of the corner of my eye, I saw something that made me freeze. Not one but three or four of the enemy no more than 20 metres away, their weapons clearly pointing towards us as they covered each other forward.

Aare houu!

'CONTACT! TWENTY METRES!' I yelled. 'GET OVER HERE! THEY'RE TRYING TO TURN US OVER!'

Moving forward, I took a grenade and hurled it in the direction of the figures I'd seen. Before it had even exploded, I pulled the pin on a second one and immediately followed on.

I don't think I hit anyone, but at least it must have forced them to take cover. Meanwhile Gaaz and Nagen brought their weapons over, and within seconds the three of us were firing down into the bazaar area. By this time we had picked up one definite enemy firing position, from the clear, steady stream of tracer coming out of the place.

But the situation was really bad now. With the other two engaging the bazaar area, we had no one to keep suppressing the enemy fire support in Smuggler's House. What we desperately needed was another GPMG.

Out here in front of the sangar, I couldn't use the field telephone, so I pressed the Send button on the PRR. I had just heard Major Rex say that he was still unable to get up onto the roof of the CT due to the weight and accuracy of fire.

'ZERO, THIS IS SANGAR ONE. CONTACT!'

'Zero, go ahead.'

'Enemy closing on my position. Three seen within twenty metres. Have got all weapons engaging likely targets on bazaar side.'

'Roger . . .'

There was concern in the OC's voice.

'Are you OK?'

'Yes, OK. But I have no one on Smuggler's side now. Any chance of reinforcement, over?'

'Zero, wait. I'll see what we can do.'

Hopefully he could send someone from the QRF.

Not very long after, I heard shouting from inside the compound. It turned out to be Rifleman Lukesh accompanied by Lance Corporal Cook, one of the signallers.

'*GURUJI!*' yelled Cookie. 'WE'VE GOT YOU ANOTHER JIMPY!'

This was great news.

'OK, COME ON UP. BUT BE CAREFUL NOT TO EXPOSE YOURSELF!'

If the enemy caught sight of them, he'd throw everything at us. There'd be bound to be a casualty.

I waited in suspense as they climbed up onto the position. Gaaz and Nagen redoubled their efforts to give maximum possible covering fire.

''Ere you are, *guruji*!' said Cookie triumphantly, as he appeared carrying the ammunition for the second jimpy.

'Quick! Get inside! Soon as you can, get some rounds down on Smuggler's House.'

A moment later, Lukesh followed him up, carrying the weapon itself. We were now five on a position that normally only had three.

'Come on then, Lukie,' I heard Cookie say. 'You give to it them *jatha* till they don't know if it's Christmas, Easter or Ramadana-ding-dong!'

He was a brilliant guy, Cookie. To have come in under those conditions was really brave, especially considering the fact that he was a signaller and not an infanteer.

Within hardly more than a minute of the second GPMG's arrival, all three machine guns were blasting away. The enemy meanwhile was nowhere to be seen, so at least we were forcing them to keep under cover. What we did not want was for them to get close enough to be able to put ladders up. If they managed to turn us over, or even just to get over a wall or in through the gate, there was going to be trouble. Then it would be hand-to-hand fighting. And that, although we would happily do it if necessary, is something you want to avoid if at all possible. Scrambling back inside the sangar, I picked up the field telephone.

'Zero, this is Sangar One. Sitrep.'

'Zero, go ahead.'

'Sangar One, reinforcements engaging known fire positions, plus I have two riflemen engaging targets on bazaar side.'

'Zero, roger. Any more on those pax you saw earlier?'

'Nothing seen since I engaged with L109s.'

'Roger.'

With the immediate threat over, I had a moment to take stock. One thing I needed to keep an eye on was the barrel on Gaaz's jimpy. You need to change it approximately every 400 rounds, and it had to be getting close now. If you don't change it, it gets so hot that it distorts and you lose accuracy quite dramatically. I also needed to keep an eye on the ammo state in both sangars. We were getting through it at a huge rate.

Flicking the switch on my PRR, I put the question to the *bhais* in Sangar 3.

'How much ammo have you got left, Lance Corporal Shree?'

There was a pause of ten or fifteen seconds before he got back to me. In that time, there was a slight lull in the enemy's fire. Instead of a torrent of tracer climbing up at us, individual streams were coming. What did this mean? Were they manoeuvring to get closer? First light would be in about forty minutes, so maybe they were looking to get in position for an assault while it was still dark.

'Ammo state is getting low, *guruji*.'

'Roger.'

'*Bhai haru!* How's your ammo in there?' It shouldn't be too bad, as Cookie and Lukesh had brought a lot with them.

'More than one box!' yelled Gaaz.

'Same!' replied Nagen.

'More than half!' shouted Lukesh.

Just as I was on the point of calling the CT, Gaaz let out a yell.

'Over there, *guruji*!'

'What?'

He was waving frantically at me to come over.

'Look! In the compound over there!'

He was pointing to a compound over the other side of the road. Squinting through my binos, I was just in time to see four or five men sprint out of the shadows and into another compound no more than 50 metres north of our position.

'How many do you say?'

'There was a whole crowd of them. At least fifteen.'

Ayee! The compound in question was out of arc to us, so there was no possibility of engaging it, but I sent an immediate contact report.

'Zero, this is Sangar One. Contact. Probable enemy FUP identified. Wait . . . ' I took a quick bearing and glanced at my map before giving the grid.

'Zero, roger. That's one for Zero One Alpha.' Zero One Alpha was the tactical air controller.

That meant air assets must be approaching. Not a moment too soon!

'Zero One Alpha, roger. AH inbound, five minutes.'

'Zero, roger. Did you copy that, Sangar One?'

'AH inbound, five minutes.'

'Correct. Out to you. Charlie Charlie One, this is Zero. Air assets inbound, less than five minutes. Out.'

A moment later, the field telephone rang and Mathers *sahib* continued.

'Sangar One, reference suspected FUP, are you able to see any pax at this time?'

'Sangar One, no, over.'

'Zero, roger. Let me know as soon as you have anything further to report.'

'Roger.'

It was a tense few minutes while we waited for the Apache to appear. In the meantime we kept our weapons trained on the compound, waiting for the enemy to show himself again. The sky was just beginning to soften from black to grey at the approach of dawn. Chances were the enemy wouldn't stick around once we had air support.

'Charlie Charlie One, air assets in thirty seconds.'

The OC's voice broke in on my thoughts. A moment later he announced what we could already hear: an Apache helicopter now approaching.

'Apache overhead in ten seconds,' he said. 'He'll take at a look at that compound and engage the enemy if he can get a PID.'

There was a roar and a clatter of blades as the heli swept down towards us.

'Pilot confirms PID! Heads down, everyone. I say again, heads down,' Rex *sahib* ordered.

'HEADS DOWN! HEADS DOWN!' I repeated.

There was a loud tearing sound as a Hellfire missile hurtled through the breaking dawn, followed by a bright flash and a stupendous bang.

A collective cheer went up from inside the sangar.

'That'll teach them a lesson!' cried Gaaz triumphantly.

It certainly was a very pleasing sight, although I had my doubts as to whether there was anyone still inside. In between looking at the target and engaging it, there was every chance the enemy could have made a getaway. It was only when the helicopter left after engaging several other targets with its Gatling gun that it became obvious that not all the insurgents had got away in time. We could hear their screams in the distance.

'Like I said, that'll teach you, you *jatha*,' said Gaaz with grim satisfaction.

I had to agree.

As the sound of beating chopper blades faded into the distance, and those of distress subsided, the tinny sound of the muezzin's address spilled from a nearby megaphone.

'*Allaaahu akbar* ... Allah is most great ... I testify that there is no God but Allah ... I testify that Muhammad is the prophet of Allah ... Come to prayer. Come to salvation ... *Allaaahu akbar* ... There is no God but Allah.'

'Come on, *bhai haru*,' I said, scrambling back into the main sangar position. 'There's work to do. We need to get this place tidied up. And don't forget your SOPs just because the shooting has stopped. There are probably snipers still out there.'

Empty 7.62 and 5.56 cases and links lay scattered all over the place, ankle-deep. We were swimming in the stuff, not to mention all the sand that covered everything.

'Here, Gaaz, Cookie, you two take a sandbag each and get filling. Lukesh, you keep covering out towards the school while I watch the street and find out what Lance Corporal Shree and the other *bhai*s are up to.'

I flicked the PRR switch to send.

'Lance Corporal Shree? You guys OK in there? See anything?'

'OK, *guruji*. Nothing seen. We were just going to start clearing up.'

'That's good. Just make sure you keep a sharp lookout. There could still be snipers.'

The words were hardly out of my mouth when a burst of automatic gunfire ripped through the air. So they hadn't all gone home for breakfast.

'*Aayo!* Where did that go, anyone?'

'That was for us,' said Lance Corporal Shree helpfully.

'Roger,' I said before turning to the others.

'Well, we have been warned, so I want proper discipline at all times,' I continued, picking up the field telephone.

'Sunray, this is Sangar One. Sangar Three reports that last contact was aimed at him.'

'Roger. We'll assume there are snipers still out there. Keep a good lookout.'

'Roger out.'

'*Guruji.* That's three sandbags,' announced Rifleman Lukesh as I returned the receiver to its cradle. 'We don't have any more and we're only halfway there.'

'Well we'll get some more later, as soon as we're stood down. In the meantime, give me a hand and we'll sweep the rest into the corner here,' I said as I got going.

Within about fifteen minutes we had the place looking quite tidy, and I stopped to wipe my brow and have a drink.

'Tiring work, *hunsa*?' I said to Lukesh as I passed him the bottle.

'Certainly is, *guruji*,' he replied with a smile.

Just then I realised I was completely exhausted. For the best part of six hours, give or take a few minutes, we'd been operating at maximum power. I doubt there'd been more than two minutes that I'd stayed in one position. The rest of the time I'd been scrambling from one side of the platform to the other, scanning with my nightsight or my weapon sight, looking,

looking and hoping. Hoping to catch sight of the enemy, desperate to get a clear shot in at him. And for much of the time, there'd been an incredible intensity of fire. It seemed miraculous that, again, no one had been hit. That talisman Mum had given me must be working.

13

Man Down

It wasn't until around 6 a.m. that we were eventually stood down. This was too late to change duties without exposing ourselves to the risk of snipers, so the OC ordered us to remain in post throughout the day. This meant we had to take it in turns to try to snatch some sleep inside the sangar – what we called chicken sleep. I organised a rota so that we each got two hours' rest to every four hours on duty. But it was too hot and we were still too pumped up from the night before to get any proper rest.

In the meantime, after clearing up, we spent quite a lot of time talking over the night's events, in particular our ambush of the three leopard-crawlers.

'I just don't get it,' said Gaaz. 'I mean, they didn't do anything to try and save themselves. They just came out, knowing we were waiting for them.'

'Maybe they were just following orders,' said Nagen.

'Obviously. But couldn't they adapt their plan to suit the new situation?'

'It is strange,' I agreed.

'My guess is they just shouted *Allahu akbar*, God is great, and off they went,' concluded Gaaz. 'Stupid *jatha*s.'

Then we were silent. I have to say that even though I wouldn't hesitate to do it again in the same situation, I did feel a bit sorry for those guys. They must have been terrified, just like we were.

Looking out over Now Zad that morning was like looking at a ghost town – except that these ghosts weren't just lost souls, they were violent, angry spirits just like those you see in religious paintings. They were hungry for blood – Afghan blood, Gurkha blood, British blood, it didn't matter whose, so long as it was human and that it was spilled, that life was extinguished, that death should rule. This feeling was intensified by the heat. Only a few scavenging flies stirred. You knew that they would feed just as happily off your maimed and broken body as off the crumbs of biscuit on the sangar floor. It was like we were the last outpost of civilisation on the edge of the world.

'Tell you what, *guruji*,' said Gaaz after some time. 'It makes you glad you're a Gurkha when you come to a place like this. I mean, look at us. Here we are, stuck out in the middle of nowhere being shot at half the time. But we've got each other and we're doing something useful. We've come to help the local people. That's got to be a good thing, even though they don't seem very grateful. And when things get really tough, we've always got something to joke about, *hunza, guruji*? I mean, every time I think back to selection I always find something to laugh about.'

We spent quite a lot of the rest of the day chatting about our first experience of Gurkha life. Of course, it wasn't the only thing we did. As section commander, I had a lot more to think about than the riflemen. For a start, their welfare was my responsibility but my welfare was not their responsibility. As a result, apart from needing to stay on top of the ammo situation and general supplies, I was thinking about them all the time. Were they getting enough to eat, enough rest, enough exercise? Did they have a good conversation when they last called home? No family worries? Are they coping with the heat? How are they coping with coming under attack? Are they getting on each other's nerves? All these concerns and more are yours to think about as section commander before you even start thinking about yourself. And when you've finished making sure you yourself are in good shape, there is the ever-present thought of the enemy. But talking about Gurkha selection was a good way of occupying the long hours when you had to keep people going.

'So come on, *guruji*,' Gaaz demanded. 'You were telling us about selection. What about the second stage?'

Having passed the first selection, I was eligible for the next stage, which took place at Taplejung, the main town in our area. All those who had passed the local selection came together about a month later to compete with each other at district level. This time there were probably a thousand-plus people for just fourteen places to go ahead to the final selection board in Pokhara.

There were two different streams: one for ordinary Guard

Duty and another for those who had achieved a higher level at school. This was EGD, or Educated Guard Duty. Thanks to my good academic results, I was part of the second stream.

As before, there was a fitness test where you had to perform sit-ups and pull-ups. I had done a lot of training since the first selection and, as before, I was one of the two or three tallest guys there, so I wasn't too worried about this. Then we were divided up and there was some marching in squads, and a run. After that, we all had to undergo a medical. Finally, there was an interview. First, they asked me about my education. This was followed by something more like a cross-examination.

'So why do want to join the Gurkhas?'

'My grandfather, he was a Gurkha. He said I should join. And my uncle too.'

'Yes, but why do YOU want to be a Gurkha?'

I thought for a moment.

'I've always wanted to be a Gurkha, *sahib*. Ever since I first heard about them when I was a child.'

'That still doesn't answer the question WHY?'

I bit my lip. What was the answer he wanted? I wondered. It didn't seem right to tell him the stories my grandfather had told me about the glorious deeds of the ancestors – the times when the Gurkhas had run out of ammunition and still carried on fighting with bayonet and kukri, or how the Gurkhas had helped the British win two world wars.

'Because I like fighting,' I replied truthfully. 'And I like guns. I want to do some proper shooting.'

These words seemed to satisfy him and he noted something down on the paper in front of him.

As before, the whole procedure was spread out over a few

228

days, after which we assembled together outside the office building. We were all very nervous, as we knew that exactly fourteen of us would be going through and no more. But again I was pretty confident of success. I managed to improve quite a lot on most of my previous scores, which was encouraging.

'OK, listen in everyone!' The recruiting officer came forward to address us. 'The following are to report to me afterwards.'

He started reading out the names of the successful candidates. As I say, I was fairly confident and in fact expected my name would be at the top of the list, or very near it. But he read out one, two, three, four, five other names. I couldn't believe it! Had I done so badly?

Six . . . seven . . . eight . . . nine . . . ten . . . I counted each one with growing desperation.

This was bad. Maybe I'd failed. Eleven . . . twelve . . . thirteen . . .

That was it. I had failed. Fourteen:

'Kailash Khebang Limbu.'

My heart missed a beat. That was me! I'd passed after all!

The relief I felt was indescribable. I had the last place! Well never mind, better last than no place!

Actually, looking back I'm not sure the list was graded at all. It could be that our names were read out at random, or according to our time of arrival. In any case, it didn't matter. The important thing was that I had got through. I was just so happy.

But of course, I still had the toughest part of the selection procedure to come. And because I could not be sure of the outcome, I took the next few days to visit the college in Dharan in which I had already enrolled. I had heard a lot of good things about it, and one of my teachers, who had earned his BSc there, told me I should go and get the feel of the place. I should talk to some of the teachers, and some of the people I knew who were already studying there.

It turned out that the college looked really good, and I decided that if I could not be a Gurkha, I would definitely be a doctor. With my mum having been ill, I still had the thought in the back of my mind that maybe it was better to be a doctor and cure people. Yet although it may seem strange to say so, on the other hand I really did want to fire guns and fight. I felt like I was standing at a fork in a mountain path. One way led to a safe place, the other went uphill and you couldn't tell where it led, only that you would be sure to have adventures on the way. For some reason I can't really explain, I wanted to take the harder road. I suppose part of it was down to what my dad had said to me.

'If you are a man, you will really enjoy the Army.'

'The British Army rules the whole world,' my grandfather added. 'And the British are so brave!'

I was really inspired by what they had told me about the Gurkhas.

Of course, as I discovered later, it wasn't really true about the British Army ruling the whole world any more. Perhaps, too, not all British soldiers are brave without any exception. But most are, and many are very brave indeed.

My life as a Gurkha really began when I left the college at Dharan for the main recruiting base at Pokhara. The distance between the two towns is 350 miles and the journey takes more than fifteen hours. I got to the bus stand very early in the morning, and because I was there in good time, I had the seat directly behind the driver. Very quickly, the bus filled up. As a result, when the last person climbed aboard there was nowhere for him to sit. The only possible place was on the engine housing, which on that old bus was on the left side of the driver. It wasn't a good place to be, as it got very hot and vibrated all the time. In any case, there were some bags on it which needed to be moved. These belonged to two guys sitting right at the front, on the opposite side of the driver. After standing looking round help-lessly for some time, the latecomer spoke very politely to the two of them.

'*Lunga*,' he said. This is a very polite word for 'friend'. 'Can I please sit there?'

But they said no – 'That's where we're putting our bags, can't you see?'

As I sat watching, I began to feel really sorry for this boy. I thought to myself, Those guys in the front can easily move their bags.

It wasn't as if they owned the bus! I couldn't see that it mat-tered where their bags went, so I spoke to the latecomer. 'Look,' I said, 'don't take any notice of those two. Just move the bags and put them somewhere else. Then you sit there. If those two guys try to stop you, I'll fight for you.'

This probably wouldn't have been a very good start to my Army career, but luckily it all got sorted peacefully in the end. It turned out that all four of us were going for Gurkha selection. However, my intervention almost cost me very dear.

As we were about to go through the main gate, one of the two boys who had been sitting in the front told the guard he should not let me through. We all had to present our Grade Pass papers at the entrance, and he had noticed that the picture on mine didn't look very much like me.

'That's just because I had long hair when I went for selection at Taplejung,' I protested. 'I look different because it's been cut!'

But the guard studied the photo and agreed it was of someone else. He accused me of stealing someone else's papers!

Luckily, the *galla*, the recruiting officer who had been in Telog and then Taplejung, was passing at that moment and came forward.

'No,' he said. 'This is the right person. He's telling the truth. It was me who told him to get his hair cut before he came here.'

So I got in.

As it happened, all four of us who were at the front of the bus passed main selection and ended up on the same intake together. One of the others became an Engineer and the late-comer became a Signaller. The third one is now a very good friend of mine. But every time we meet – the last time was in Afghanistan on Op Herrick 9 – he always reminds me of how we nearly ended up in a fight together.

'You're a hard man, Kailash,' he always says.

But actually he is himself now a Commando, after passing their selection test, so I would say that he is quite a hard man too. It would have been a good fight, although being quite a lot bigger than him, I like to think I would definitely have won.

It was late evening now, and after finally getting past the guardroom, I joined the other potential recruits as we waited to see what was going to happen next. Later, we were told to form an orderly queue and we were all given our basic kit issue. This consisted of a kitbag, two blankets each, a plate, knife, fork and spoon, a mug – for no particular reason that I could see, some of us got tin ones, others got plastic – and we were then shown to our accommodation. This was in several long, single-storey buildings where the beds were arranged in parallel lines. I don't know how many we were in each building, but at the time it seemed like there must be at least two hundred of us.

I remember spending the first night wondering whether I was really in the right place. Was I going to be selected? Some of the other guys looked really tough and fit, and they seemed clever as well. It looked like quite a few had had a really good education. But even so, I felt reasonably confident. Our intake was approximately fifteen hundred in all, and I knew that there were roughly two hundred and fifty places, so now that I had got this far, I felt there was quite a good chance of success. What I lacked in any department, I would make up for with determination. I hadn't realised at the time, but actually my chances of getting through the first and second rounds had been much smaller.

Altogether the selection process at Pokhara took four weeks – if you lasted. On the first day after our arrival, we were given a number of talks about what we were going to be doing over the next month. This all sounded very exciting, but what really impressed me was the *gurujis* themselves. When I first saw our instructors, I thought Wow, I really want to be like that! They were quite small, most of them smaller than me. But at the same time they had really big personalities, and they looked seriously strong as well.

At the outset, we were told that, besides Gurkha selection, we were also being assessed for the Singapore police force. Those who didn't get into the British Gurkhas still had the chance of joining the police. But although nobody said so, we all thought that going into the police was definitely second best. For myself, I decided I would be a British Army Gurkha or nothing at all.

'But why?' they wanted to know. It was the first question they asked when I went forward for my induction interview.

'Look,' I said – I don't think I even said *guruji*, because I did not yet understand Army ways – 'my grandfather was a British soldier in India and my uncle is a Gurkha in Singapore. But what I really want to do is get a gun and fight!'

They really laughed when I said this. They must have been thinking, Who is this person? But it was the truth.

It was more than twenty-four hours before the next major engagement, and the following morning, after the usual checks, we carried on the conversation.

'The first week was really tough, wasn't it, *guruji*?' Gaaz demanded.

It certainly was, and after only three or four days, people started to leave. We all wore chest numbers, and if your number was called out on parade, you had to fetch your kit and report to the guardroom straight afterwards. That was the end for you. Because of this danger of being told to leave, I decided straight away that I would keep out of trouble. I didn't want to be caught fighting in case that was a reason for losing my place. Some of the guys were quite aggressive, I noticed, but I made sure I was polite to everyone. For that reason my nickname to begin with was Khebang-*solti*. *Solti* is a Limbu word meaning 'friend', so together it means something like 'Mr Nice Guy from Khebang'.

But this nickname didn't last long. I have always been quite a good volleyball player, and whenever I spike it, I really hit the ball hard and shout out 'Yaah' at the same time. I soon became known as 'Yaah-*solti*'.

All in all, after the first few days I felt I was getting along OK, but then at the end of our first week we were told there would be a *doko* race the following morning. Now a *doko* is a special kind of basket which is used for transporting things in the mountains. I knew how to carry one – I had often used a *doko* to collect hay for the cattle, or to carry rice or logs in. But I had never tried to run with one uphill. And for this race, we were told, part of the course would be up a steep hill. To make things worse, we would be carrying 30 kilos. Now the thing about carrying a *doko* is that you have to hold it high on your shoulders and keep it there with a strap that goes round your forehead, leaving your arms free. So it's all about balance. But because I had never tried running with one, especially not uphill, I was very nervous about this race.

I also heard that lots of people who did well on other things failed on this race.

Furthermore, unlike me, a lot of the other guys knew about it and had already practised for the race a number of times before they came.

As the time drew near, I began to get really anxious. I just didn't know what it would be like. The *doko*s could so easily get unbalanced. It would have been fine if there wasn't much in it. I knew I could cope with that. But with half your own body-weight on your back it would be a lot different from what I was used to.

So finally the moment arrived and the *guruji*s came round checking the weight – we had to pack them ourselves – and the British officers were there too. Well, I thought, I will just have to try my hardest. There was nothing else I could do. We were all called to line up and then one of the *gurujis* began counting down.

'ARE YOU READY?' he yelled. I was as ready as I was ever going to be.

'THREE … TWO … ONE … GO!' he shouted, and off we went.

To start with, the course was flat, but after about 300 metres we began to run downhill into a valley with a small stream to cross at the bottom. To my surprise, things felt OK. Although the load was heavy, I found I could keep it in balance all right so long as I took care to keep my stride even. But after the stream there was a paddy field to cross. The rice had been harvested, which meant the surface was really uneven and difficult. There was nothing for it but to just put everything I had into it. I so badly wanted to do well because I was desperate to be selected.

As I crossed the paddy field, I glanced either side and to my amazement, I realised I was in first position! I was still out ahead when we got to the end of the field, where we had to scramble over the long mound of earth which had been built up to retain water. Thereafter, the course turned uphill. Now it began to be seriously steep. I was pushing hard when I noticed on the hillside a small shrine that we were going to pass and as I did so, I prayed to its god to help me.

'Give me some power!' I said gasping under my breath. 'Help me beat these guys, please.'

I was still out ahead as we began the climb, but as we got higher, a few people started trying to pass me. I had to push even harder.

'Oh god, please don't let me down.'

But eventually some of them did manage to get through. I was really sweating now. I'd never done anything so hard in all my life. I told myself I had to win otherwise I might not be selected, and yet although I was running as hard as I knew how, it seemed like it wasn't enough.

When we reached the top of the hill, the course ran in a long loop. Somehow I had to find more energy from somewhere. Where was the god when you needed him?

The main thing, I realised, was just to keep going, and not to take the pressure off – even though the hardest part was now behind us. Redoubling my efforts, I managed to catch up a few of the guys who had passed me on the hill. It felt like sweet revenge. Finally, as we staggered over the finishing line, I knew I had done my best. That was the main thing. The guy who won was a long way ahead, but still I managed fifth or sixth out of the forty in my group, so that wasn't bad. Actually, considering it was my first attempt at running with a load, I feel quite pleased with the result even today.

Unfortunately, those who did not do well on the *doko* race were dropped the next day. One of those who went was Chudpe, a boy who was always telling jokes. This was a great loss to us all, as he was always laughing and telling funny stories. He was a huge asset to our collective morale. People used to laugh as soon as they saw Chudpe. He was very intelligent and well-educated and good at everything he did, but he just did not have the required level of fitness. One interesting thing I learned from him was that it is actually possible to over-laugh. On one occasion, he said something to one of my friends that was just so outrageous – I forget what it was: just one of those things that seem really hilarious at the time – that we were all bent double with laughter. I remember seeing tears in the eyes of one of the lads. He had to go outside to calm down and recover. But another boy actually fell on the ground and started having trouble breathing. We had to throw water on him because it began to look as though he really might die!

I don't know what happened to our joke teller. I didn't hear whether he was one of the ones who came back the following year. All I know is that we missed him a lot.

Throughout the course there were parades when those people who did not make it were sent down to the guardroom, where they were given some money and sent back to their families. You never knew until the moment your name was called if it was going to be you. We all went on parade with our kit ready and packed in case it was us. First there was roll-call, then the *gurujis* gave us a talk. Finally, a long list of chest numbers was called out.

'Those of you whose numbers have been called, well done. Anyone whose number has not been called out, report to the guardroom.' Each time, there would be ten, fifteen, twenty people whose names were not called out, and they would fall out and often that was the last we would see of them.

Not long after the *dokos* race, we had another race. This time it was a straightforward running race, without any load, on the flat. The distance was over something like 2.5 km. Again I was a bit nervous, as I hadn't done much in the way of athletics before. There wasn't much flat ground near to Khebang. What made me really anxious, though, was noticing as we went down to the start that some of the guys had bare feet.

'Where are your boots?' I wanted to know.

'It's easier without,' they told me.

This put me in a dilemma. My boots were old and in poor condition. Maybe it would be easier without them. On the other hand, I'd never tried running barefoot. I couldn't decide what to do. As it turned out, however, I didn't have time to take them off. We were called in to line up as soon as we got there. This time there were about twenty in my group and I managed third or fourth, which again I felt was quite good for a first attempt.

Our routine every day was to wake up, wash, shave – if we needed to – use the toilet then go to breakfast. When I first saw people shaving, I was amazed.

'What are you doing?' I wanted to know. 'And why?'

At seventeen and a half, I didn't have anything to cut. Like most Limbus, I don't have much facial hair. Back home, if anyone could grow a beard they did. Either that or they would pull out individual hairs with a pair of tweezers. I'd never seen a razor.

After breakfast, there was a parade and the roll was called. The *gurujis* would then tell us what we would be doing that day. On one occasion, I recall, the *guruji* said that he had seen one of us praying at the temple the previous evening. I realised he must be referring to me, as this was something I always did, though I didn't think anyone ever noticed.

'That boy has got a lot of sense,' he went on to say. 'Your future life is going to depend on what happens here, and you're all going to need as much help as you can get.'

As if to emphasise his point, he then called out the next batch of numbers of those being returned to civilian life.

*

The next time we came into contact with the enemy, it was in the form of sniper fire. I was in Sangar 3 when, towards the middle of the day, I heard the unmistakable sound of a rifle shot landing a short distance away.

Aayo! Who was that for? I wondered.

'CONTACT! Wait out.' Lance Corporal Shree's voice came up over the PRR a moment later.

'Can either of you see anything?' I yelled to Nagen and Gaaz.

'No, nothing,' they replied in turn.

'All right, keep a good lookout. There could be more than just one.'

For what seemed like ages we crouched down, waiting for the follow-up, but nothing came.

'What about we try putting a helmet up and see if they fire at it?' said Gaaz. 'You know, like they did in the First World War? That way we might be able to identify their position.'

'All right, Gaaz. Not a bad idea,' I said. Apparently that was exactly how the infantry in the trenches would find out whether their position was fixed by enemy snipers. 'Let's see how good they really are. But we won't use a helmet. It would be stupid to take your helmet off. We'll use your water bottle instead.'

'Good point, *guruji*. But why mine? I had the idea. Surely it should be Nagen's?'

'No,' I said. 'You had the idea. You can have the privilege of getting yours shot to bits.'

Without further complaint, Gaaz reached for his water bottle and, after emptying the contents down his neck, held it out to me.

'What shall we use for a stick?' he demanded.

'Here, this will do.' I took down one of the arc markers, judging we could do without it for a few moments.

With the three of us huddled together on the floor of the sangar, I lay on my back and carefully raised the bottle to just above sandbag height.

TING!

Sure enough, the sound of a round landing on the sangar followed almost immediately.

'*Aare hou!*' we all exclaimed together, looking at each other in wonder.

'These boys are certainly on the ball today,' said Gaaz as I leaned over and grabbed the field telephone.

'Zero, this is Sangar Three. Contact. Enemy sniper. Location unknown but probably somewhere to the east of my position. Observing.'

It was a few seconds before I realised the line was dead.

'Nothing heard. Will try on other means. Out.'

Other means is the correct way of referring to another method of communication when using proper radio procedure. It's a way of masking your intentions to anyone listening in.

I followed up with a call on the PRR while Gaaz put the arc marker back in position.

'Zero, this is Sangar Three. Contact. Sniper, possibly in a position somewhere to the east. Am observing, over.'

'Zero, roger. Out to you. Sangar Six keep a good eye out on AOI Three. Sounds as if they could be using that building on the roof of the compound we identified earlier.'

'Sangar Six, roger. Looking. Out.'

I checked the field telephone again, but with the same result. The wire must be broken somewhere between the sangar position and the CT. Perhaps it had even been hit by a stray round. I needed to let the OC know.

'Zero, this is Sangar Three. It looks like our field telephone has been taken out. Will be using this means for the time being, over.'

'Zero, understand your other means knocked out. I'll get back to you. Out.'

A few minutes later, we heard a shout from down below. I looked out and there was Cookie.

'*Guruji!* I'll come up and fix your phone. I've got a fresh reel of Don Ten.'

'Not now, Cookie,' I replied. 'It's too dangerous. There's a sniper.'

'It's all right. It needs fixing and it won't take a moment.'

'If you're sure . . .'

I liked Cookie a lot. I'll always be grateful to him for bringing up the GPMG during that first night attack. He was a really smiley guy, thin and wiry and very friendly. In short, an excellent soldier. I'm afraid it's true that often we infanteers think of signallers as being not always quite up to the mark when it comes to front-line soldiering, but Cookie proved that theory wrong. Even though he didn't have an infantry background he was really proactive and helpful. In fact I'd have been very happy to have him as my section 2 i/c. What made him even more of an asset in Now Zad was that he mingled really well with the *bhais* – especially the younger ones. He was a good joiner-in and always asking to share Gurkha food.

Without saying any more, Cookie climbed up to the sangar and began tracing the wire from the phone out through the sandbags and onto the roof of the building.

'Easy,' he said after a few moments. 'I can repair this.'

'You be careful,' I replied.

Hardly were the words out of my mouth when there was a crack of rifle fire followed by a scream.

'SHIT! SHIT! I've been fucking hit . . . '

Jatha! They'd got Cookie!

'ZERO, THIS IS SANGAR THREE, CONTACT! MAN DOWN! WAIT OUT.'

'Zero, roger. Who is it? Can you help him?' I could hear the concern in the OC's voice.

'It's Cookie!' I said, slamming the receiver onto its cradle.

Cookie had already started to climb down, so he could obviously still move, but I thought I'd better go after him. In the first few minutes after getting hit, you don't always realise how bad it is.

Grabbing my rifle, I called out to the *bhai*s.

'Gaaz! Naagen! Cover me, OK? I'm going down.'

I realised there was a good chance of being hit myself, but put the thought out of my mind. You just do.

The two riflemen did as they were told as I scrambled out of the sangar and over to the ladder. Cookie himself had managed to get off the roof, and I caught up with him at the bottom.

'You OK, Cookie?'

Of course I knew he wasn't, but what else was I going to say? Looking into his eyes, I could see immediately that he was in a bad way.

'I'm OK . . . *guruji*. I'll be fine . . . '

I did a quick check to see where he'd been hit and saw a small patch of blood on his side in between his front and rear body armour.

'All right, Cookie, we're going to get you sorted,' I said as we hobbled towards the CT. 'The doctor will put you right,' I went on, not sure if I really believed what I was saying.

There was intermittent fire coming from each of the different sangar positions.

At the door to the CT, the two medics were waiting. I watched as they laid him out on a stretcher.

'OK thanks, Kailash. You can go now,' said the MO as I took one last look at the casualty.

'See you later, Cookie.'

'Cheers, Kailash,' he said weakly.

Climbing back up into the sangar position, I was more conscious of the danger than on the way down, but luckily I made it back in without incident.

'Zero, this is Sunray Sangar Three. Back in position.'

'Zero, roger. Well done. Keep a good lookout and let us know if you see anything.'

This hardly needed saying, because of course that was all we could do – all we could ever do. Just watch and wait and wait and watch. It was so frustrating.

The *bhai*s were seriously upset.

'Is he going to be OK, *guruji*?' they both wanted to know.

'He should be fine. You can't be absolutely sure, but I reckon,' I replied, hoping to sound more optimistic than I felt. The truth was, I was really worried for Cookie. It quite often happens that to start with after being hit you can still function but then the body shuts down. I just hoped it wasn't going to be the case with him.

'*Jatha!*' exclaimed Gaaz. 'Don't they realise he's one of us? He's a Gurkha too.'

Gaaz had turned angry.

Unfortunately, as we both understood in our hearts, it was unlikely we would see anyone now. The Taliban knew what they were doing. Having scored a hit, they'd most likely leave us alone until they saw another time we were vulnerable.

It was about half an hour after Cookie got shot when I had a call from the OC.

'Sangar Three, this is Zero.'

'Go ahead, over.'

'I need you down here for a detail, please.'

I guessed at once what that meant. Cookie was being casevaced and the OC wanted me to command one of the WMIKs.

'Roger. Coming now, out.'

I grabbed my rifle and my map and turned to go.

'OK, *bhai haru*. I need you to cover me again. The OC wants me to go down. Probably Cookie's being casevaced.'

'You be careful, *guruji*,' said Gaaz.

'Thanks. I will.'

Down on the ground, Rex *sahib* explained the situation in more detail.

'Captain Martin assesses Lance Corporal Cook a P2 casualty. We need to get him extracted ASAP,' he began. A P2 casualty is one with a non-life-threatening injury but cannot walk. A P1 is someone who is either in need of immediate medical attention and unable to walk or is unconscious, while a P3 is a walking casualty. I nodded.

'Yes sir.'

'There's a Chinook on its way and I want you to be ready to command one of the WMIKs to take him down to the HLS.

Mathers *sahib* will command the other one. So go and sort out a crew and be on five minutes' notice to move.'

'*Hasur, sahib.*'

'Any questions?'

'No sir. But I suppose there won't be anything coming in on the helicopter?'

'Good point, but no, this is the IRT. It's not actually coming from Bastion.'

IRT stands for Immediate Response Team – basically a dedicated air ambulance based at Bastion in full-time support of the various troop dispositions round Helmand province. Its aim was to get any serious casualty off the battlefield in what we called the Golden Hour.

'Is that everything?'

'*Hunza, sahib.*'

'OK, thanks, Kailash. By the way,' he added, 'how are things up on the position? Have you got enough *pani* up there? I don't want people getting dehydrated.' This part, the OC spoke in Gorkhali. He spoke the language very well and, except when giving orders, used it most of the time when speaking to us.

'We're fine for water sir, thanks.'

'OK good.'

I really admired the OC in that moment. He could easily have sent someone else out to give me my orders, but he wanted to do it himself. I could sense that he was really tired, even more than me probably. He had so much on his shoulders. But as well as being brave – he spent a lot of time when we were not actually in contact walking round the positions checking up on everyone, while during the contacts he was mostly on the roof of the CT itself – he really cared for the men under his command. I had the impression he never took his boots off.

The first thing I did when I went over to the accommodation block was to tell one of the riflemen to take a mug of tea over to Rex *sahib*.

'And put extra sugar in it, OK? He looks really tired.'

'*Hasur, guruji.*'

'Any news on Cookie?' demanded the other off-duty riflemen as I went over.

'Is he OK?'

'Are they sending a heli for him?'

Several voices joined in together.

'He's OK, according to Rex *sahib*. But yes, they are sending a heli. Keep that to yourselves, though,' I said, glancing towards the ANP block. Actually not many of the ANP guys were to be seen at this time of day. When it got really hot, they mostly stayed inside, sleeping I suppose.

I looked at the duties list. I wanted to take Nani *guru* with me, of course. As he was the best driver, I wouldn't have wanted anyone else. But who was I going to take to man the .50? Normally I would have taken Gaaz, but as he was manning the .50-cal in Sangar 3 right then, I felt that was the best place for him for now.

At that moment, Rifleman Lal appeared.

'Lal *bhai*!' I said. 'Good. You can come with me.'

'*Guruji?*'

'Lance Corporal Cook is being extracted back to Bastion. They're sending a Chinook and I want you on top cover. Nani *guru* will drive.'

'*Hasur, guruj.*'

Lal had yet to leave the compound since we had arrived, and I could see that in one way he was very excited. But he was clearly nervous too. When one man goes down, everyone gets nervous.

'What about your rifle? Have you cleaned it yet today?'

'Yes, *guruji.*'

'Show me.'

Lal handed me his weapon.

'Well done, *bhai*. That's excellent,' I said, quickly looking at the gas plug.

One thing you have to be careful of when you are using your rifle a lot is carbon building up on the gas plug, and I always insisted that the riflemen treated weapon cleaning as seriously on operations as on the parade ground. More so, in fact.

'You've got to be a perfectionist,' I would say.

By adopting an attitude of perfectionism, you give yourself a bit of leeway. I always think that if your weapon is only 99 per cent perfect, you've got a 1 per cent chance of it letting you down when you need it most. I've heard of lots of instances of weapons misfiring at a crucial moment. In fact, it happened to one of our officers, Lieutenant Hollingshead on Op Herrick 4, who was a member of the 10 Platoon team we had relieved in Now Zad. During the action, he found himself face to face with a Taliban fighter about 15 metres away. Taking aim, he pulled the trigger but his rifle misfired. Then the Taliban had a shot at him but his weapon misfired too.

Now I'm not saying Mr Hollingshead's weapon was dirty. Or if it was, it was because he'd been several hours in contact. The point is, you want to minimise the chances of having something like that happen to you. That way you don't have to rely on miracles.

After talking to Rifleman Lal, I went and found Nani *guru*, gave him a quick brief and told him to get his gear. Not long afterwards, Mathers *sahib*'s voice came crisply over the air.

'Two One Charlie, this is Zero.'

'Two One Charlie?'

'Zero, report to CT soonest, over.'

There must be news of the Chinook.

'OK, *bhai haru*. All ready?' I said. 'Let's see if you can break your previous record,' I went on, looking at Nani.

'Hopefully without killing the patient,' added one of the other riflemen within earshot.

I wondered how Cookie was doing. Although he'd managed to get himself down from the sangar and over to the CT, he hadn't looked at all good to me. He might only be a P2, but he could go into shock at any time, and shock is a killer. People die from perfectly survivable injuries because of shock.

Mathers *sahib* stood waiting outside the CT. Even now we'd given no indication that we were about to go anywhere, in case anybody might be thinking of telling one of their friends on the outside.

'OK, so have you got your map with you? Good, so the HLS is here. It's well within arc for the section on ANP Hill, so we'll be covered by them as well.'

I checked my map against Mathers *sahib*'s and marked the HLS on it.

'Cookie will be in your WMIK, I suppose?'

'Yes, so you'll need to get there first. You'll need to cover us as we unload.'

'Yes *sahib*,' I replied. Nani *guru* would like that. He could pretend he was driving in a grand prix.

'And he's still a P2?'

'Yes, although he's not actually walking at the moment. He's been on oxygen and he's on a drip now, but the MO thinks he'll pull through OK.'

'*Hunza, sahib.*'

'So what we'll do,' Mathers *sahib* continued, 'is mount up right away and go straight out as soon as the casualty is loaded. Once in the HLS, secure the position and wait for the Chinook to touch down. The medic will go on with the patient, but as soon as he's handed over, he'll come back out. As usual there'll be a sixty-second turn-round. Any questions?'

'No sir.'

I was used to these excursions by now, although I have to say on this occasion I was very nervous. It was still less than an hour since the incident and there was a good chance the enemy was still in the neighbourhood.

At once I ran over to where Lal and Nani were waiting.

'Time to go, *bhai*s,' I said, and once I'd quickly checked their equipment, the three of us headed for the WMIK. Just as we got there, Cookie was being carried out on a stretcher. He was on an IV drip but still obviously conscious, as I could see him saying something to the medical orderly. While the others were mounting up, I went over to say a few words of encouragement.

'Hello Cookie,' I said. 'Don't worry. You'll soon be all right. You'll be back in Bastion in less than hour. Probably in England by tonight.'

He looked towards me as I spoke.

'Cheers, Kailash *guruji*.' I could hardly hear his voice, and as

I looked into his eyes, I could see he was in a bad way. He was trying to be cheerful, but in that second, I was very concerned for him. He looked more like a P1 casualty to me. I even thought he might die.

Nani *guru* was already revving the engine by the time I was on board, and less than half a minute later our wheels were spinning as the gates opened and we blasted through. I had the GPMG ready to fire and my rifle just next to me for short-range targets. My head was spinning too. What would happen if we were ambushed? If one of the WMIKs was disabled? Maybe we'd have to fight our way back in. At the same time I couldn't help thinking about poor old Cookie being thrown around in the back of the other vehicle. I wondered what sort of state he'd be in by the time we got to the HLS. With one hand on the wheel and his rifle in the other hand, Nani drove like he'd never driven before. Down the road we went, past the shops now all shut up and abandoned, and out into the desert, skidding round the corners and bouncing over every bump. But we couldn't go any slower. Although the enemy probably wouldn't be expecting us to go out like this, it would only take a lucky throw of a grenade or a fortunate RPG shot and we'd be in big trouble.

Within less than five minutes, we were skidding to a halt on the flat ground directly between ANP Hill and the edge of town. Nani kept the engine running while I debussed and, after quickly clearing the ground, threw myself down about 20 metres away. The second WMIK followed close behind, and soon after it halted, I heard Mathers *sahib* on the PRR informing the OC that the HLS was now secure. Less than a minute later, you could hear the sound of the Chinook beginning its descent.

So far, so good, but now we were at our most vulnerable. The enemy would surely have seen us go out and would easily have time to get in position. There was a building we knew he used regularly which would give him the ideal place to engage us from, and I kept it firmly in my sights.

'Lal, reference building four hundred metres!' I yelled up at him, pointing. 'Any sign of trouble and you are to engage, OK?'

'*Hasur, guruji.*'

'But don't just stare at it. Remember to keep looking through three-sixty degrees.'

'Three-sixty, *guruji*,' he replied, swinging the .50-cal slowly from left to right and then behind.

By this time Cookie had been unloaded, and as soon as the chopper touched down, the medic and the stretcher-bearer ran into the swirling dust.

Sixty seconds from now.

But what if they hit the helicopter with RPG? They couldn't miss. I strained my eyes, looking for any movement.

Sixty seconds and—

The engine note changed to a whine and the dust enveloped us. It was up to the gods now.

'Everybody mount up!'

There was unusual urgency in Mathers *sahib*'s voice. He was obviously feeling nervous too.

As I got up, I could just make out one man carrying an empty stretcher running in the direction of the other WMIK.

So where was the other one?

'Move now!'

Nani dropped the clutch and with a lurch as the tyres fought for grip, we tore off.

The medic must still be on the chopper!

He must have gone on and not got off in time. Mathers *sahib* wouldn't have just abandoned him.

Sixty seconds. That's all they give you, and that was all he got.

As we roared back into town, I noticed the wind on my face. But this pleasant feeling was mixed with real anxiety. We were approaching another maximum-stress point. With the gates opening to let us in, we were vulnerable to a lot of different scenarios – snipers, RPG, grenades – any one of which could spell disaster.

But nothing happened. Within no more than twenty minutes of leaving, we were back in the jittery calm of the DC, two men down. The medic we could maybe live without, but Cookie was a real loss.

The medic reappeared, together with Cookie's replacement, on a resupp a few days later. I teased him that he must have felt like taking a rest, but he explained that there had been something wrong with the drip, and while he was trying to fix it, the heli took off. Cookie himself has since made a full recovery and gone back to work, although he is no longer in the Army. That is the Army's loss, as he's a top man. I hope to meet him again one day.

Back inside the compound, I have to say I felt a big relief. It seemed hard to believe we hadn't been contacted and I wondered how long our luck could last. For sure we hadn't heard the last of the Taliban. Later that afternoon, as we ate a meal, there was a lot of talk about whether there was going to be another big contact that night.

'According to ops, it's going to be overcast again,' said one of the riflemen who had phoned home. 'He said he'd checked the weather forecast with the aviation guys.'

'You can never trust those met forecasts. They're always getting it wrong,' said another.

'They're usually quite good over here,' said someone else. 'The weather's more stable than it is back in England. It's more predictable.'

'Well,' I interjected, 'you don't want to rule anything out just on the basis of a weather forecast. You just never know what the enemy is going to get up to next. He could have got hold of some night-vision equipment for all we know. And there's no saying he hasn't got hold of some parachute flares. When I was inspecting General Dostum's arms dumps, he had plenty, I can tell you.'

'But General Dostum was Northern Alliance, wasn't he, *guruji*?' said Gaaz, who was just finishing his meal. 'Aren't they the sworn enemy of the Taliban?'

'That's true, but my point is you never know what the Taliban might have been able to capture,' I replied.

We did have a quiet night in the end, and as usual it was mostly sleepless for me. But I was used to it from my days with Recce Platoon and didn't feel it too much. As soon as I got up on the position, I would be fully alert again. The biggest danger came from boredom, which is partly why I was always checking and rechecking our kit the whole time. It is also why I never minded when Gaaz resumed his questions about my early life.

'Sorry, *guruji*, but I want to come out top of my JLC. I want to be a lance corporal by the time I'm twenty-one, same as you.'

JLC stands for Junior Leaders Cadre, the course everyone eligible for promotion to lance corporal must pass. So I didn't mind at all.

'Tell us some more about final selection, *guruji*.'

Once a week at Pokhara, they gave us a day off. We would all leave the camp and go down to a river nearby to bathe and to do our *dhobi*, or laundry. On these days we would kick a ball around, or just sit around laughing and talking about our villages. And of course we talked about what might be coming next. We also discussed our chances of staying the course, or whether we would be one of those who had to make the long journey home.

When people did leave, it was the custom of any friends who remained behind to give them something – a T-shirt or a bag or maybe a pair of boots or shoes. To start with, it was just something insignificant, but by the end, we had given almost all our belongings away. Eventually, I even gave my watch to one guy I knew who was leaving. It was a really nice one which my dad had given me, and I was a bit nervous of giving it to him as it still wasn't certain I would be staying. But I was so sorry for this boy. He was crying a lot and he had tried so hard. It hurt me to see people carrying their bag out through the gate. Like me, they had dreamed of becoming a Gurkha, and I felt really bad for them.

In fact, as we got nearer to the end of the month, the *gurujis* told the people leaving they shouldn't worry too much. They had only just missed out and they would have a good chance if they came back next year. In fact, I know some guys who went back three or four times before they eventually got in.

I often thought it would have helped me a lot if I'd had a bit more experience in life before I went to Pokhara. For one thing,

I might have done better at the command tasks. As it was, I was completely unprepared for these. To start with, I didn't even realise that they were part of the testing – and nor for that matter did anyone else who hadn't done one before. We just thought they were part of the ordinary training.

What happened was that one of us would be selected to be section commander for a team, and that person would have to work out a plan and then give orders to the others. I'll never forget the first time I was given a command. We were formed up alongside the swimming pool and split into groups of six or seven.

'Right, Eight Nine Two. Fall out for a briefing.'

That was me. I was already really nervous as, like everyone else, I didn't know how to swim.

'OK, the scenario is as follows: one member of your team is wounded. You can choose which one. The swimming pool represents a stream. Your task is to use this equipment to get him, and each member of your team, across from one side to the other, keeping within the boundaries you can see marked out.'

The *guruji* then showed me my equipment. There was a sheet of corrugated iron, several planks of wood and some lengths of rope lying in a pile.

'You've got two minutes to work out a plan. You'll then give your orders to your team and you'll have fifteen minutes to complete your task. Understood?'

'Yes, *guruji*.'

My mind went blank. I had no idea what to do. Not only could I not swim, but the boundary marker showed that we had to stay at the deep end. It occurred to me that there was a good chance of me drowning, along with everyone else. But there was nothing for it, so I lined everyone up and gave them their orders.

'Look guys,' I said. 'Number Four Three Six, you're wounded so you can't do anything. What the rest of us have to do is get you across to the other side. And we have to take all this stuff with us.' I pointed to the tin and the rope and the planks. 'Does everyone understand?'

There was silence as the seriousness of the situation sank in.

'So what we are going to do is this. On my command, we all jump in. Then we'll cross to the other side. Have you got that?'

The guys nodded uncertainly.

'OK. Go!'

Some of them then grabbed the planks of wood and the rope. I took the tin. Then we all jumped into the pool. Even today I have no idea how we managed to get to the other side without drowning! Actually several of the guys had to be pulled out by the PTIs (the Physical Training Instructors).

By this time, all the *gurujis* were laughing their heads off, and so were we. Only then was it explained to us that we were supposed to make a raft. But of course, we had no idea. I certainly had never seen a raft in my life. My only thought had been to get across.

'So what did the *gurujis* have to say about it?' Gaaz wanted to know as I finished telling the story.

'Luckily they thought we were really brave just for having a go, so the result was good.'

'*Hunza*. They were actually all right, the *gurujis*,' said Gaaz good-humouredly. 'I remember one time we had to put up a nine-by-nine tent. They gave us fifteen minutes to complete the task, but by the end of our time, we had got nowhere. We were pulling on ropes and tripping over poles with the canvas on top of us and laughing our heads off. It was total chaos!'

'So what happened?'

'Eventually, one of the British officers came up to us. "*Saare noramro*," he said. "That's REALLY bad." He was laughing too. Then he showed us how to do it.'

It wasn't until later still that I discovered nobody minded whether you actually succeeded in carrying out the task. The result didn't matter. What they wanted to see was how you tried and how you reacted when things went wrong. But although these command tasks seemed like a fun part of selection, they were taken very seriously by the officers, and if I'd realised, I'm sure I'd have been more worried by them. As it was, of all the things we did during selection, they were the thing that bothered me least. In fact, if I am honest, the only thing that really scared me was the night-time entertainment. Even today, I think I would rather face another night attack by the Taliban than endure the terror of thinking I might have to perform.

Not every night, but once or twice a week, the *gurujis* would come down after evening roll-call just before bedtime and call out several names. Those who were picked had to sing a song or tell a joke or, in the case of those who had them, play their musical instrument. I dreaded having my name called more than anything. We had to give presentations during our education sessions in which we had to introduce ourselves and tell people something about our village. I didn't find this a big problem. But as a simple country boy, I had no jokes, and my singing voice is really bad, so every time the *gurujis* came down, I used to pray that my name wouldn't be called. Luckily, it never was, though I'm not sure why. It may be because I was a favourite of the *gurujis*, because I was always so respectful towards them. Or maybe they thought that because I was from a really remote village I wouldn't have much to say. If so, they were quite right. Even now I am not good at remembering jokes, and when my children ask me to make up stories at bedtime, I am never very successful. I find it difficult to make things up, and the only stories I have are the ones I remember my mother telling me about the tiger in the jungle.

'There was once a tiger . . .' I say, but immediately my children interrupt me and say they have heard it all before. They want new stories of course.

Finally, the two weeks came to an end and the day of the final selection arrived. As I said, we actually took our bags on parade with us, not knowing if we were going to survive it.

On this occasion, the DRO (Director Recruiting Officer) came down to announce those who had passed and those who had failed. He was assisted by a QGO who stood on the steps to call out the numbers of about half of the platoon. He did so with the words '*aayo babu*', a very polite form of address.

'*Aayo babu* Four,' he began. '*Aayo babu* Seventeen . . . *Aayo babu* Twenty-eight . . .'

As their numbers were called, these people had to fall out and stand in a group over to one side of the parade ground. It was a very poignant moment. We all knew that if you had your number called, it was all over.

Then, somewhere near the end, my own number, 892, was called. I couldn't believe my ears. It seemed that despite all my hard work, I had failed.

But then again, I thought, this form of address is unusual. Perhaps it's going to be different this time.

I was completely confused and nervous.

In the end, about half of us were now in one group, and half in the other – with about eighty in each group, as I recall. The *guruji* now began talking about the future, and what it was going to be like in the Army for those who had passed. Only at the end of this did he announce that those whose numbers had *not* been called out should take their kit and go down to the guardroom. So I had passed after all! I said a prayer of thanks.

The next moment, our world was turned completely upside down. When those who were leaving had fallen out, and the officers had gone inside, suddenly the *guruji*s completely transformed. During the parade, they had been so polite, and even on a day-to-day basis they had been quite friendly. But from this moment on, they were like tigers.

'Congratulations, you are in the British Army now!' the sergeant major said. 'But this is when the REAL hard work starts! So get down and give me ten press-ups – NO! make it twenty – NO! make it thirty!'

At first, everyone was too shocked to move.

'I said GET DOWN you useless *jatha*!' the *guruji* shouted. 'You're not civilians any more, you know! YOU'RE IN THE ARMY!'

For the next twenty minutes, we were running on the spot or doing sit-ups and press-ups or star-jumps, with the *guruji* shouting at us and calling us really bad names. Then all at once, they began to drill us. Nobody had any idea how to march, and we were all over the place, completely uncoordinated. But instead of telling us what to do, the *guruji*s just shouted at us, calling us bad names.

'*Tongrut horu!*' they shouted every time they saw us. This is an insult meaning something like *You bunch of idiots*.

'You're going to be wearing the cap badge of the Gurkhas from now on. You've got to be perfect!' the sergeant major yelled.

After some time, we were called to attention.

'RIGHT, ALL OF YOU, YOU'RE MARCHING LIKE A LOAD OF GIRLS BECAUSE YOU LOOK LIKE GIRLS! When I fall you out, you're all to get yourselves down to the barber's shop and get a haircut. After lunch, there will be kit issue at the RQMS store.'

The parade then dismissed and we all hurried off. But one of the guys, I remember, just broke down in tears. He was totally traumatised. One of the *guruji*s immediately went up to him.

'What's the matter with you, man?' he wanted to know. 'Can't take it? Do you want to leave?'

'Yes, *guruji*,' he said, still crying. 'I want to leave.'

'Well you just go away for a bit and think about it. Then come back and tell me.'

Needless to say, when he'd calmed down, the boy went back and said he wanted to stay after all.

In the meantime, we went for our haircuts and the kit issue, where we were given a complete set of Army uniform. Of course, although we were completely shocked by the sudden change in the *guruji*s, we were also really happy.

It wasn't until the next morning that we were finally told which of us had been successful for the British Army and who would be going into the Singapore Police Force. I remember sitting on the ground as our names were read out. I have a lot of connections with the Singapore police. My mother's brother served with them, as did one of her sisters' husbands. But I had heard from my grandfather that there wasn't much going on in Singapore, so there wouldn't be much chance of seeing action. That was my main reason for hoping I could join the Army.

Again, the split was approximately fifty-fifty. So of the five or six hundred of us who came to Pokhara, just about forty made it into one of the British Gurkha regiments.

That night I wrote a letter to my family.

'Mum! Dad! I got selected for the Army!'

I don't think it's possible for a human being to be prouder or happier than I was in that moment.

That morning as I lay with Gaaz and Nagen looking out over the desolation that the town had become, I have to admit that that moment of joy seemed a long time in the past. Now, there was less to see than ever. These days there was no *disha* patrol, and the only sign of human activity was the call to prayer at dawn.

'*Allaaahu akbar* . . . Allah is most great . . . I testify that there is no God but Allah . . . I testify that Muhammad is the prophet of Allah . . . Come to prayer. Come to salvation . . . *Allaaahu akbar* . . . There is no God but Allah.'

'You know what, *guruji*? I've got a feeling that's where they get their orders for the day,' said Gaaz, gesturing towards the mosque. 'I reckon we should take it out.'

'It's tempting, isn't it?' I agreed. 'But then again, who's to say it really isn't the good guys who go to pray every day? You just don't know.'

'Come on, *guruji*. They're just like us. We pray to Kali when we go into battle. They pray to Allah. The Christians pray to their God. When it comes down to it, all wars are religious wars if you ask me.'

'Why don't they abolish religion altogether?' said Nagen. 'That's what I'd like to know.'

'Except look at Chairman Mao,' Gaaz replied. 'He didn't have any religion. Nor did Stalin, or Hitler. That didn't stop them going to war. They made a religion out of not being religious! So abolishing it isn't going to help. Like I said, all wars are religious wars one way or another.'

I shrugged my shoulders.

'The main thing is to be ready for them whoever they are,' I said. 'It doesn't matter to me what they believe. Our job is to support the local population and keep the peace, so that's what we'll do. Nobody said being a Gurkha was going to be easy.'

14

A Moment of Madness

I was in Sangar 3 with riflemen Lal and Baren when Baren fell
back with a cry.

'What happened? What happened? Are you OK?' I shouted,
even though he was only a few feet from me.

'*Guruji*,' he gasped, breathing heavily. 'I've been hit.'

Aaye! We were in trouble now.

'Lal! Just keep firing, OK? Keep going!' I said as I scrambled
over to where Baren was lying, his head surrounded by empty
cases.

We'd come under serious attack from Sniper's House
moments after an ANP patrol was ambushed on the other side
of town. This was a building we'd come to realise was a real
danger point.

'*Guruji*, I think I'm going to die,' Baren said quite quietly.

'Where? Where have you been hit?' I demanded. 'Don't

worry. You're not going to die!' I was shouting as I grabbed the telephone.

'Sangar Three CASUALTY! Wait out.'

Lal turned round to look.

'Keep firing!' I shouted. 'Don't worry what's going on over here. He'll be OK.'

I said that but really I was very afraid. Baren didn't look at all good. But it was strange, as I looked him over quickly I couldn't see anything. Nothing that was obvious anyway.

'Are you sure you've been hit?' I exclaimed. 'I can't see anything.'

'Yes. Definitely,' he groaned. 'It's here.' He pointed to his thigh.

Looking down, I saw blood. Not much, but the fact that it was only a small quantity doesn't necessarily mean anything one way or the other. It could have exited somewhere else, which would be where the real damage was done.

The phone rang. That would be the OC wanting to know the situation, but I ignored it. I needed to know how badly Baren was injured.

There was still a huge weight of fire flying around in all directions. Sangar 1 were engaging the enemy, as was the CT behind, and I could hear the other .50-cal in between the bursts of GPMG being fired by Lal, but I was more concerned about Baren. I was afraid I was about to find something really bad. When you get hit, it can take some time for the wound to show much. It could be that if I turned him over I'd find half his back missing. I also knew that even after a direct hit, it can take three or four minutes for a man to die.

I looked into Baren's eyes again and I could see he was thinking the same thing. They were full of fear.

'OK, I'm going to take a look,' I said.

I jerked his trouser leg out of his boot and pulled it up to where he was pointing. But although there was a bright red mark and my hand was quickly covered in blood, I couldn't see a puncture wound.

'It's just a graze,' I said, shaking my head. 'You're fine.'

Taking a field dressing out of the first-aid kit, I tore the pack open, placed it over the wound and bound it up tight. Baren groaned.

'You're in shock,' I said. 'But you're fine.'

'No, I think it's here, *guruji*. My side,' he said now in a whisper. His breath was short and shallow and he was obviously in a lot of pain. 'Yes, it's gone into my side.'

Now I was really scared. It could be the round grazed his leg and entered further up. So I pulled his trouser leg back down and examined his shirt. He'd got his body armour on of course, so if he'd taken a bullet it was going to be somewhere he wasn't covered. Again I didn't see anything at first. But then I noticed a small tear in his shirt, and a bloodstain. This could be bad after all. As I pulled it up carefully, Baren gasped in agony.

Sure enough, there was the wound. But to my relief, I understood what had happened. Again, it was just a graze, that was all. There was no puncture of the skin, just a bright red line a few inches long. Baren had had an incredibly lucky escape. The round had skimmed his thigh and then his side, without actually penetrating.

I got him to turn over so that I could be certain.

'You're OK, *bhai*. You aren't going to die. You're fine. It's just a graze. It's nothing.'

Baren's breathing was still shallow.

'Are you really sure, *guruji*?'

'Listen,' I said. 'Am I your *guruji*?'

'Yes,' he replied. 'You are my *guruji*.'

'Right, well as your *guruji* I'm telling you you're fine. So come on, get up. Get stuck in.'

Baren looked down and ran his hand over the wound. It was still hurting him and he winced in pain, but the realisation that it wasn't serious brought him back to life with a start.

'*Aare jatha!* I really thought I was going to die! The dirty *dusman horou*!'

And now he was really angry. From being certain he was going to die, he had turned into a wild animal – furious.

'*Jatha haru!*' he shouted, shaking his head and crawling back into position, where he opened up immediately with the .50-cal.

A few seconds later, there came a loud shout from down below.

'STRETCHER!'

'NOT NEEDED!' I yelled in reply.

'IT'S OK. WE'RE COMING UP.'

'NO, DON'T!' I yelled. 'HE'S OK!'

I looked down. There were the medic and Rifleman Prakash attempting to hard-target their way up into the sangar.

'No need!' I shouted. 'Get back down!'

'Are you sure?'

'Yes! He's fine. It's just a graze.'

After a second's hesitation, the two of them turned round, flung the stretcher down and threw themselves off the roof and back down the ladder. Some of these medics are seriously brave,

I thought to myself as I reached for the field telephone. Seeing the stretcher had reminded me I needed to call the tower and give them a proper casrep – a casualty report, that is.

'Sangar Three, CASREP, over.'

'Go ahead.'

'It's Baren, but he's OK.'

'How bad is he?'

'I say again, he's OK. Completely fine. It's just a graze. He's on the .50-cal right now.'

'We'd better extract him anyway,' replied the OC – I guess he didn't want to take any chances – but I declined.

'Better not to extract right now,' I said. 'We're still getting a lot of small-arms. It's just too risky.'

'Roger. But you're sure he's all right? No shock?'

'He was a bit shocked,' I said. 'But he's OK. Fully recovered. He's got a field dressing on. I'll send him over as soon as it calms down.'

'All right, so long as you're sure. But keep me informed.'

'Roger.'

In fact, Baren wasn't only fine, he was exploding with rage. He and Lal were getting angrier and angrier and they were swearing a lot. They were desperate to actually see the enemy, but all they had to go on was the bit of smoke Lal had seen earlier.

'I just want to be able to see the *jatha*, *guruji*,' said Baren as I took up position next to him. 'I want to kill that *muji* who shot me.'

This is just about the worst possible word in the Nepali language, and I must say that setting it down like this embarrasses me. As I have said, Gurkhas do not swear much, and when they do it is quickly forgotten. But it is the reality. On this occasion, the air was black with foul language.

'We've got to kill them, *guruji*,' said Lal fiercely. They were both really mad now. Totally frustrated.

The *bhais*' anger was infectious. We knew the enemy were somewhere close. But where were they exactly?

'OK. Wait there!' I said, grabbing my weapon and my binoculars and climbing out of the sangar position onto the roof. Although this meant I was again relying on just the camnet for cover, I wanted to be able to see inside the next compound. The rounds were still flying up at us, but I didn't care. I too just wanted to kill now. I wanted the *jatha* dead.

Suddenly I saw something. *Aare!* They were right next door to us! Poking out from a hole less than 50 metres away was the very thing I was looking for. The muzzle of a gun barrel with a wisp of smoke curling from it.

'OVER THERE!' I yelled. 'Reference doorway in left-hand wall of compound next door. Go right two metres. Hole in wall. There's a gun barrel! There are people in there!'

At this, Baren and Lal both jumped up and brought their weapons out of the sangar onto the roof.

'We'll get them, *guruji*! We're gonna kill those *jatha*!'

Balancing the GPMG on his hip, Baren began to fire, with Lal joining in on the Minimi. We were all out on the roof now, all three of us fully exposed and still with a massive amount of fire coming up at us, mad as anything.

After a few seconds I realised this was all wrong and I hit the deck hard.

'*Bhai haru!* Get down!' I yelled. 'You need to get down!'

'Not until I've killed them all!' Baren shouted.

He was totally pumped up now, no longer a human being but a vicious animal intent on destroying its prey.

'ENOUGH!' I shouted. 'Get down both of you! NOW!'

Their aggression was good. They were being brave, sure. But there comes a moment when bravery and aggression tip over into something else. Something that isn't really brave but is in fact stupid. And I could see that Lal and Baren had both reached that point. It was essential I control them or we really were going to take casualties.

But they ignored me.

'GET DOWN!' I yelled, even louder. 'BOTH OF YOU!'

This time they obeyed.

They were just in time. A second later, I spotted a man, dressed in the typical loose brown clothing of these parts, wearing a grey turban and carrying a weapon. I couldn't say whether it was an AK47 or an RPG, but he was running in our direction across the compound of the clinic.

'*Guruji!* Did you see that?' Lal exclaimed.

But I was already halfway back into the sangar and didn't stop to reply. Grabbing three grenades, I stuffed one into my webbing pouch and held on to the others, one in each hand as I climbed back out onto the roof.

'OK, Lal, you take this,' I said, giving one of them to him. 'Baren, CHECK FIRE!' I shouted as, pulling the camnet aside, I extracted the pin on the first grenade.

I have quite a good throw, and by taking a short run I was able to get it well into the compound. It exploded almost immediately, though of course I couldn't tell if it actually got anyone.

As soon as I'd thrown mine, Lal threw his, and Baren opened

up again. As he did so, another figure flashed across the corner of the compound.

'CHECK FIRE!' I yelled again, pulling the pin from the second grenade. This one I dropped right into the corner. It must have been close, but again I didn't have the satisfaction of seeing anything.

I glanced at my watch. The OC had mentioned calling up air support. It couldn't be long before it got here. In the meantime, the key was to keep the enemy pinned down inside the compound so that when the Apache or the A-10 did get here, we could actually destroy them.

'OK, guys, keep suppressing!' I shouted as I crawled back inside the position. I needed to give a quick sitrep to the OC, also to grab more belts for the GPMG and some more magazines for the rifles. A few more grenades would be good too.

'Zero, this is Sangar Three. Contact! Enemy position identified in next-door compound. Approx fifteen metres. Have thrown three grenades.'

'Zero, roger. Well done. We should have Apache overhead in minutes five or less. Can you give me an exact grid reference of their position?'

'Roger. Wait out,' I replied, slamming the receiver down and grabbing my map.

When I had passed the location on, the OC announced that he was sending two more men over as reinforcements until the air support arrived.

'That'll give you an extra Minimi and another SA80,' he said.

'Roger. But tell them to be very careful getting up. We're still getting a lot of accurate fire on the position.'

A short time after, Riflemen Lukesh and Purna appeared, bringing with them a second GPMG and more ammo. It was very brave of them to come up, as we were being engaged at that very moment. You could clearly hear rounds striking the sandbags. My assessment now is that we were being engaged by a fire-support group while raiding parties were forming up in the clinic and in the bazaar.

Baren and Lal were back inside the sangar by now, and with five of us, it suddenly became very crowded. But it was too dangerous to stay outside for any length of time. Unlike in Sangar 1, there had been no possibility here for us to build a second wall of sandbags for protection further in front. There wasn't room, and anyway, I doubt the roof would have held the extra weight.

Because it was essential not to forget the bigger picture, I put Lukesh and Purna to cover our eastern flank, looking out towards what was left of Sniper's House and down into the bazaar, while I kept Baren and Lal together looking out over the clinic next door.

'Just watch for any movement and engage immediately, OK?' I said to the newcomers.

'*Hasur, guruji.*'

A short pause in the enemy fire gave me the opportunity to send another quick sitrep.

'Zero, this is Sangar Three, over.'

'Go ahead.'

'Reinforcements now in position observing. Enemy fire is a bit less.'

'Zero, roger. Out.'

The incoming fire was definitely a bit less, but why? I put the field telephone down and resumed scanning the local area, first on one side, then the other. The town itself was completely quiet, and yet you just knew that death was out there, lurking hidden in the alleyways and abandoned buildings.

Moments later, another blizzard of accurate fire engulfed the position.

For thirty seconds or more, we were completely unable to move. Rounds were entering the sangar above our heads and the place was thick with dust as they punctured the sandbags.

Then the field telephone rang.

'Air support in less than one minute.' I had never been more glad to hear the OC's voice.

'Roger. At present unable to return fire. Sustained accurate fire on my position.'

'Roger. Will inform pilot.'

Slamming the receiver down, I turned to the others.

'Air support approaching, *guruji bhai haru*!'

This was a massive morale boost, and we heard the beautiful sound of rotor blades slicing through the early evening air.

'Apache!' the *bhai*s all exclaimed simultaneously.

It's hard to explain what that sound meant to us. It was just so comforting. From feeling like you are totally vulnerable, totally at the mercy of the enemy, the next moment you feel completely safe. You feel that everything's going to be all right now – even though of course it might not be.

With the helicopter overhead, the incoming fire stopped and we were able to get back in position. But our troubles were far from over. Seconds later, we started coming under fire from the other side of the sangar.

'Quick, *guruji*! There's enemy down there!'

Lal was pointing in the direction of some buildings on the western side of the bazaar.

'Where those shops are! I saw movement!'

Sure enough, I spotted not one but several flashes and some gunsmoke as I scanned the area with my binos.

'Zero, this is Sangar Three, CONTACT! Area to western side of bazaar. Enemy movement. Looks like they're trying to turn us over!'

You had to admit, these *jatha* were brave. Very brave. They were trying to turn us over even though we had air support right on top of us – which was of course the right thing to do. They knew that if they could just get close enough, the helicopter would be useless. Blue on blue.

'Down there, *guruji*!' yelled Baren. 'There's four of them – maybe more! Heading for the clinic!'

'OK, guys, fire at will,' I said, forcing myself to stay calm. 'Fire at will!'

The time for restraint had passed. I don't mean that we were out of control again. We weren't just spraying rounds down without any discipline. On the other hand we needed to get as much weight of fire onto the enemy as possible, even if we couldn't see him except in glimpses. We knew pretty much where he was, so it was a question of forcing him to stay back. In these situations, you have to do anything to prevent the enemy from gaining the initiative. You need to get the rounds down so he daren't expose himself. You have to deprive him of the opportunity to launch a full-scale assault.

'Zero, this is Sangar Three. CONTACT! Movement seen in clinic again. Engaging!'

'Zero, roger. I'll ask the pilot if he can help.'

There was tension in the OC's voice. Normally you wouldn't attempt to use air support to take on targets at such close range, and it was a big risk to do so. But the situation demanded it.

Within seconds there was another Charlie Charlie call on the PRR.

'Ready, Kailash?'

'OK ready.'

'Roger. Charlie Charlie One, Apache will engage target in old clinic. HEADS DOWN! I say again HEADS DOWN!'

The sound of the heli changed to thunder as it headed in towards us. At less than 50 metres' range and practically overhead, he opened up with his 30 mm cannon.

BRRRRB BRRRRB BRRRRB

Cautiously, I poked my head up to see where the rounds were falling. He was about 20 metres too far to the right, the rounds falling harmlessly on open ground.

'Did he get them, *guruji*? Was it a target?' the *bhais* all wanted to know.

'He was twenty metres off.'

'*Aaye!*'

'So now what?'

They were bitterly disappointed. It was so frustrating, but you couldn't blame the pilot. The helicopter had come under heavy fire itself.

'Quiet, you guys! I need to send a target indication,' I shouted, pressing the Send button on my PRR. 'Zero, this is Sangar Three. Rounds fell approximately twenty metres to right of target.'

'Zero, roger. He's coming round again. HEADS DOWN! HEADS DOWN!'

Again came the thunder of blades and the deep burble of the cannon.

BRRRRB BRRRRB BRRRRB

Aaye jatha! This time he was on target OK, but now several rounds fell just a few metres short and the whole sangar shook.

'WOW, *guruji*! That was too close, wasn't it?'

'Listen, *bhai haru*, this guy's taking serious risks for us, OK? Now be quiet a moment. Zero, this is Sangar Three. That was a target. But a bit close to my position.'

'Did he hit you?'

'Not quite.'

'OK. This time he's going to come in at right angles. HEADS DOWN! HEADS DOWN!'

A third time, we heard the clatter of blades and the roar of the engine as the helicopter swept down towards us. There followed a loud crackle of small-arms fire as the enemy switched their attention away from us and onto the chopper. But the next thing we knew, the helicopter's cannon fire was actually striking the corner of the DC and the sangar was vibrating violently.

'CHECK FIRE! CHECK FIRE!' I yelled over the PRR.

Thankfully the pilot must have seen what was happening and his gun went silent.

'*Hernuhos, guruji*! He's trying to kill us!' exclaimed one of the riflemen.

'Look out, you stupid man!' yelled another.

We were all a bit shaken, I have to admit.

'At least he didn't hit the sangar,' I said. 'Be thankful he's here. Now come on, let's keep at it.'

The truth of the matter was, the enemy was in a very good position. It was going to be almost impossible to hit him where he was. The only thing likely to cause him serious trouble would be a Hellfire missile, but that would have been way too risky in these circumstances.

We continued engaging the clinic while the Apache adjusted his line of attack.

Swinging round low, the helicopter came in for another run. This time his rounds slammed into the southern corner, exactly where I expected the enemy to be.

BRRRRB BRRRRB BRRRRB

'That'll teach you for shooting at me!' yelled Baren.

Yet again, the Apache banked steeply round with a clatter of blades, dust and smoke partially screening him. This time he flew off towards the north, and as the sound of the machine faded, it gave way to the sound of loud cries coming from the clinic.

'Listen! Did you hear that, *guruji*?' said Lal.

The screams got louder.

'Got the *jatha*!' cried one of the other riflemen.

'That sounds like a target all right,' I said

I picked up the field telephone.

'Zero, this is Sangar Three. That was a target. Screams coming from inside clinic area.'

'Zero, roger. Will relay to pilot. But don't take your eyes off the place, OK? They might try to reinforce it.'

'Sangar Three, roger out.'

Grabbing some bottles of water, I threw one to each of the *bhai*s. We'd been in contact on and off for nearly two hours now and we were all badly in need of a drink.

'Drink all of it, *bhai haru*. You don't know when we'll get time for another one.'

Shortly after, the OC was on the air to say that the ANP

convoy that had been ambushed earlier in the morning was still on the far side of the bazaar near the graveyard, and reporting squirters (suspected enemy) running between the clinic and the petrol station.

'It looks as though they are withdrawing from the bazaar area. The MFC will try to cut them off,' he announced.

Not long after, the 81 mm tube burst into action, and we watched as the impact of successive rounds erupted in cascades of white smoke.

'Wow! Take a look at that!' said one of the *bhai*s.

'I bet they weren't expecting mortar!' said another.

But we were continuing to take accurate fire on the sangar position. Although it wasn't coming from the clinic any more, the enemy still hadn't given up.

Suddenly a shout went up from Baren.

'Need more link, *guruji*!'

Oh no! This was something I'd been dreading hearing. I knew we must be getting low, but right now there was no way we could get anybody up onto the position to resupply us. They'd just have to try and throw it up.

'How much have you got left?' I demanded, looking over at him. To my horror I saw that the barrel of the GPMG was glowing a deep red. He urgently needed a barrel change too.

'Less than half a box.'

Roger.

'Zero, this is Sangar Three. We need more link for the GPMG, but it's too dangerous to come onto the position. They'll have to try and throw it up.'

'Okay. I'll get some over to you right away.'

Less than a minute later a cry came from down below.

'RESUPP!'

I knew Gaaz's voice at once.

'OK. LET'S HAVE IT,' I replied, scrambling out onto the roof.

Gaaz's first two attempts failed, but eventually he got the measure of it and first one, then another, then three, then four boxes skidded towards me.

'LET ME KNOW IF YOU NEED MORE.'

'OK. SHOULD BE ENOUGH FOR NOW.'

At least, I hoped so. I was just focused on keeping the enemy from getting any closer.

'OK, *guruji bhai haru*, we've got to try to work out where these positions are,' I said. 'So I need for you all to be looking, looking. There's still half an hour of daylight left. That's time enough for the enemy to launch another assault.'

I said this because I didn't want the *bhai*s to give up, just because we had air support. Besides, it was true.

The likely places were the same today as the other days. The treeline to the east, Smuggler's House and just about anywhere in between. Every so often, I would hear the OC on the PRR acknowledge one or other of the sangars giving the grid of another fire position. But it was one thing to identify them and quite another to knock them out, even with a helicopter on station. One big problem was that if they thought the helicopter was on to them, all they had to do was put down their weapons and walk away. They knew they wouldn't get attacked. The pilot wouldn't just hit random people. He had to be sure they were enemy. So although it was great to have air support, we still needed to find the enemy positions in order to give the pilot targets to engage.

The other thing we had to be alert to was the possibility of the enemy regrouping and having another go at turning us over. It was clear that he had routes in and out that enabled him to get very close to us without exposing himself. We never discovered what or where these were. My own conclusion was that there must have been some sort of tunnel system. But I doubted they could have been dug recently. More likely they went in long before the present conflict – maybe back when the Russians occupied Afghanistan during the 1980s.

In any case, our attention was soon back on the clinic when there was a sudden shout from one of the *bhai*s.

'CONTACT! IN THE CLINIC AGAIN!'

This was followed with an immediate burst of fire from Baren on the GPMG.

Just at that moment, Mathers *sahib* sent out a call on the PRR.

'Charlie Charlie One, A-10 on task.'

Thank the god.

'A-10, *guruji bhai haru*. A-10!' I said to the riflemen.

Normally they would cheer, but this time things were so close they didn't even look up.

I looked down into the street below, half-expecting to see a ladder. But there was nothing.

'A-10 approaching ten seconds.' Mathers *sahib* now began the countdown over the PRR.

'A-10 in ten seconds!' I repeated.

'Now see what happens, you *jatha*!' said Baren, only now looking up from the GPMG.

'Hey! Keep your eyes on the clinic and the sniper holes!' I shouted.

The A-10 roared in low overhead. I have heard that the American air force makes jokes about the type as being the only aircraft capable of suffering birdstrike at both ends – a reference to its relatively slow speed. I know some people call it ugly too. All I can say is that to us, it was the most beautiful flying machine ever built. The enemy seemed also to have strong opinions about the A-10, as from the moment of its arrival, things quietened down dramatically. It seems they didn't quite dare to close with us and instead withdrew the way they'd come.

We watched as the aircraft took on targets around the town. When you are as busy as we were, it is easy to lose a sense of the bigger picture, but while we were fighting our own bit of the war, the other sangars had been fighting theirs and relaying contacts to the CT. As a result, the OC was able to give the pilot multiple target indications, and it was these he began to engage. We watched with huge satisfaction as the A-10's cannon ripped into successive positions.

After some time, the A-10 departed, and suddenly I noticed how quiet it was. For the next half-hour, the only sound came from the five of us moving round inside the sangar, interspersed with the occasional radio transmission. After another half-hour, I called for some food to be brought. We were all really hungry by now. It was still too dangerous for anyone to come up, so I told the *bhais* they should throw it. But after several attempts, we realised it just wasn't going to work. Even though the riflemen on the ground secured the mess tins by putting two together and tying them, the contents spilled everywhere.

'FORGET IT!' I shouted. 'Just bring some biscuits, OK?'

We would just have to wait until after dark for a proper meal. That would be soon now, though there was still plenty to do.

The ANP convoy that had been ambushed in the morning was still stuck on the other side of town. They hadn't taken any casualties, but they needed extracting. The OC's plan, delivered individually over the field telephone, was to provide them with an escort of the two WMIKS after a resupp he had arranged which would be brought in by Chinook.

'Be advised, the 2 i/c will take the WMIKs down to the HLS. He'll resupply ANP Hill and then escort the stranded vehicles back to the DC. Meanwhile the sangars are to remain on high alert. Radio intercepts suggest the enemy has not left the area. Also be advised we have another Apache due in figures five. He will be clearing the route to the HLS.'

'Sangar Three, roger out.'

With Mathers *sahib* and the two vehicles out of the DC while ANP Hill was resupplied, and with the ANP themselves still not back, we were going to be seriously short of manpower in the event of more big contacts, so it was another anxious twenty minutes.

The muezzin's call to evening prayer was drowned out by the sound of the helicopter arriving. The pilot then proceeded to loiter overhead while he waited for the arrival of the Chinook. In the sangar, now that it was getting dark, I took the opportunity to stand Baren down so that he could at last be examined by the medics.

'I'm fine, *guruji*. I'll stay,' he said. But I insisted. Gaaz could take his place.

'You need to get those wounds dressed. We don't want you to get an infection.'

Reluctantly, Baren left the position just as the two WMIKs burst out of the compound and headed down to the HLS. Gaaz then came up, and soon after we heard the sound of helicopters in the near distance. It turned out there were not one but two Chinooks, and they were accompanied by another two Apaches.

'*Namaste, guruji bhai haru!*' exclaimed Gaaz on entering. 'It feels like Christmas! But instead of Santa and his reindeer, our presents are coming by helicopter.'

We all laughed. It was so good to have Gaaz back with us. He had been resting and was full of energy.

My main concern now was for the stores. With the light fading fast, the vehicles were going to be even more vulnerable than usual. It would be harder than ever to spot the enemy.

I needn't have worried. Within less than ten minutes of the drop, the OC came up on the PRR.

'Charlie Charlie One, this is Zero. Zero Bravo reports all stores accounted for.' That was a big relief. 'But be aware,' he went on, 'there are reports of suspected enemy observed two kilometres east.'

'Did you get that, *bhai haru*? It's not over yet.'

Even though we still had air support in the form of an Apache helicopter, it wasn't many minutes before we saw flashes of tracer and heard the familiar sound of rounds thudding into the sangar position.

'Zero, Sangar Three, CONTACT, wait out!'

'Zero, roger.'

Seconds later, an arc of tracer lit the sky as the helicopter itself came under attack.

'*Aaye!* Did you see that, *guruji*?' demanded one of the rifle-men.

'Looks like they must have got hold of an anti-aircraft gun from somewhere!' said Gaaz.

There followed an immediate burst of cannon fire from the helicopter. Then another, and another.

BRRRRB ... BRRRRB ... BRRRRB

Several flashes lit up the sky as the rounds found their way onto the target.

'Charlie Charlie One, this is Zero. For your information, pilot confirms that as a kill.'

'That'll teach you, *jatha*!' came Gaaz's voice through the gathering dark.

Five minutes later, there was a loud explosion as a Hellfire missile tore into a building on the southern side of town, while almost immediately afterwards the ANP convoy, escorted by the two WMIKS, burst back into the compound.

'Look! It's Father Christmas!' exclaimed Gaaz.

15

Night Attack

We all agreed that the enemy had given us a good fight that day.

'I just wish the *jatha* would come out and show themselves occasionally,' said Nagen, as we sat down to our first full meal in almost twenty-four hours.

'And it would be good if the Afghans here joined in sometimes,' said one of the other riflemen.

Actually, this was a bit unfair. The ANP had twice been ambushed patrolling. It was the local police who did nothing.

'What I'd like is if the Taliban just came round and we could fight it out hand to hand,' said someone else.

'They know we'd beat them. That's exactly why they wouldn't,' replied Nagen.

After eating, those of us who had been on duty all day went for rest, though I can't say I got much sleep, and I don't suppose the others did either. There was too much adrenalin in our veins. But the night was a quiet one.

Sometime the following morning, I had a strange conversation with some of the local police. When the Apache was firing into the old clinic, one of the rounds that had almost taken us out must have struck the ground near to the police pick-up. Some shrapnel had smashed the windscreen and one of the wing mirrors and the police were all really frustrated and angry. The leader came up to me and started shouting threateningly as if it was somehow my fault their vehicle was damaged. But, speaking in Urdu, I tried to convince them it was a Taliban mortar that had done it. I thought that might encourage them to fight.

'Look, brother,' I said. '*Taliban nikya hal kyi*. The Taliban have done this. *O Taliban marna porega*. We have to kill the Taliban.'

Although I did finally manage to persuade him that what we were looking at was the effects of enemy action, I still had the uneasy feeling the local police blamed the Gurkhas for what had happened. To their way of thinking, if we hadn't been there, there would have been no attacks and they could have had a nice quiet life.

Because of the resupp the night before, we spent part of that morning sorting out the stores. We'd been getting low on ammo and water, so it was reassuring to have got our supplies back up to full strength. We had also taken delivery of more ILAWs, so that was good for morale too. Plus there was a letter for Gaaz which I took to him later.

I found him lying on his bed, gaming and singing a song I'd often heard him sing to himself. I can't remember what it was, though he did once tell me who it was by. Somebody Adams, I think. But I don't take much interest in modern music. I prefer traditional Nepalese folk songs.

'Gaaz! There's a letter for you.'

'Oh thanks, *guruji*!' he exclaimed, jumping up. 'I wonder who it's from . . .'

I think it must have been from his parents, as he wasn't too excited when he saw the envelope.

'Gaaz, I don't mind you reading it straight away,' I said. 'But when you've finished, I want to see your bedspace tidied up, OK?'

'Yes, *guruji*,' he replied, a bit embarrassed.

The one area that I could always find fault with Gaaz was his personal admin. You could tell him to tidy his things up and he'd do it. But less than twenty-four hours later, it would be just as bad or even worse than before. I didn't really mind, but I pointed out to him he would need to get a grip at some point.

'Just remember that when you're an NCO, you'll have to lead by example.'

'Yes, *guruji*.'

He looked at me as if to say he was sorry I'd said that. He knew it was his one weakness and he didn't like to be confronted with it. But after a moment, he brightened up.

'Hey *guruji*! When I've done it, will you give me a game of *bagh chal*? You can be the tiger.'

'Sure,' I replied, knowing full well that his strongest game was when he played the goats. I made sure I won all the same.

At the O-group later that day, Rex *sahib* gave us a heads-up on the general situation. 3 PARA were back in Bastion, and we shouldn't now expect to be relieved for at least another ten days, possibly two weeks.

'It looks like the enemy has decided that it's make or break time for him in Helmand. He's throwing everything he's got into it, so we're just going to have to dig deep.'

The OC looked a bit fed up as he said this, as if he felt that we'd all done enough. I was even a bit concerned for him. He took his command so seriously, and cared for the men in his charge so much. But he must know that we Gurkhas would carry on fighting right down to the last man. And even if we ran out of ammunition we wouldn't give up. We'd use our kukris. And if we lost our kukris, we'd fight with our bare hands.

When I got back to the accommodation block afterwards, I told the *bhai*s they were to take extra care to look after the OC.

'Make sure you give him plenty to eat,' I said.

I had maximum admiration for Rex *sahib* and the way he was leading us and I wanted to make sure the *bhai*s didn't take him for granted. We should be grateful we had such a fine officer commanding us. The reality of it was that these were tough times. We'd been in major contacts now for four out of the past five days, and there was no indication that the enemy had run out of either manpower or energy for the task. It had become clear that we had landed up right in the heart of a Taliban stronghold and our presence here was unbearable to them. They were going to get rid of us if they possibly could. No price was too high to pay.

That night there was another good moon, and back up in Sangar 3 again, the atmosphere was pretty tense. We were just waiting for things to kick off.

'So what do you reckon, *guruji*?' demanded Gaaz. 'Before midnight or after?'

'Same as usual,' I replied.

'You mean before?'

'No. I mean just when you think he's stayed in bed.'

Gaaz laughed.

'Good one, *guruji*.'

As it turned out, we had a wait of several hours, and after the usual chat about how things had gone the day before and what we could expect tonight, we got round to talking some more about our training days at Pokhara.

For the next two weeks after selection, we worked unbelievably hard – mainly at drill. I found this really difficult. I just couldn't get my arms and legs to do what they were supposed to. Every night when I went to bed I had the words 'Right arm, left leg! Left arm, right leg!' ringing in my ears. But because there was so much shouting and confusion on the parade ground I hardly knew what was going on and my mind was all over the place.

'COME HERE! DO THIS! DO THAT!'

'GET DOWN AND GIVE ME TEN!'

It only came back to me when I said my prayers in the evening.

We even had to shout ourselves. Every day during our drill sessions, one of the *gurujis* made us march up to a tree and shout. He said he wouldn't let us go until we had shouted so loud that a leaf fell off the tree! Of course, we were never successful.

We had to learn new things all the time. On one occasion early on, the CSM (Company Sergeant Major) came down to give us a lesson in how to eat the British way.

'You use the knife like this. For cutting. Do you understand? You don't pull your food apart like a monkey. And this is how you use a fork.'

After this introduction, he demonstrated how to use the knife and fork together to eat rice.

'So from now on I don't want to see anyone using their hands to eat.' We all nodded in agreement.

'The next thing,' he announced, 'is toilet training. From now on you are going to be using one of these.'

At this point, a Western-style toilet was solemnly brought in to the classroom.

'That means, when you have a piss, you have to lift up the seat. And make sure you aim it in properly.'

Next, he demonstrated how to sit on the thing. Up until then, not many people had even seen a modern toilet. We just used to squat down.

'And I don't want to catch anyone with their feet on the seat!' said the CSM. 'If I catch anyone squatting with their feet on the toilet, you will get such a rifting your toes won't even touch the ground! Does everyone understand?'

Again, we nodded furiously.

'And don't think this doesn't matter. You will be responsible for keeping the toilet block clean. I want to be able to eat my breakfast off the floor in there. So if I find it's a mess, that's where you will be eating *your* breakfast. Do you understand?'

There followed several more days of drill, before we were taken down to the pay office for our first pay. This was another new experience for us. We were told we must march in and halt correctly in front of the pay clerk and salute him.

'Kailash Khebang Limbu, ready for pay, SIR!'

You had to say 'sir' to the pay clerk, and salute him even though he was not an officer. This, we were told, is the tradition, and in fact if you go to the Gurkha Welfare offices in Nepal, you will see even some really old soldiers doing exactly the same when they come in to collect their pension, even though they are no longer in the Army and even though they may be far senior to the clerk handing out their money.

I will always remember my first pay. It was the first money I had ever earned and it gave me such a good feeling. The ten thousand rupees handed over seemed like an enormous fortune to me. At the time, it was probably worth about £120 – enough to keep a family living in a remote village like Khebang for many months. But although I was going to send most of it to my family, I also wanted to give some money to the *galla*, the recruiter, who had come down from Taplejung and was still waiting to see if any of his candidates had been successful. I gave him two thousand rupees and told him to go off and have a good drink at my expense. I asked him to take the rest of the money back to my family. In a note accompanying it, I explained that two thousand should go as a present to my grandfather and grandmother, while the rest was for my parents.

This *galla* was a retired Gurkha from a village near to Khebang – at least, near on our terms: it was maybe four or five hours' walk between the two. He had been the one responsible for taking me down to the first selection in Telog and then for sponsoring me, along with several others, as a candidate in Taplejung. It was the *galla* who was the person who told us where we had to be at what time on which day. He was also the one who told us what we needed to bring in the way of boots, clothes and so on. There were no formal joining instructions, just the verbal ones he gave us. He had travelled down to keep an eye on his candidates at Pokhara, the tradition being that if you are successful, you will reward him. There was also a prize from the Brigade itself for the one who brings the largest number of successful candidates, so it could be quite a lucrative position.

The final event of our time at Pokhara was the *khosm khane* parade. This was when we finally passed out of Pokhara, after which we would be taken to Kathmandu, and from there by aeroplane to England to start our basic training at Church Crookham.

On this final parade, we all had to place our hand on the British flag and swear the oath of allegiance to the British crown.

Swearing the oath was the easy part, of course. The hard part was doing the drill. It was our first-ever formal parade and we were all in our best uniform. But although we were all very nervous, somehow we got through without any major disasters. This was just as well, as there were a lot of spectators. Many people's families had come to see them, and beside all these family members, a lot of the locals from the town also turned out to watch, either through the fence or standing on their balconies nearby.

It was a great occasion and I was sad that my own parents weren't there to watch, though I wasn't the only one on their own. There were one or two others from really remote areas like mine whose families couldn't make it. In fact, it is quite possible that my parents still didn't know that I had passed. The *galla* might not have reached my home with my letter yet.

Fortunately, the parents of one of my friends were very kind to me and, as well as offering their congratulations, asked me to join them for the show that was taking place on the evening after the parade. This was one of the most memorable events I have ever experienced. There was singing and dancing and fireworks and a lot of beautiful girls in amazing costumes. It felt like a really good reward after such a hard month and I loved every minute of it. My dream had come true and this was the final, wonderful climax.

The next day, we all had to parade in travelling uniform. This consisted of a blazer and a shirt with collar and tie. Naturally, I had no idea how to tie a tie, but a few people – the ones who came from the cities – did, and they helped the rest of us. When we were all lined up, I was so proud as I thought back to my village. As a child, my uniform had been just a T-shirt and shorts, with flip-flops on my feet. But now I was a member of the British Army and looking as smart as ever could be. It was an incredible feeling to have come so far.

Many parents came back on this final morning to say a last goodbye to their sons. Lots were crying, and again I felt quite sad to be on my own. But before we knew it, we were on the bus and on our way to Kathmandu, with hundreds and hundreds of people lining the streets to wave.

As soon as we reached Kathmandu, we started attracting attention there too. A lot of people came up to us, asking where we were from. They saw our uniform and thought we must be from some school or college. When they heard we were Gurkha recruits, they became even more interested. We became very popular with the girls. Some of them even came up and handed us letters proposing marriage.

For myself, I was actually rather scared of these girls. I liked the idea of girls, of course, but I never knew what to say to them. Even at school, there were some who used to come up and try to talk to me, but when I saw them head in my direction, I always used to divert. It seemed to me they were much more advanced than I was. Besides, I didn't really have any interest in love and marriage at that age. I wasn't yet eighteen after all. In fact, rather than spend my time with these girls in Kathmandu, what I wanted more than anything was to get some sleep.

At about 10.30 p.m., the field telephone rang.

'Kailash, be advised that int has picked up threat of imminent attack. Be on high alert.' Mathers *sahib*'s voice was calm and reassuring, despite the news. 'Everything OK with you?'

'Everything's fine. We're ready.'

'Well done.'

The 'int' the 2 i/c was referring to was intelligence picked up by scanning the radio waves. I subsequently heard that the Taliban's code for action was 'Cooking meat now'. We change our codewords on a regular basis, but because they hadn't bothered to change theirs, our interpreter must have realised immediately what was about to happen.

Almost as soon as I had put the receiver down, Nagen called out to me:

'*Guruji!* Do you see those lights over there?'

I looked out in the direction of the wadi – the dry river course that ran to the east of the town – and saw several vehicle lights.

'Got them,' I said, switching on my night-vision sight. 'That was the 2 i/c by the way – saying there's been int of imminent attack.'

'*Hunza, guruji,*' said Gaaz.

'So it must be the enemy,' said Nagen.

We watched as the vehicles parked up together. I could see several people getting out, but it was impossible at this stage to say whether they were definitely fighters or not, and until we had confirmation we would have to hold off engaging them. After a few minutes, however, their headlights were switched off, and almost immediately there were three explosions in the distance. We quickly discovered this was the mortar base plate up on ANP Hill firing the 81 mm tube. It turned out they'd got sufficient evidence that it was indeed the enemy and had opened up. The first round landed some distance from where the vehicles were, but the second was closer and the third was just a few metres away.

'Looks like the MFC's creeping rounds onto them!' I exclaimed as we waited to see if there was going to be a fourth explosion. Sure enough, after a short delay, another round detonated right on top of them.

'Well that makes a nice change!' said Gaaz happily. 'I reckon that's the first time we've had the initiative of the *jatha haru*. I bet that gave them a surprise.'

The OC came up on the PRR.

'Charlie Charlie One, be advised that we've got positive ident of enemy in those vehicles. MFC will fire for effect.'

I heard afterwards that the ANP really earned their stripes that evening. They were the ones who had picked up the Taliban signals and, by speaking on their own frequency, had tricked the Taliban into identifying themselves to us. The ANP had discussed the position of the headlights with the local police on the radio, fairly certain that the enemy would be listening in on the local police frequency. As soon as the enemy realised the ANP were on to him, the vehicle lights all switched off simultaneously – proving that it was him. Of course, this also shows the treachery of the local police who must have told the enemy what frequency they would be operating.

Five more explosions went off in the distance.

For the next hour, the MFC harassed the enemy as the Taliban tried to get his vehicles into town. It was clear that even if some had been damaged in the first barrage, several had survived and more were heading towards us using a different route. Meanwhile, the OC kept us informed of what was going on by a mixture of PRR and field telephone.

'The MFC will be engaging vehicles in the vicinity of the Coliseum. Let me know if you see any squirters.'

The Coliseum was another AOI where the enemy had been sighted during previous contacts, and several more explosions followed soon after this broadcast.

'Looks like the vehicles are withdrawing, *guruji*!' said one of the riflemen.

'That doesn't mean we've heard the last of them,' I warned. 'Could be he was just dropping people off.'

Sure enough, just a couple of minutes later Gaaz shouted excitedly, '*Guruji!* Quick! Two of them! In the bazaar! Looks like they're carrying RPG. Can I engage?'

'You're sure?'

'Definitely.'

'OK, but hold your fire.'

I relayed the information back to the CT immediately.

'Zero, this is Sangar Three. Contact. Two pax with RPG in bazaar area. Am I clear to engage?'

'Zero, roger. You're quite sure they're armed and threatening?'

'Yes, definitely armed. And threatening.'

'OK, you are clear to engage.'

I turned to Gaaz.

'Which way did they go?'

'East. Towards the burned-out building in front of Sangar One.'

Jatha! That meant they'd closed to within 50 metres.

'Nagen. Take the Minimi over next to Gaaz and get some rounds down, OK?'

Within a few seconds, both machine guns were spitting fire.

'Zero, this is Sangar Three. Pax observed heading for reference point two. Engaging target area.'

'Zero, roger.'

Almost immediately, we came under sustained fire ourselves, as did both sangars 1 and 2, together with the CT. It was clear the enemy had managed to get into position, despite the best efforts of the mortars.

'Where's it coming from? Where's it coming from?' I shouted. The usual question.

'I can't see, *guruji.*'

'No idea, *guruji.*'

The usual answers.

As soon as there was a slight let-up in the thud of rounds into the sandbags, I flung myself out of the main position and onto the roof outside. By scanning with my HMNVS, I gradually began to see we were being engaged from positions to the north-east, round to the south. Brief flickers of light on our left side and ahead of us, in other words – the telltale sign of muzzle flash.

'FIRE POSITIONS AHEAD AND TO NORTH-EAST!' I yelled to the *bhais*. Using short, controlled bursts, they began to engage the target area. It was hard to be certain, but it was likely the fire positions themselves were outside of town providing support for the enemy who were now inside.

'Still can't see anything, *guruji*!' shouted Gaaz.

'Keep engaging known positions!' I replied. That was all we could do at this stage. Mainly this meant the treeline approximately 300 metres distant to the north-east and the area around the football pitch to the south.

Scanning continuously, I suddenly noticed the lights of several more vehicles approximately 3 kilometres due north of the DC. Using the PRR, as I was by now on the platform outside the sangar itself, I called the CT at once.

'Zero, this is Sangar Three. Vehicles moving approx three thousand metres to the north. Am observing, over.'

'Zero, roger. Seen. Out to you. Mike One Zero Alpha, do you see them?'

This was one of those occasions when we could clearly hear the radio traffic between ANP Hill and the CT over the PRR. A lot of the time, you couldn't, perhaps because of atmospheric conditions or because the aerials were not in line of sight.

'Yes, I've got them too.'

Mike One Zero Alpha was the callsign of the Mortar Fire Controller up on ANP Hill.

'Zero, roger. Keep observing. I may ask you to engage. We just need a PID.'

'Roger, understood. Stand by mortar.'

Minutes later, the 2 i/c reported another convoy of vehicles on the same road, but further away, heading towards us. It looked as if the enemy was going to launch a serious assault. Probably those we had seen earlier had been sent to provide close support for a raiding party. I wondered how long it would be before we had air cover. I felt sure that the OC must have asked already. What I didn't know at the time was that, due to multiple contacts elsewhere, there would be a delay in getting aircraft out to us.

After about ten minutes of heavy fire, things quietened down a bit. That didn't mean we could afford to rest. Most likely it meant the enemy were just about to launch their attack.

'Keep observing, *bhai haru*,' I said. 'They're out there somewhere.'

Another burst of fire came streaking in at us almost before I'd finished speaking, again from the direction of the treeline. It was almost as if the enemy had heard me and wanted me to keep my head down because of what was about to happen. Several more minutes passed in an agony of expectation.

Suddenly a shout went up from the CT.

'ENEMY STRAIGHT AHEAD! IN ALLEYWAY!'

This was followed by a long burst of 7.62 as the GPMG opened up.

'Sangar Three, this is Zero. Not sure if you saw that but pax seen in alleyway are on direct axis to CT. Keep your eyes peeled, OK?'

Mathers *sahib*'s voice was as clear as ever, but I could tell he was seriously pumped up.

'Sangar Three, roger out.'

I strained my eyes searching for movement, but there was

nothing. Everything had gone eerily quiet. If you didn't know the circumstances, you would have said it was a beautiful night. The moon was bright and the stars sparkled with an intensity you just don't get in England. As I lay in my forward position on the roof, I allowed myself a moment to think about my wife and family back in Nepal. It was hard to imagine I should be joining them in less than twenty days from now, and I asked God to look after them for me until I could get home – whenever that turned out to be. And yet, almost as soon as the thought came, I banished it. I couldn't afford the luxury of even five seconds' dreaming. This was the time to be switched on. If you give in to thoughts about home when you're as exhausted as we were, there's a danger you're going to fall asleep, and that's the single worst thing you could ever do. If that happens, someone's going to die for sure, and when they do, it'll be your fault. I reminded myself there were enemy out there. They could be just a few metres away, getting ready to lob a grenade up onto the roof.

'You OK in there, *bhai haru*?' I wanted to know.

'Fine, *guruji*.'

'Just thinking about what a nice place this would be to come on holiday, *guruji*.' That was Gaaz, of course.

Satisfied they were fully alert, I was just about to send a sitrep to the tower when something flashed in a blaze of intense white light across the corner of my field of vision.

RPG!

A split second later, it exploded against the wall directly below me.

'I've got him! I've got him!' cried Nagen, opening up with the Minimi. He was quickly joined by Gaaz on the GPMG while

I reached immediately for the UGL. An instant later there were two more explosions as first one then another RPG round exploded behind us somewhere in the compound. Straight away both Sangar 1 and platoon HQ'S GPMGs burst into life as the two positions erupted in fury.

Above the clatter of small-arms fire, I heard the 2 i/c come up on the PRR. It seemed the mortar team had spotted the contact.

'MFC will engage with both systems,' he announced. That meant he'd be deploying both mortar and sustained-fire GPMG. I lay watching – a bit nervously, I admit – as his tracer arced through the air towards us. The target area was less than 100 metres from the sangar position, so there was very little margin for error.

To start with, the rounds landed a good distance away, but successive bursts came closer and closer.

'*Aaye guruji!* You'd better look out!' yelled Gaaz from inside the sangar.

He was right. Although the rounds were not actually striking the sangar, the ricochets were, and in a way that was even more dangerous. At least when you are being engaged directly, the rounds fall reasonably predictably, but a ricochet has a completely random trajectory. You could easily lose an eye if you were trying to watch the fall of shot.

'Zero, this is Sangar Three, CHECK FIRE!' I shouted. 'I say again, CHECK FIRE!'

'Zero, roger. GPMG to check fire. Was he getting close?'

'No but his ricochets were.'

'Roger.'

'Good call, *guruji*,' said Gaaz. 'I don't mind dying, but I'd rather not be taken out by our own side.'

Not long after, Rex *sahib*'s voice came up on the PRR. He reported that he had instructed the MFC to prepare to target the area of the football pitch and be ready to creep rounds back onto the DC in the event of a major attack developing.

The words sound quite ordinary, but I could tell at once what was being said. If a serious action developed, the OC wanted the mortars to fire right up to the DC. And if the enemy got over the walls, they were to drop rounds inside. You don't call for indirect fire on your own position unless you think you are in danger of complete disaster. It looked as if we were going to have to face the possibility of blue on blue whether we liked it or not.

'Roger so far, over.'

Each of the sangar positions acknowledged the call in turn.

'Zero, also be advised we are getting reports of enemy mobile mortar base plate being moved up. So all of you keep a good eye for any further vehicle activity and let me know.'

How the OC knew this, I'm not sure, but it could possibly be int from a high-flying spy plane. This was one big advantage we had – the ability to get intelligence from the air.

'Charlie Charlie One,' the OC continued, 'Emerald Thirty-Three confirms air support en route. Should be overhead within the hour.'

Emerald 33 was the callsign of the 3 PARA Battlegroup commander. Well, that was good news. But it was bad news too. It meant that we had another sixty minutes without air support. Air int was great, but what we needed was weapons delivery systems – A-10 or Apache or even B-52. If they were delayed, this must also mean there were other major contacts going on which prevented them getting here sooner. Where could these other contacts be? Probably 3 PARA themselves were having a rough time of it too.

It was around 3.30 a.m. when the Apache finally arrived but, strange to say, there were no further contacts before it did so. And apart from one brief sighting of movement at the end of the alleyway opposite Sangar 1, there weren't any more afterwards either. I heard later that our interpreter had been listening to the enemy radio broadcasts throughout the night and it seemed they had taken some casualties. Maybe that was why they hadn't in the end come in with a full-scale attack on the DC.

The sound of the muezzin's loudspeaker calling people to morning prayer coincided with a realisation that the enemy had almost certainly dispersed.

'*Allaaahu akbar* . . . Allah is most great . . .

'I testify that there is no God but Allah . . .

'I testify that Muhammad is the prophet of Allah . . .

'Come to prayer. Come to salvation . . .

'*Allaaahu akbar* . . . There is no God but Allah.'

'That's so wrong!' exclaimed Gaaz. 'If there's one god, there's hundreds of them. If not thousands. You know what, *guruji*, that *jatha* is really starting to annoy me. I swear I'm going to accidentally drop a UGL on him one of these days.'

I knew he was joking and I knew what he was getting at, but I couldn't let this go unchallenged.

'If you did, I'd have to charge you,' I replied. A charge, in this case, meaning to bring a charge for behaviour unbecoming of a British soldier, leading to a court martial.

'You would too, wouldn't you, *guruji*?'

'Definitely.'

303

'You're a hard man, *guruji*. But that's why we look up to you and all the other *gurujis*. You're completely honest.'

I shrugged. The point is, as an NCO you have to show the riflemen how to behave. You have to lead by example, and they have to know exactly where they stand. They have to know that you would be willing to give up your life for them. That way they can trust you. But it is also important for them to know that you would not hesitate to punish them severely for wrong-doing – most especially if it brought the Brigade of Gurkhas into disrepute in any way.

In this we are perhaps a little bit different from other parts of the Army. As I have said, for us, to be a member of the Brigade of Gurkhas is like being a member of a family. We look out for each other as if we were all members of the same family. So if somebody does something that could harm the good name of the Brigade, it is as if they did something bad to their own brother. More importantly, this is also the way we fight. We fight as members of a family. If someone gets hurt, it's like you yourself get hurt.

Our attitude is also what makes us different from other Nepalese too. Back in Nepal, this kind of deep feeling extends beyond your own immediate family to other members of the same caste. But it doesn't go further than that. In Nepal, whether you are a Rai or a Limbu, a Gurung or a Sherpa, it really matters. On the other hand, once you are a Gurkha, there is no caste or even class distinction at all. The only distinctions we make are based on rank and experience.

The sound of the muezzin gave way to silence. The eerie silence of a graveyard. What we didn't know at the time was that that night's contacts were the last serious action we were to see in Now Zad. From this time onwards, our main problem would be just sniper and occasional mortar fire.

We remained stood-to well into the next day, however, and it was not until around noon that I was called down off the position for a resupp of ANP Hill. They were getting low on ammo and water.

As before, it was really nerve-racking to go out of the compound so soon after a major engagement. We couldn't be sure there wasn't a stay-behind party lying in wait for us, knowing there must be a good chance we'd be going out at some point. On average, we went out of the DC once every forty-eight hours either to collect stores or to take stores up to ANP Hill. The Taliban knew this perfectly well by now, and it wouldn't have been at all difficult for them to ambush us just as they had ambushed the ANP twice already. In fact, thinking back, it seems strange they never did.

16

Extraction

The next real excitement the enemy had in store for us was a return to indirect fire. Last night's intelligence about a new base plate was obviously spot on. This time he aimed at the DC instead of ANP Hill and several rounds fell just outside the compound to the north-east and south-west. The shout went up around the compound.

'IDF! I-D-F! TAKE COVERRRR!'

I was on duty in Sangar 1 when the rounds landed and immediately started looking with my binos for the tell-tale smoke and dust of the round being fired. There was a pause before the next rounds came, and this time they fell within a few metres of the CT.

'*Aaye, guruji!*' exclaimed Gaaz. 'The next one's gonna be right on top! *Jatha!*'

By that time, of course, everybody on the roof of the CT was safely inside, but even so a direct hit would have been a big nuisance. It would definitely destroy the HF (high frequency) and satellite radio antennae. If that happened it would massively disrupt our ability to communicate with the outside world, and we'd be in a really bad way. No outside comms would mean no air support.

But at that point the enemy stopped.

'What was that all about?' demanded Gaaz. 'Just when he'd got us bracketed, he stopped. D'you reckon he just ran out of ammo?'

'Unlikely,' I replied. 'More likely he was just setting up his base plate. As soon as he saw what the final correction was to get on target, he stopped. Any more and there was a chance he'd give his position away.'

'So what you're saying is he'll be back. And next time he won't miss.'

'That's my guess.'

'You know what, *guruji*? You have a really good military brain. I am impressed.'

'Thanks, but it doesn't take genius. I'd say the Taliban have a good military brain. They saw what happened last time when they attacked us with mortar. They might not realise it was the bomber that picked up the heat source. They might think it was just luck in spotting the base plate. Either way, they know they daren't risk identifying their position to us. Besides, by doing this, they keep us guessing. We don't know when they're going to hit us next.'

'You mean they're trying to make us afraid?'

'Of course! And they hope they can wear us down by keeping us always on the lookout. They want us to have to be extra careful as we move round the compound. Never to walk, but always to run. Never to leave your helmet off. We'd do exactly the same.'

'You're right, *guruji*. You have to give the *jatha* some credit, don't you?'

Our other big problem from now on was highly accurate sniper fire. As I knew from my previous stay in the country, there was still a good supply of Dragunov rifles in Afghanistan, and we assumed that this is what the enemy were using. Luckily, we managed to identify several of his fire positions, and by patiently waiting in his own pre-prepared position, Corporal Im Ghale, who was universally recognised as the best shot in the whole company, was able to take out a number of them.

A nervous calm descended on the DC and we began to notice other things more. The heat, the dust, our exhaustion. Strangely, it was during these periods of inaction that it became more important than ever to keep morale up among the *bhais*. I did this by a combination of attention to detail as to SOPs and drills, and taking advantage of the opportunity to get everyone properly rested. I even took up smoking as a way of relaxing myself. A lot of the *gurujis* and *bhais* also smoked, and I must say that I found it very enjoyable to chat and puff away as the sun went down in the evenings and the heat began to get a little less intense.

Although I never slept very much, it was good, too, to go and lie down. Sometimes I used to carry on thinking about the conversations about basic training I'd been having with Gaaz. They were hard, but they were such happy days.

*

From Pokhara and Kathmandu, we flew to Church Crookham. Arriving after a twelve-hour flight, it was snowing and really cold. Even though it was only late January, I did not expect this. I expected weather something like it was in Pokhara – warm by day and cooler in the evening. The other unexpected thing was the attitude of the *gurujis*. I thought that now we were starting basic training, they would be kinder. In fact, as soon as we arrived the first thing they did was to advertise each other's bad qualities.

'You want to watch out for So-and-So. The man's a tiger.'

'Don't mess the short one around. He's a karate black belt. Last year he knocked down six recruits in a single day.' Of course, they weren't being quite serious. They just wanted to put us on our guard.

As at Pokhara, there was a lot of drill, but here it was even harder. Every morning there would be a parade with lots of shouting as we were taken through the different routines, first with no weapons, then with wooden ones to familiarise us with the movements, finally with actual rifles. We all hated it. Luckily for me, because of my height I was always put in the back row, usually at the end to act as anchor.

One difference from Pokhara was that at Church Crookham the *gurujis* expected 100 per cent respect for authority at all times.

'Yes, *guruji*. No, *guruji*.'

Whenever we spoke to them, we had better be sure to remember our manners. The result was that I hardly ever opened my mouth without using the word '*guruji*' to everyone except my intake – including, to her surprise, one rather stern aunt I had! After a few weeks in England we were allowed to phone our families back in Nepal. When she answered, I found I couldn't stop myself.

One other big difference from Pokhara was the frequent kit inspections. Every morning and every evening, as well as after practically every activity, we had to stand to attention while our stuff was examined by one of the *gurujis*. I swear they could smell it if anything was out of place. Occasionally you might try to hide an unironed shirt underneath a pile of ironed ones. But somehow they would always sniff it out.

'You can't fool me,' they'd say as they handed out a punishment – an extra duty, say, or twenty press-ups on the spot.

Another big difference – and, as it turned out, a big help in Afghanistan – was the lack of sleep. Every day we were woken early and then kept up very late. And as in Now Zad, when we did get to bed at the end of the day I was often so keyed up that it took me ages to get to sleep. I used to lie there thinking about my home and my mum and dad and my sister. I remember feeling sorry for the times I had told little Gudiya off, and I regretted my hard words.

We slept twenty to each block. Every morning it would be the same. The alarm sounded and someone switched it off. Nobody moved. Then one of the *gurujis* would march in with a stick and start poking our feet with it.

'Get up you lazy w*nk*rs!'

While in Pokhara, whenever the *gurujis* swore at us, it was in Gorkhali, but at Church Crookham it was generally in English, so this was one way we expanded our vocabulary.

'If you *jathas* aren't out of your lazy beds in the next five seconds there's going to be trouble.'

Fortunately for me, my place was at the end of the room,

furthest from where the *guruji* came in. If I was really quick, I could get up as soon as he entered and be dressed before he reached my bed.

One result of having so little sleep at night was that we were always falling asleep by day. Given the smallest opportunity, at least one person was bound to be caught out. Never during drill or PT or sports or on parade, of course. But in any classroom activity, even weapon training or first aid, there was always the danger. English classes were the biggest problem of all, with guys falling asleep the whole time. Luckily the lessons were given by civilian teachers, and they weren't so strict. There would even be occasions, if a lot of people were struggling, when they actually stopped the class.

'Right, everyone. Five minutes' sleep!'

Then we would all collapse on our desks. These teachers were really nice, though sometimes they did lose patience.

'Come on, guys, if you don't pay attention I'm going to have to report you.'

This meant trouble, so we really tried hard. As a result, you'd see people running out of class every few minutes to splash their faces with water. Another technique we had was, as soon as we felt ourselves going, to start chewing the chillis we always carried round in our pockets. Unfortunately, this only worked for about the first ten minutes.

If you did actually drop off, the first thing that happened was the person next to you would be told to give you a slap. When you had come-to, the *guruji*s would have a few choice words to say before making you do some press-ups or a run round the block outside.

'Kailash. If you don't pay attention, I'm going to rip your

arms off and beat you round the head with the wet end.'

'Kailash! Wake up or you'll have to go home! We're obviously depriving your village of an idiot!'

One thing that made keeping awake extra difficult was whenever the *gurujis* switched the heater on. For the first few weeks, this happened a lot because of the time of year, and I myself was one of the most frequent offenders. To make matters worse, I usually sat next to a recruit called Jit.

Now Jit and I were very different. His nickname was *Bhagawan*, which means god in Gorkhali. This was because he understood very little. I could always answer the questions, but he never could. Unluckily for him, his education was quite poor and he found it difficult to follow anything that was being said because all our instruction was in English. But although he often didn't know what was going on, he never fell asleep. He would sit to attention throughout all the classes and it became his job to wake me as soon as I started snoring – which I always did. As soon as this happened, the *guruji* would shout 'SOP, Jit' and that was his signal to smack me on the head.

I don't know if it was because he didn't like me, but whenever he did so, he hit me very hard. I longed for the day when I could get him back, but somehow it was always me and never him who got into trouble. This really annoyed me. Then at last, one happy day, it turned out that it was him and not me. I was just waking up as he fell asleep and the *guruji*, seeing this, pointed at me.

'Now's your chance for revenge, Kailash.'

I stood up and whacked Jit so hard that he woke up crying. Seeing this, I was horrified at what I'd done and started to apologise and try to comfort him while everyone else had a good laugh.

On the whole, though, we recruits got on well together. Occasionally there would be scuffles in the accommodation blocks, but people quickly made up afterwards. For myself, I made sure that I put my love of fighting behind me. The only other time I remember coming close to hitting someone was one time when I was made RPS (Recruit Platoon Sergeant) for the weekend.

One of my responsibilities was to make sure the toilets and shower rooms were clean. The idea was that we should all do the job together, but there was this one person who refused to help.

'Where is he?' I wanted to know.

'Still in bed.'

'Still in bed?'

'Yes, but he's from a really good family. He's not used to this sort of thing.'

'I don't care who he is, or where he's from,' I said. 'He should come anyway.'

Luckily he did, because I'd already decided that if he gave me any trouble I was going to knock him down.

Of course, weapon training was the thing we most enjoyed at Church Crookham. I was really excited to start as soon as possible. I remember, though, that when I first held the SA80 rifle, I was a bit disappointed. It was much lighter than my grandfathers's old gun, and much smaller. It also had a lot of plastic on it, which didn't seem right. It looked a bit fragile and I was worried that I might break the thing if I wasn't careful. I was wrong of course, but that was my impression.

The first actual shooting we did was with a .22 rifle, and this was even more of a disappointment. The actual gun was quite a bit bigger than the SA80 but it didn't seem to have any recoil. I couldn't understand this at all and I called the *guruji* over.

'*Guruji*, this doesn't feel right. I've fired my grandfather's gun and it gave a huge kick when you pulled the trigger. I think there must be something wrong.'

But the *guruji* laughed.

'Don't worry,' he said. 'There's nothing wrong. You don't get much of a kick from such a small rifle bore, that's all.'

Fortunately, when we started training on the GPMG, it was fully up to my expectations. Not only did it look really nice, but it felt and sounded just right and I loved everything about it. For me at seventeen it was a dream come true.

After five weeks, we were allowed out of camp for the first time. One of the *guruji*s took us into town, where we had to go in pairs. I remember having exactly a hundred pounds in my pocket while the friend I was with had about forty. We walked around together for some time before eventually deciding to go for something to eat. There was a Kentucky Fried Chicken restaurant which we thought we would try.

We went inside.

'So what about it?' we asked one another in Gorkhali. 'You gonna do it?'

'You do it.'

'No, you do it.'

We went on like this for some time before giving up. We just couldn't think what to do or what to say. It was two very hungry recruits that went back to barracks at the end of the day.

Things improved slightly when I went down next time, on this occasion with a different friend. Again we walked around a bit before eventually arriving at the KFC. This time, my friend went in and when he got to the front of the queue he asked very nicely for what he wanted. I was so relieved. But now it was my turn, I froze.

'Same one!' I said at last.

Although I was always top of the class in school at Khebang, this did not mean very much. The standard of teaching in my village was not very high, unfortunately. Furthermore, a lot of the other recruits, especially those from the cities, had taken more English lessons after passing the School Leavers' Certificate. Some had gone to private schools where the standards are a lot higher, and a few had even studied in college for two years or more. Not only that, but some of the other recruits were as much as five years older than me and some had gone through Pokhara three times. So these people had a big advantage. But I always tried my best and didn't let my lack of a good education hold me back.

The other thing I found was that I was not so fit as some of the other recruits. In our races, I could manage to come in somewhere between tenth and fifteenth place out of forty in our intake. However, as the course progressed, my fitness improved, so that by the end of nine months I could sometimes manage first place and I usually came in the first three or four.

As at Pokhara, command tasks were an important part of our training, and I was one of the first people to be given a chance, perhaps because I was so keen. Unfortunately, it was a total disaster. I was made section 2 i/c while one of the *gurujis* acted as section commander. When he set off towards the objective, I had no idea I was supposed to follow him. When I eventually caught up with him, he started shouting at me.

'Kailash, where the hell have you been all this time? What took you so long?'

I just stood there, not knowing what to say.

At the end of our time at Church Crookham, there was a final parade when our *gurujis* announced which unit we would be in. I desperately wanted to be an infantryman. Besides the two infantry battalions, I knew that there were Gurkha Engineers, Signallers and Logistics people too, but I really didn't want any of these things. I prayed they would just make me an ordinary rifleman.

'21126684, Rifleman X Rai. Gurkha Signals.'

'21170907, Rifleman Y Gurung. Gurkha Logistics.'

'21124393, Rifleman Z Tamang, First Battalion.'

As they read the names and numbers out, I became more and more tense until at last my turn came.

'21170101, Rifleman Kailash Limbu, Second Battalion.'

I was so happy when the announcement came, so relieved. I'd made it.

Sometimes as I lay on my bed in Now Zad, I used to ask myself what my life would have been like if I'd become a doctor instead of becoming a Gurkha. I think I would have enjoyed it. I'd certainly be having an easier time of things than we were having in this safe house. On the other hand, for all the danger, I wouldn't have wanted to miss this for the world.

The big turning point for us came during the final week of the month when the CVRT of the Household Cavalry suddenly appeared. The funny thing was, we'd been talking a lot about tanks, partly among ourselves and partly over the PRR. We thought there was a good chance the Taliban were listening in to our radio broadcasts, just as we listened in to theirs. They could get hold of ICOM scanners over the internet just like anyone else could. So we used to joke among ourselves over the PRR, sometimes in English, sometimes in Urdu, sometimes in Gorkhali, that there was a whole regiment of cavalry on its way.

'Gonna be two hundred of them, any day now.'

'In brand-new tanks.'

'Yeah, I think it's today in fact.'

In reality, we had no idea. We were just trying to make ourselves feel good and the Taliban feel bad. The OC had mentioned the possibility of a small detachment of Scimitar armoured reconnaissance vehicles being sent by Battlegroup HQ, but as a section commander, I did not know the full details.

The arrival of these vehicles was a turning point in another way too. The OC had the excellent habit of going round the whole position at least once every day when we were not in contact. On his rounds, he would go up into each sangar, partly to check our equipment and supplies, and partly to make sure everyone was all right. It wasn't exactly an inspection, and he used to chat about the usual things – girlfriends, family and so on. He made jokes about the Taliban too, speaking in Gorkhali the whole time. But as well as doing these routine checks, he also made it his habit to take a good look with his binoculars at the surrounding area. If we had seen anything new, such as a firing position the enemy had not used before, we would show him and he would mark it on his map. Sometimes, too, he would point things out to us – things that we might have missed through overfamiliarity with what we were looking at day in, day out.

What happened on this particular day was that when the OC went up onto the roof of the CT shortly after dawn – this being always the first place he visited – he was scanning with his binos when he suddenly realised that he was staring down the barrels of an improvised rocket-launching system positioned in a bunker not more than 100 metres away.

Probably the most dangerous weapon the Taliban had in their armoury was their version of the Katyusha rocket. This was first developed by the Russian Army at the beginning of the Second World War. They used it during the capture of Berlin in 1945. During the Cold War, the Chinese got hold of the design and eventually exported it to the Middle East. I suppose the ones the Taliban had came in from Iran. But whereas most people who use these rockets deploy them using proper launch systems mounted on the back of lorries, the Taliban just laid them carefully on the ground and sighted them manually. Although it might not sound likely to be very effective, we knew this enemy to be brilliant improvisers. They had people who could set them up just as well as if they were using the most modern laser-guided systems, by using nothing more than line of sight. If they'd managed to launch them before we got onto them, the result was bound to be very bad for us indeed. Each rocket carries more than ten pounds of high explosive. If only one of them hit the CT, it would cause mul-tiple casualties. If two – wipeout. And there were at least six launchers.

As soon as Rex *sahib* realised what he was looking at, he called me over.

'Kailash, I've got a job for you.'

'*Hasur, sahib*.'

'I want you to go up into Sangar Six with Nabin and to engage the bunker you will see straight in front of you.'

'*Hasur, sahib*.'

He then showed me its exact location marked on his map of the local area.

'It's a rocket launcher,' he went on. 'And I think we'd better hit it before they decide to hit us. Quick as you can, then!'

Ordinarily, I'd have saluted, but we didn't do any of that on operations and I just nodded and ran off to carry out his instructions. We now had the other .50-cal mounted on top of an ISO container, and within a matter of minutes I had emptied half a belt of ammunition into the target. So far as we could tell, there was no one on the position, but that wasn't the point. The point was to immobilise the weapon system.

I definitely hit the target, but we could not be sure it had been completely destroyed and the rockets knocked out. So the first thing the OC did when it was confirmed the tanks were actually en route to us was to give them orders to engage the same position as soon as they came within range.

Just like the enemy, the first thing we knew about the tanks' arrival was when the Scimitars fired their 30 mm guns at the Katyushas from a position up on ANP Hill. It was in the evening and I was up in Sangar 3 at the time. I'd just heard on the PRR that they would be arriving any moment.

'Hey guys! Great news! Tanks! The cavalry is on its way!'

'Tanks?'

'Yes, for real. CVR. From the Household Cavalry.'

The *bhai*s were overjoyed. It was the best news we'd had for a long time, a huge morale boost. Although having air support was great, having armoured vehicles on the ground was in some ways even more comforting. There was a huge cheer throughout the compound as their rounds tore into the launch pad.

'Take a look at that, *guruji*!' said Gaaz delightedly. 'I bet the Talibs weren't expecting that, the *jatha*!'

Within minutes, you could see the whole position had been completely destroyed.

That night, the CVR got down to work. Rex *sahib* wanted to give the impression that there were more of them than there really were, so he got them to spend several hours just manoeuvring round the town, paying special attention to all the AOIs and known fire positions. We watched them through our nightsights as they went about their business from up in the sangars.

'That should make the Talibs worried all right,' remarked Gaaz.

'Well yes, *bhai*. That's the idea.'

'Wow, just look at them,' he went on, admiringly. 'I'd just love to be inside one right now.'

'Not if it got hit by RPG you wouldn't,' I said.

'True. But I'd really like to see what goes on behind Smuggler's House and places like that.'

'Probably not a lot.'

'What I'd like to see is those positions up in the treeline,' said Nagen.

'That would be more interesting,' I agreed.

Every so often, one of the tanks let rip a burst of fire from its GPMGs as they cleared their way forward.

'Pity we haven't had them with us all along,' observed Gaaz, admiringly.

It certainly would have been a big plus.

Later, after we changed duties in the early morning, the 2 i/c called me over.

'Kailash, there's going to be a resupp of ANP Hill. We'll also be bringing the tank troop leader into the DC for a meeting with the OC. I want you on one of the WMIKs, OK?'

'Yes sir.'

'Same detail as usual. Fifteen minutes' notice to move from now. No indication that we're going until I give the order. Mount up straight away, gates to open on my signal. Then it's high speed out of town and follow me round to where the CVRs were parked up, here.'

He pointed the position out on his map and I marked mine up as he continued.

'In the event of contact, usual routine. We cover each other and extract back to the DC if less than halfway out or extract back to ANP Hill if that is closer. Maintain radio silence unless in contact. Any questions?'

'No, that's absolutely fine, sir.'

'OK, go and tell your *bhai*s and listen out for my signal.'

I ran straight to the accommodation block to tell Gaaz and Nani.

'Gaaz! Nani *guruji*! Wake up! We're going out.'

The two riflemen were both fast asleep, Gaaz among the jumble that constituted his bed space and Nani *guruji* tidy in the corner.

'What's that, Kailash *bhai*? Where are we going?' demanded Nani, bleary-eyed.

'The 2 i/c has to pick up the tank troop leader and bring him back to the DC.'

321

'He does?' he said, jumping up.

'That's great, but when? When?' said Gaaz, fully alert. 'I really want to take a look at those tanks. Do you think there's any chance of a go in one?'

'Unlikely,' I replied.

A short while later, the three of us were mounted up, engine running as the gate opened. This time, although there certainly was the ever-present danger of ambush, I felt a lot less nervous going out than usual. The thought of a troop of CVR within half a kilometre of the DC was very reassuring.

Another ten minutes and we were skidding to a halt along-side the CVRs where the troop leader sat waiting for us.

'Say, *guruji*, check out the commander! Now that's what you call a British cavalry officer,' exclaimed Gaaz excitedly.

I saw exactly what he meant. The person whose tank the 2 i/c had pulled up next to was sitting in the turret, with a large map spread out in front of him. Giving a very relaxed wave to Mathers *sahib*, he climbed unhurriedly down and they shook hands. After a few moments of serious talk, the two men started laughing together and I could see that there was an instant con-nection between the two officers.

Later, I learned that the troop leader's top priority was to get hold of a goat. He had heard about Gurkha goat curry and wondered if we could make one for him and his men if he sup-plied the animal. Unfortunately, our source had long since left Now Zad and there was no chance. In fact the ANP themselves had lately been reduced to looting the local shops, as they had completely run out of stores. But the idea appealed to the *bhai*s a lot. It increased their good opinion of the Household Cavalry Regiment even further.

That night, as a result of the CVR patrol, we had a completely quiet time of it for the first time in almost a week, and the next day was quiet too.

The tanks remained with us for around seventy-two hours, during which time, apart from some isolated sniper fire, the enemy kept a low profile. When eventually the HCR left, we were very sorry to see them go. The good news, however, was that the 3 PARA Battlegroup was by now getting very close. Just two or three days away. We were told they would be conducting what in military terms is called a 'relief in place'. Basically, this meant they would be clearing the town on foot and then covering our extraction out. But this had to be kept top secret. The ANP weren't told; not even the *torjeman*, our interpreter, was told. And of course the local police were not told either. As a result, we had to carry on as if nothing was happening. One thing this meant was that, although we would have liked to tidy the place up properly for the Paras coming in, we couldn't, as it would have alerted the Afghans. We had to leave things more or less as they were.

'But that doesn't mean you don't have to sort out your bed space, Gaaz. For the third time of asking.'

'Yes, *guruji*. I mean, no, *guruji*.' The only time I saw Gaaz lost for words was when I was telling him to tidy up after himself.

We were hit once more after the tanks left, but the engagement did not have the intensity of the earlier ones and my assessment is that the enemy realised the game was up. There was no way he was going to dislodge us before the battlegroup arrived.

Our first sight of the incoming troops was just after first light on the morning of 31 July. I was up in Sangar 3 when, out of nowhere, three Chinooks appeared to the south of the DC. They made hardly any noise, as they were flying tactically, and it was only when they landed no more than a few hundred metres away that you would have known anything about them if you weren't expecting them.

As it was, we watched delighted as the Paras disembarked and began to patrol towards us.

'Check it out, *guruji*!' exclaimed Gaaz. 'That's got to be at least a hundred men! There's gonna be some very worried Talibans round these parts,' he continued. 'That's enough to clear them all the way back to the mountains! Wish I could go with them, *guruji*. I really do.'

I knew how he felt. The worst thing about our situation in Now Zad had been not having the manpower to be able to mount fighting patrols. There's nothing I would have liked more than to go hunting for the enemy. Just to be able to have the chance of seeing them right up close. As it was, 3 PARA were going to have that satisfaction.

'I'd still like to see what they've got in that training area,' said Nagen, as we watched the first of them start to clear the buildings on the edge of town.

'Yeah,' agreed Gaaz. 'And I'd like to be able to see what's left of those rockets after the tanks hit them.'

After maybe an hour of slow patrolling, the first of the troops entered the compound. In fact I thought they were going to clear all the way out as far as the treeline, but they stopped on reaching the DC. The Para Commanding Officer then came forward. I noticed that he was quite short – Gurkha height – but he had a very impressive bearing. He and Rex *sahib* spoke together for some time while the sergeant major talked to Corporal Santos. Soon after, I was called down together with Lance Corporal Shree to brief the incoming section commanders.

On climbing back up into Sangar 3 with some of these NCOs, a bit of a tense atmosphere developed. The incomers didn't seem that much interested in what I had to say.

'It's all right,' said one of the Para section commanders. 'I've been here before. I know the area.'

I suppose he must have been on Operation Mutay, when 10 Platoon of 2 RGR under Major Murray *sahib* deployed to Now Zad alongside B Company of 3 PARA.

Well, you obviously think you're a top guy, I thought to myself. And indeed you are. But the enemy doesn't know that.

'Look,' I said, 'I've done P company too and I'm telling you, you need to get down. There are snipers out there.'

No sooner were the words out of my mouth than TIKK! – a round embedded itself in one of the wooden arc markers. He got down very fast after that and started paying much closer attention to what I was saying as I pointed out the arcs of fire and the various places we had identified as enemy fire positions.

But the atmosphere was still a bit uneasy, and as we came down off the sangar, one of the Para sergeants pointed to a pee bottle lying on the ground and demanded to know what it was. I suppose it must have been kicked over the side during one of the contacts and lain there unnoticed until this moment. Normally we took them down with us and threw them in the latrine. When I told him, he exploded.

'You don't fucking piss in the sangar area! You should know better than that.'

'Listen,' I said to the Paras. 'We haven't peed *except* lying down for the last three weeks. We haven't been able to move out of the sangars all day from dawn to dusk.'

But this guy just ignored me.

'Dirty bastards,' said one of the other Paras under his breath.

This was a bit insulting but I decided to ignore it. He'd find out soon enough the reality of the situation.

Meanwhile, Rex *sahib* was busy showing the Commanding Officer and the Platoon Commanders round the position. I noticed that he took care to point out the strikes on the two .50-cals and to show them Nabin's helmet where it had been struck. Also the CWS broken by a round in Sangar 3 and the many ammo boxes that had been hit.

'I reckon those Paras think they're coming in to sort things out because we couldn't handle it, *guruji*,' said Gaaz later. 'Well good luck to them is all I can say.'

I agreed.

'Sometimes people have to learn the hard way.'

We were in Now Zad for exactly thirty days. According to the official report, we were in contact twenty-eight times over just eleven days, during which time we expended in the region of 30,000 rounds of 5.56 mm ammunition, 17,000 rounds of 7.62, more than 2000 rounds of 12.7 mm (.50-cal), threw 21 grenades and fired three ILAWs – not to mention all the air ordnance. It is uncertain how many enemy we killed for only one of our men wounded, but the figure usually given is around a hundred, and this seems realistic to me. It was to all intents and purposes an old-fashioned siege – not unlike the siege of Kalunga, where British troops first encountered Gurkha soldiers back in 1814.

Looking back, there are moments when I am amazed we survived – let alone that we took no significant losses. One breach of the compound wall would have been enough to have turned it into a disaster zone. As it was, my big memories are just of the time spent up in the sangar positions, waiting and watching – long periods of anxiety broken up by prolonged periods of intense, accurate enemy fire and wondering how we could possibly get the initiative back and survive to fight another day. But above all this, I remember the *sahibs*, the *gurujis* and the *bhais* who I fought the Taliban insurgency alongside. Each of them was, in my view, a hero, a warrior in the true Gurkha tradition. So when, as I occasionally do, I ask myself whether I could face another operation like the one we fought over those four weeks back in July 2006, I answer:

So long as I am with the officers and men from the Brigade of Gurkhas my answer is yes, I would. Any time.

Epilogue: After Now Zad

The Paras stayed in Now Zad just thirty-six hours before handing over to the Royal Regiment of Fusiliers. 3 PARA themselves went on to Sangin and Musa Qala, where they had a very rough time of things and took quite a few casualties. As for myself, I was back in Nepal just a few weeks later. The subsequent days I spent with my newborn son were among the happiest of my life. Now I had a boy I could bring up and teach to be a man. Hopefully he will carry on the traditions of our family and do something good for his people.

My Army career since Now Zad has been one of steady progress. After Op Herrick 4, I returned again to Afghanistan in 2008–9 on Op Herrick 9 and again in 2011 for Op Herrick 14. Each of these were hard tours, very kinetic, and we lost men on both of them.

By the time of Op Herrick 14, I was a Platoon Sergeant in Tamandu Company. At the time of writing I am a Colour Sergeant. I hope eventually to become a late entry officer.

As to the other men, Nagen went to the Gurkha demonstration company at the Royal Military Academy Sandhurst, where he remains. Baren continues to serve in the first battalion RGR and is presently based in Brunei. Cookie, as I mentioned, recovered and has now left the Army. Nani has also left the Army, made redundant a few years back. He is living and working in the UK. Lance Corporal Shree was promoted Corporal and went to Catterick as an instructor of Gurkha recruits. Corporal Santos is now also a Colour Sergeant, presently instructing at the infantry school in Warminster.

Of the officers, Mathers *sahib* first became Adjutant and is now serving as a Major. The OC, Rex *sahib*, later became an equerry to Her Majesty the Queen. He is now a Lieutenant-Colonel and is Station Commander at the Royal Military Academy, Sandhurst.

And then there is Gaaz. At the time of the Now Zad tour, Gaaz was a member of 12 Platoon, having come into my section as a recruit. After returning to Shorncliffe he got an attachment with the Yorkshire Regiment in Germany. After some time, he came out to Brunei, where I, as a newly promoted platoon sergeant, was on the staff during his Junior Leader Cadre for promotion to lance corporal. It was so good to see him again and I was really pleased he did well. He got his promotion soon after returning to the Yorkshires in Germany. He was just twenty-one, exactly as he hoped he would be. I later heard that Gaaz so impressed his platoon commander that he was being considered for entry to Sandhurst and possible commission as a regular officer. Of course it wasn't just his great sense of humour and his intelligence but his enthusiasm and forcefulness in command that people noticed.

Like the rest of us, Gaaz had several more tours of Afghanistan, returning there for the last time on Op Herrick 15 in the autumn of 2011. Just as at Now Zad, his platoon was sent to take over a compound. They were helicoptered up and then had to patrol in. They were taking a lot of fire on the position, both direct and indirect, and he'd responded by firing UGL. Later on, they were building up the position with sandbags – again just as at Now Zad – when there was a sudden burst of machine-gun fire. Everyone took cover but Gaaz, no doubt remembering the enemy's tactics, quickly got back up to return fire. He was struck by a single bullet that caught him between the eyes.

Gaaz died a hero's death, in the arms of his platoon commander.

When I think of this, I am filled with sorrow – not just for him, but for each of the Gurkhas who fell during the recent Afghan war, and for all their families and friends. My only comfort is that each and every one who did so died a true Gurkha's death – full of courage, never failing, good-humoured, resourceful, noble to the end. True warriors all. But as Gaaz was my friend, and is the one I knew best, it is to him that I wish to dedicate this book, the gift of one soldier to the memory of another.

May his deeds never be forgotten.

Jai Gurkha!

Glossary

ANP Afghan National Police

AOI area of interest

Browning .50-cal heavy machine gun

casevac casualty evacuation

casrep casualty report

CSM Company Sergeant Major

CT control tower

CVR(T) combat vehicle reconnaissance (tracked)

CWS common weapon sight

DC district centre

DRO Director Recruiting Officer

EGD Educated Guard Duty

FIBUA fighting in a built-up area

FOO Forward Observation Officer

FP fire position

FUP forming-up place

GPMG general-purpose machine gun

HLS helicopter landing site

HMNVS head-mounted night-vision sight

IA immediate action

IDF indirect fire

IED improvised explosive device

ILAW interim light anti-tank weapon

IRT Immediate Response Team

ISAF International Security Assistance Force

jimpy general-purpose machine gun

JLC Junior Leaders Cadre

J Tac tactical air controller

LSW light support weapon

MFC mortar fire controller

MID Mention in Dispatches

Minimi machine gun

OC Officer Commanding

O-group orders group

pax personnel

PID positive identification

PKM Russian 7.62mm machine gun

PRR personal radio relay

QBO Quick Battle Order

QGO Queen's Gurkha Officer

QRF Quick Reaction Force

resupp resupply

ROE Rules of Engagement

RPG rocket-propelled grenade

RPS Recruit Platoon Sergeant

RRF Royal Regiment of Fusiliers

sitrep situation report

SOP standard operating procedure

UGL underslung grenade launcher

WMIK Weapons Mount Installation Kit: an armoured Land Rover

Index

A-10 aircraft, 120–1, 171–7, 280–1

Afghan National Police (ANP): on ANP Hill, 186–7, 188; evacuation of casualty, 185–6; firing of random rounds by, 7, 118; *hajira* hill people in, 76; interception of Taliban signals by, 176, 295–6; in Now Zad compound, 42–3, 44, 49, 73, 74, 76, 85, 89, 90, 123, 247, 322; patrols, 7, 74–5, 156–8, 264, 277–8, 282, 284, 285; suspicion of, 49, 85, 247, 323

Afghanistan: dietary rules in, 189; earlier conflicts in, 77–8, 95, 143; Helmand province, 2, 30, 37, 55, 84, 90, 246, 288; marriage customs, 123; rich and poor in, 93–4; 2003 tour, 91–6, 203; Op Herrick 4 (2006), 47, 248; Op Herrick 9 (2008–9), 232, 328; Op Herrick 14 (2011), 203, 328; Op Herrick 15 (2011), 330; *see also* Now Zad compound; Now Zad town and district; Taliban insurgency

alcohol, 17–18, 19

Ambika (Gurkha), 29

ammunition, 57, 81–2, 165–6, 184–5, 219, 278–9

Amrit (Gurkha), 29

Apache helicopter gunships, 45, 76, 186, 221, 271, 273–7, 283, 286, 303

Atta Muhammad, 92

B-52 bombers, 131–2

bagh chal ('the tiger game'), 88–9, 100, 287

Baren (Gurkha), 5–6, 7, 10, 70, 98, 101, 268–71, 272, 274, 277, 280; army career since